The Guardian Directory of Pressure Groups & Representative Associations

THE GUARDIAN DIRECTORY OF PRESSURE GROUPS

& REPRESENTATIVE ASSOCIATIONS

Research by Chris Bazlinton and Anne Cowen
Edited and with an Introduction
by Peter Shipley

GALE RESEARCH COMPANY : DETROIT : MICHIGAN

*First published in the United States
of America, 1977,
by* Gale Research Company,
Book Tower, Detroit, Michigan

*First published in Great Britain
by* Wilton House Publications Ltd.

Printed and bound in Great Britain
at The Pitman Press Ltd, Bath

ISBN 0 904655 00 8

CONTENTS

EDITOR'S NOTE

The idea for a *Directory of Pressure Groups* came from Chris Bazlinton. He drew up a list of potential entrants, devised the questionnaire, despatched it to over 600 national organisations and, with Anne Cowen, prepared the first draft. He also obtained the support of *The Guardian* newspaper and, in this connection, the interest and co-operation of John Ryan is much appreciated.

Although fifty percent of the questionnaires were completed and many additional entries have been compiled, the variety of pressure groups, the impermanence of many of them and the daily appearance of new ones, together with the inevitable changes that have occurred among some entrants in details such as the appointment of new officers, does not allow the production of a definitive work. The amount of information given varies from organisation to organisation, but was governed largely by the quantity and quality of material supplied, and not by any intended bias on the part of Researchers and Editor. Nevertheless, it is hoped that a worthwhile source of reference and information has been produced, covering twelve major areas in which pressure groups operate.

The Researchers and Editor would like to thank all the organisations who replied to the questionnaire and in many cases provided additional information; to Sue Daniels who typed much of the early drafts; and to Fiona Shipley who typed the Directory and accompanying material in their final form.

Peter Shipley
March 1976

vi

INTRODUCTION

I — INTERESTS AND CAUSES: THE ANATOMY OF PRESSURE

Who runs Britain? In any answer to that much debated question the part played by pressure groups would loom large. Their material interests and ultimate aims are varied, their activities extensive and their influence can be far reaching. They range from the giant organisations that represent industrial and commercial interests, national campaigns that seek urgent solutions to social problems, to countless local groups locked in battle with bureaucracy over the level of rates or the proposed route of a new motorway. Pressure groups reach into every area of social and political life and the voices of the most important are essential to the smooth working of government.

An historical perspective suggests, however, that the contribution of such groups to public affairs has long been a central one. The British have traditionally been a highly organised people, and their history is the elaborate evolution of sectional interests — craftsmen's guilds, companies of merchants and manufacturers, associations of scientists, artists and professional men, mill owners and railway developers, unions of artisans and labourers — reconciled to each other and to a greater, public good. It is also a history of the pursuit of ideals and causes, when self-interest has been tempered by conscience: in campaigns to abolish slavery or to end the exploitation of child labour, or in the efforts of Chartists and Suffragettes. Each group has been able to protect and promote its particular claims, and compete with others for economic resources, social status and government favour, while the political system has been able to

1

adjust and satisfy their sectional aspirations without causing any threat to the foundations of its own existence.

Given this background, what is striking about group interests today is the apparent explosion in the number of active organisations, certainly during the last fifteen years and comparatively over the last fifty; the diversity of their motivation; the extent of the influence some enjoy with governments in which has been detected the unaccounted exercise of political power; the influence also some have in moulding people's attitudes and behaviour and in shaping social change; and the complex machinery of bargaining, lobbying, and persuading that has grown up with the increased tempo of pressure group activity, together with the accompanying apparatus of bureaucracy, information and protest.

The world of pressure groups is one of some intricacy, a labyrinth that is also a minefield, that before venturing to explore such doubly hazardous terrain, some essential instruction in map reading is advisable, if only to draw attention to some of the more prominent features on the land ahead.

Pressure groups are first and foremost organised sections of the community looking after their own interests. But many bodies that behave in this way could not be termed pressure groups: a local cricket club or a history society are not pressure groups, even when the one holds a raffle to raise funds for a new pavilion, or the other stages an exhibition of ancient maps and prints, and they come into contact with the public. If however a proposal to build a new motor-way threatens to cut across the cricket pitch and would entail the demolition of an historic building, both organisations are likely to oppose the plan: they may write to the local newspaper, lobby councillors, hold public meetings, and perhaps, realising their common interest, join together for a campaign of protest; they may even send a deputation to London to put their case to government officials or a minister. In such a situation the cricket club and history society would both be pressure groups.

For the purposes of this Directory, however, such organisations will be excluded, because the application of pressure is a secondary

2

reason for their existence, and arises only occasionally. Our interest is in bodies, which, although they may engage in a wide variety of activities, find themselves regularly putting their case to authority or to public opinion, with the objective of securing changes that are beneficial to their group and preventing those which are detrimental. It is the concentration on actively seeking (or preventing) social and political change that distinguishes the pressure group from other organised, self-interested groups. A pressure group therefore is an association of individuals joined together by a common interest, belief, activity or purpose that seeks to achieve its objectives, further its interests and enhance its status in relation to other groups, by gaining the approval and co-operation of authority in the form of favourable policies, legislation and conditions.

Many students of British politics have found the term 'pressure groups' inadequate. They consider it to be misleading, emotive or, even, disparaging, a generally unsatisfactory description of the kinds of groups they are describing and of how these groups set about their tasks. Terms such as 'sectional groups', 'interest groups' or simply 'organised groups' have been used to denote the nature of the organisations concerned, while Professor Finer's phrase 'The Lobby' has described more effectively than 'pressure' the style and methods of such groups in a representative democracy. 'Pressure groups' can still be applied as a generic term, covering two main kinds of organisation: 'interest', 'spokesman' or 'representative' groups, and 'promotional' or 'cause' groups. Most bodies that would otherwise be called simply 'pressure groups' fall under one or other of these headings, although some fall under either one or between them both.

Interest groups

This term covers those organisations which represent and act as spokesmen for distinct economic and social interests of the community. Among these are some of the most influential 'pressure groups' and representative associations in modern Britain: employers' organisations, from the Confederation of British Industry as the leading spokesmen of businesses and manufacturers of all kinds, under public ownership as well as in private enterprise, to bodies which uphold the interests of one industry, such as engineering or

3

shipping, but which encompass powerful interests in their own right. (Examples of these types of interest groups are found in Section 1 of the Directory.)

The other, equally important kind of pressure groups that represents a distinct economic interest is the trade union movement: the Trade Union Congress with its 10,000,000 affiliated members together with individual unions that comprise nearly half of that total are listed in Section 3 of the Directory.

Thirdly among the interest groups are those representing professions or occupations that fall outside the orbit of either employers' or employees' organisations. Many of these are ancient with considerable influence that affects society in far reaching ways — such as that exercised by the British Medical Association, the National Farmers' Union or bodies for lawyers, engineers and scientists.

All of these interest groups, employers, trade unions and professions, occupy key positions in the processes of decision making in Britain. They have access to government departments, ministers, backbench Members of Parliament, international agencies, local authorities, and the media. Most have extensive facilities for research and providing information and advice on which governments rely, and which can be turned to campaigns intended to influence public opinion. All can, if so determined, employ 'pressure' on the rest of society or on governments in such a way that the line between influence and the direct use of power is blurred and indeed crossed.

Yet with them all, pressure, in all its forms, is only a part of their work. They provide their members with benefits and services, in legal, financial and insurance matters, safeguard professional standards, standards of safety and the health and welfare of their members; provide technical training and education, and engage in many other activities which serve the interests of their members in an unspectacular day-to-day manner.

By comparison some other interests are much less well organised and represented. Only in the present generation have consumers become aware of their identity and their potential. Now a number of distinct consumer groups exist (see Section 4 of the Directory) who watch over the decisions not only of governments, but also of those mightier interests of producers and organised labour. The accelerating rate of inflation in recent years has given an urgent impetus to the creation of a consumer interest, in which governments themselves have taken a hand. Its late emergence was due partly to the generality and vagueness of the concept itself in that at some point in everyday life we are all consumers, and the idea lacks the sense of a combined purpose that holds together other economic group interests.

Similarly some organisations that purport to represent a particular social category find their efforts diffused by lack of cohesion: women's organisations for example (see Section 7 of the Directory) do not so much represent a distinct 'interest' common to all women, but express needs and aspirations of individuals. Besides those who are specialised groups that concentrate on particular areas, the home, or work or health, and which may complement each other, there are groups whose values conflict: organisations seeking to enhance family life and motherhood on the one hand, and those radical feminists attempting to escape those traditional roles on the other. The collective expression of women's identity is a force in society real enough, but this is quite different from the existence of a common all-embracing 'interest'.

Difficulties arise also in relation to other organisations that wish to represent the views of particular sections of society, such as bodies for the homeless or the old, the lowly paid or other deprived groups. Here the social problems experienced by each group may be more clearly defined and their solution lend itself to campaigning through a 'pressure group'. But the organisation itself may have very few low paid or old members, and it may consist instead of younger or middle class activists who assume responsibility for the deprived and act as their spokesman. 'Representative' or 'spokesman' organisations of this kind are not strictly speaking 'interest' groups, but would be more accurately included in the category of 'cause' or 'promotional' pressure groups.

5

Promotional groups

These are bodies united by a belief, a cause or the desire to solve a particular problem. They are not defined by the interests they represent but rather by their style and approach to the issues which engender them.

Firstly are *ad hoc* groups that spring up in reaction to a specific situation and may combine a number of differently motivated sections for a limited time and for a clearly defined objective. At a local level, organisations that campaign to prevent a road building or property development scheme or the siting of an airport, are pressure groups of this sort. Nationally, a body such as the 'Stop the Seventy Tour' — the campaign against the South African cricket tour of 1970 that propelled Young Liberal Peter Hain into the headlines — was an *ad hoc* grouping of limited objectives. Similarly many other radical or left-wing propaganda campaigns, on Vietnam or for the withdrawal of British troops from Northern Ireland, are promotional groups of this nature. More broadly based *ad hoc* promotional groups have been concerned with the introduction of commercial television in the 1950s, the abolition of capital punishment, and, more recently, pro- and anti-Common Market organisations.

Some organisations ostensibly concerned with single issues in fact acquire a permanent structure, either because the problems to which they address themselves will not go away, or because the 'cause' implies and represents a much broader set of problems. The Campaign for Nuclear Disarmament, the Anti-Apartheid Movement or Shelter (the National Campaign for the Homeless) each in its own way has ramifications beyond its own specialist field.

Not all promotional groups are 'issue' centred, but aim to improve the welfare and conditions of specific groups or society in general on an open-ended basis. The Howard League for Penal Reform, Age Concern and the Human Rights Society are all concerned with problems whose solution could not be guaranteed by the passing of an act of parliament or by conducting a publicity campaign.

Promotional groups frequently direct their efforts firstly against other pressure groups, and voices raised in support of a cause can prompt the formation of a rival body to put the opposite point of view. Thus environmentalist groups may aim their fire onto 'interest' groups representing major industrial or commercial concerns. And as a specific example of chain reaction among promotional groups, the successful efforts of the Abortion Law Reform Association, culminating in the Abortion Act of 1967, gave rise to the Society for the Protection of Unborn Children opposing the reform measures.

A great deal of the recent growth in pressure activity has occurred in the category of promotional groups. In particular those concentrated on social concerns — housing, poverty, problems of ethnic groups and minorities, young people and deviancy. Their structure is fragmented and may operate on a local level only with few funds and no national organisation to support them. These smaller, newer, diffuse or *ad hoc* 'promotional' groups cannot aspire to the privileges of direct access to senior civil servants and government ministers (should they wish to channel their efforts into the official machine). Instead, those engaged at a community level concentrate on helping those people on whose behalf they are campaigning and on pressing local councils. Otherwise 'promotional' groups must compete for public attention through the media, publishing literature, setting out their case, holding meetings, conferences or demonstration (see Section II of the Introduction for methods and avenues of pressure). Promotional groups can acquire the expertise, reputation, contact with official bodies and consequently influence, associated with some of the older and more powerful 'interest' groups, but this is rarely achieved overnight. Alternatively they can turn to the political arena or seek charity status, two fields which play an important part in campaigning and representation.

Political organisations

Political parties seek power, and in this fundamental respect differ from either 'interest' or 'promotional' pressure groups who do not aim to take power themselves. The major parties are also more broadly based than any single sectional interest or pressure group in that they are coalitions of several interests and philosophies. Political parties therefore have a wider outlook, appeal and a larger purpose than any one pressure group. Conversely many sectional groups prefer not to become too closely identified with just one

7

party as they hope to deal equally with governments of any complexion.

Despite the differences of character and the reason for a separation of activity between political parties and pressure groups there are some significant overlaps. First and foremost is that certain economic interests are linked with particular parties: the trades unions and the Labour Party are connected for reasons of history and ideology, and the link is close and formal; between the Conservative Party and big business it is less formal but, given the funds donated by the latter to the Tory Party, a crucial one. There are also overlaps of member- ship between promotional groups held together by a belief or ideal and supporters of political parties who share that view: between for example the Anti-Apartheid Movement and members of the Labour and Liberal Parties. Such connections often remain however on a purely personhl plane and do not necessarily lead to formal association between the party and the group. This is especially the case with an organisation that hopes to win sympathisers from a number of parties as means of advancing its status and securing voices for its cause at Westminster.

Political parties are in a sense pressure groups for at least part of their existence, when they are in opposition; individual politicians likewise can have the effect of acting as a pressure group, in the case of a body of backbench opinion trying to influence the decisions of its own, governing, front bench, or through some more formal grouping of like-thinking party members. An increasing number of factions and ginger groups have emerged within the major parties to become political pressure groups in their own right, and not always operating strictly within the context of the party. To add to the older Fabian Society and the Tribune Group, the Labour Party now has the Manifesto Group and the Social Democratic Alliance. One strand of opinion, Dick Taverne's Social Democrats, could not however be kept within the confines of the party, and likewise, the interests of Scottish self-government have precipitated the break-up of the Labour Party in Scotland and the creation of a rival organisa- tion. The Conservatives now have the Bow Group and the Tory Reform Group on the left-wing of the party and on the right the Monday Club, the Selsdon Group and the Trident Group.

8

That Labour and Conservative Parties have proved resilient enough to encompass widely differing views within their respective ranks is part of the secret of their continued predominance. Each generation has its own intra-party feuds, but the process of fragmentation has accelerated in the last ten or so years, both within the parties where there has been a tendency for divisions to become sharper and translated into organised factions, and outside them. Most important has been the rise of Welsh and Scottish Nationalism, and the prospect of extensive devolution will have the profoundest impact on the Englishman's conception of his own political representation.

And on the fringes of the political spectrum are numerous independent groups who aspire to power but who lack the means and support to achieve it yet. This goal is as remote for the National Front as it is for the Communist Party or the International Socialists. Can many of the fringe organisations be called political parties, so narrow is their appeal? Could they be better described as pressure groups? Few actually represent social or economic interests, although they may claim to speak for the working class for example. They are at the stage of promoting causes, but ones which are not negotiable within the present system, and in this they do not conform to the basic definition of a pressure group, which entails the reconciliation of sectional claims to the general interest. Many of the techniques employed by the political fringe are, however, recognisable as 'pressure group' tactics in the broadest sense.

For these reasons and not least that most 'interest' and 'promotional' groups come into contact at some time with political parties and Members of Parliament and the legislative or electoral processes, the political spectrum is included in the Directory in Section 1. There remains in our discussion of the structure of 'pressure' activities, the category of charitable status.

Charities

The relationship between pressure groups and charities is a sensitive one. There were 115,000 charities in Great Britain in 1975, who were registered with the Charity Commissioners, a body established in 1853. Besides maintaining the official register, the Commissioners promote the effective use of funds raised, hold (in the hands of an

Official Custodian), investments made by charities and remit income to them and generally administer the law relating to charities. The law's main benefit is to confer upon charitable organisations tax repayments that add £75million to their total income of £300 million. But it is ambiguous and antiquated, dating back over 350 years.

To qualify as a charity an organisation must carry out works that are to the public good, but do not involve political activity. To define these imprecise concepts is the Commissioners' task and it is causing them considerable discomfort. The report published in the autumn of 1975 by the House of Commons Expenditure Committee on the Charity Commissioners and their Accountability criticised their 'backwater image'; it hoped that legislation would be introduced to permit political activity by charities so long as this remained subordinate to their main purpose, which charities should be required to show was 'beneficial to the community'.

The problems of the present laws were highlighted by the fact that a number of charities expressed fears to the researchers of this Directory that inclusion would jeopardise their status. Many, however, who pursue their aims openly and vigorously, such as Oxfam or Age Concern, were happy to be included. Other organisations, such as the Disablement Income Group and the Friends of the Earth, have set up separate bodies to distinguish between their promotional, propaganda work and their charitable activities. All organisations that are registered charities, and they are found throughout the Directory, are included as bodies who by their work represent or act on behalf of an interest or cause, and their status is clearly indicated.

II — ACTIVITY AND RESPONSE: AVENUES OF PRESSURE

No organised body is a pressure group unless it is active in seeking ways of influencing authority, directly or indirectly. And no pressure group will be successful unless its activity elicits a favourable response, by using the right methods, applied in the right quarter at the right time. The means to this end are varied.

Pressure groups and parliament

One of the traditional avenues open to groups trying to put pressure on governments or to translate their aims into legislation is to enlist the support of Members of Parliament. The House of Commons is itself a bundle of assorted interests, as Sir Winston Churchill described:

> Everybody here has private interests, some are directors of companies, some own property which may be affected by legislation which is passing and so forth . . . Then there are those people who come to represent public bodies, particular groups of a non-political character in the general sense, and there again we must recognise that as one of the conditions of our varied life . . . We are not supposed to be an assembly of gentlemen who have no interests of any kind and no association of any kind. That is ridiculous. That might apply in Heaven, but not, happily, here . . .
>
> (Quoted in Finer, *Anonymous Empire*, pp 46–47.)

Besides the associations that arise even before a member is elected, as a result of his earlier business or professional background, organisations frequently enlist the services of a sympathetic backbencher as an honorary vice-president or committee member, or pay him a fee to act as its representative and spokesman in the House; this adds prestige to the pressure group and goes some way to ensure that its interests will not altogether be neglected in parliament. On a more formal basis a body can sponsor the candidature of a prospective member, as is the case with over a hundred Labour MPs, who are sponsored by trade unions and a handful under the sponsorship of co-operative societies. Members backed in this way are, however, expected by the parties to follow the party whip rather than support the union's line should the two conflict. As Yorkshire miners' leader Arthur Scargill was sharply reminded by the Commons in 1975, sponsored MPs are not delegates of single organisations appointed to carry out their wishes above all else, but are representatives of

11

whole constituencies. The distinction does indeed underline the whole concept of democracy and representation in Britain.

Since Churchill's day the public attitude to the outside interests and connections of a number of prominent politicians, the practice of MPs being retained by public relations firms employed by foreign governments to improve their images, the danger that some politicians would use their public positions to advance private interests, combined to produce a demand for a register of members' interests, the first edition of which was published, with few surprises, in 1975.

Having overcome the initial hurdles, what does a pressure group expect from its parliamentary supporters? This depends on the relationship: obviously a sponsored MP will be expected to do more for the organisation concerned than a member who is an informal, sympathetic contact. Whatever the terms, the member's cooperation will be sought to defend the group's interests if legislation that affects them is introduced. In this defensive role an MP will be provided with briefing material and possibly suggested amendments to a bill. A pressure group with adequate research and information facilities can play a constructive part in adding to the pool of informed opinion, either in the debate on second reading where the whole principle of a bill is thrashed out, or in the committee stage, where minute examination of the bill is undertaken, clause by clause, and where amendments and new provisions can be introduced. Technical advice to an active member at this stage of the legislative process is precisely the kind of well-timed and directed activity that can ensure some success for a pressure group working within the system.

In a more assertive way, groups — and it is very often those in the promotional category — can lobby a backbencher about to introduce a Private Member's Bill and try to persuade him to adopt their proposal. Some organisations, such as the RSPCA and the National Council for Civil Liberties, with their own lawyers drafting bills, play a very positive part in advancing their causes in this way, although a relatively small number of Private Members' Bills reach the statute book in their intended form.

Additionally an MP pledged to help a pressure group can be prompted to ask questions of the appropriate minister, either orally if he is challenging a policy, or in writing if he is seeking factual information buried in a government department; or to speak on behalf of the group in debates, in party committees, or put his name to motions. For the well-organised pressure group the parliamentary representative is a reliable contact to whom they have guaranteed access as and when the need arises. The MP can also be an avenue through which ministers may be approached; the tendency is, however, increasingly for pressure groups to approach government departments independently, cutting out the backbench MP.

Pressure groups and government

It is the aim of all pressure groups to see its aims translated into action by government. Pressure through political parties and in campaigns to arouse public opinion are means to this end. One of the most striking features in the development of the pressure group in modern times, however, has been the growth of direct contact between interest groups and Whitehall departments. As the task of government has become more complex and technical, and its involvement in economic and social affairs ever more extensive, the liaison between the machinery of bureaucracy and technocracy has grown closer.

This growth has been two-way: interest groups seek favourable policies and information on decisions affecting their spheres of activity; departments, weighing up priorities and advising ministers, seek expert advice, and, in the administration of laws, depend upon goodwill and cooperation of industrial and professional organisations.

The intricate web of relations has many aspects, informal and formal. Bodies such as the TUC and the CBI are consulted at the highest levels, while they and their individual member organisations contribute to a wide range of government work, with representatives on committees, working parties and specialised study groups. Single organisations, such as the British Medical Association or the National Farmers' Union, working with the Department of Health and Social Security and the Ministry of Agriculture respectively, have been involved at the centre of policy making. They have indeed been indispensable to the work of government; as one former Conservative minister remarked of the role of interest groups, although they were 'formed as a weapon of offence and defence against government, they have now become a necessity to government, so much so that where a group does not exist, the government finds it necessary to invent one'. (Ian Gilmour in *The Body Politic*, p 346.)

The inevitability of close contact between government and certain interests contains some dangers; firstly, that the authority and expertise of an organisation lead to its participation in official business in a way that changes its function from being a pressure group to a part of the bureaucracy itself; secondly, that an organisation enjoying such a position may only have regard to its own interests at the expense of a full consideration of wider, public interests. In this context, pressure group politics are as Ian Gilmour observes 'closed politics' that have the effect of 'extending the field of government secrecy and scarcely adding to the field of public controversy'.

The claims of no sectional interest can be incorporated into government machinery without some degree of political or public debate. For powerful established groups, propagandist campaigning is very much a second line of approach; for promotional groups, however, who with some notable exceptions do not enjoy such intimate relations with government departments, it is the main avenue of pressure.

Publicity and campaigning
One of the keys to success for any kind of pressure group today — and this applies as much to interest groups as to promotional ones — is the purveying of information. For specialist requirements this means research documents, background information, briefing materials, technical journals, and the giving of advice when and where it is needed. For mass communication, information means press conferences and releases, advertising (for those who can afford to pay for it), newspapers, magazines and pamphlets for general consumption, and through spokesmen and interviews on radio and television.

14

The communications media, academic or popular, are vitally important to group interests competing for the attention of those in
authority and position of influence, and of the public. President
Giscard d'Estaing recently drew attention to the influences of French
pressure groups in mass communication, and sounded a warning:

> ... I do not think television directors and journalists say to themselves:
> I will say this or that because a pressure group asks me to do so. On the
> other hand, you can be influenced by pressure groups because they are
> very skilled. They spread information or create an atmosphere, and from
> time to time we perceive the echoes of campaigns which in fact reach as
> far as information. (*The Times*, 8 January 1976)

To find its way into the mass media a story must have impact: the
dramatic, unusual or controversial will catch the eyes of news editor
and reader alike. In this competitive world pressure through publicity
is subject to commercial rather than strictly moral criteria. Alone it
may not be enough. Organisations such as Shelter, particularly during
the latter half of the 1960s, produced publicity and advertising of
considerable emotional power, depicting scenes of poverty and homeless families. Yet although this did much to arouse widespread public
concern, action by central government to eradicate the problem did
not ensue, and Shelter's results were achieved through the use of
funds donated by the public in local initiatives. Thus despite the
initial impression made by Shelter and the public's reaction, the
national total of homeless people has increased in the years since its
formation.

Pressure through mass publicity therefore needs supplementing in
other ways. Here specialist information, to convince government
departments, ministers, and MPs directly, plays an important part;
but this too is a competitive business for vast amounts of material
arrive each day on the desks of MPs and officials. Trite handouts
find their way into waste-paper baskets, while well-documented
reports, authoritatively researched, professionally produced, and
perhaps covered by a forceful, factual summary of the main points,
demand attention. The ability to produce material of this kind is as
important to an industrial concern or a trade union as it is to a
promotional group attempting to alleviate a social problem. The
academic disciplines employed may be different but it is the
intellectual quality that counts, 'guaranteed' with support or

contributions from distinguished figures in an appropriate field. As one student of pressure groups has said: 'Some social and intellectual prestige is necessary to ensure that your information is what the best people believe to be the best'. (W J M Mackenzie, 'Pressure groups in British government' in Richard Rose (ed), *Studies in British Politics*.)

In the context of appealing to public opinion more direct methods can be adopted, in meetings, rallies, marches and demonstrations. The less sympathy a group has in Whitehall, the more likely it is to embark upon a mass campaign of this sort. When an interest with established access to official circles sets itself on such a course, it is usually a sign that the normal channels have failed. Whether an organisation has the inclination or capacity to mount a large scale public campaign depends on many variable internal factors. An industrial or professional body has identifiable degree of support in its existing membership; it will also probably be blessed with a London head office and a regional or branch structure through which it can mobilise its members. It is in these ways easy to measure whether the organisation truly represents its industry or profession or not, and although the public may not be invited to join the organisation, the degree of the representativeness will have its effect on public opinion and on authority. The established interest group also has a head start in finding funds for publicity and advertising. Indeed the same resources that had previously enabled it to speak with authority directly to government will now enable it to put pressure on them with the additional weapons of public support from other groups and the media.

The situation is however very different for the group attempting to promote a cause. It will probably depend on the energies of a few individual activists, probably located in a London office close to the centres of power and the media. It will probably be relatively short of funds and its 'grass-roots' membership scattered. It is also impossible to measure how representative an organisation is that protests against cruelty to animals or opposes the relaxation of censorship in the cinema. They do not speak for a definable social or economic interest and theoretically the whole population could join them. Such groups must attempt to enlist the support of celebrities and distinguished people from many walks of life, and to

16

capture the imagination of press and public with a central message. If support is numerically significant or socially prestigious, and the media sympathetic, then authority may be forced to take account of a powerful current of opinion. Public campaigns are not however divorced from other areas of activity.

The Campaign for Nuclear Disarmament offers one of the most famous examples in modern times of a promotional pressure group attempting to influence government through a mass movement, while at the same time trying to work in the political arena through the Labour Party and trade unions. The latter met with temporary success, but both wings of the CND have failed to produce the desired response and since the mid 1960s the movement has faded in the public consciousness. Public campaigns of a different kind by various industries to prevent their nationalisation have also met with failure; the two pronged attacks of massive and expensive press publicity combined with lobbying through conventional political channels have been unable to sway governments set upon a policy. The fate of such campaigns and movements demonstrate that promotional pressure groups can rarely overturn the pledges of a government to the electorate, or replace people's loyalty to a political party by an allegiance to one cause or section.

A pressure group faced with intransigent authority and without influence at court, but possessing a definable degree of active support, may be tempted to embrace direct action. Other factors may also lead organisations into activities such as the occupation of offices or empty houses, sit-down demonstrations, daubing walls with slogans, digging up cricket pitches or disrupting meetings. They may have become impatient with the lethargy or unresponsiveness of bureaucracy or feel that the conventional channels of negotiation and discussion have been exhausted; alternatively, as is the case of many radical groups, direct action appeals for ideological reasons.

Its purposes are often symbolic, to capture the headlines or to make a gesture of defiance, but direct action can be turned to obtain concrete results where other methods have failed. Local community action groups have found this to be so, and the squatting movement in particular has mushroomed from its ideologically inspired beginnings in 1968 to include 30,000 people living as squatters, some with the recognition of councils who acknowledge squatting as a short-term remedy to homelessness.

One of the facts of life in modern industrial societies is the capacity of concentrated, organised groups of workers in essential service industries to put pressure on government, employers and the public by use of the strike weapon, with effects no section of the community can escape. It surpasses all other forms of direct action used by pressure groups and sectional interests; it raises the whole question of the balance of power and influence between component sections, on which representative democracy rests.

III – THE ROLE OF PRESSURE GROUPS

Pressure groups exist to speak for sectional interests or associations of like-minded individuals, to influence government policies, either by direct contact, or indirectly through political parties or the effect of public opinion. Such freedoms of association, discussion and lobbying do not exist in totalitarian states, and the diversity of interests is lacking in more primitive societies. Pressure groups are therefore characteristic of open political systems in the process of change.

What their present-day level of activity tells us about the state of democracy is, however, a subject for debate. One extreme view is that sectional interests exercise too much influence, and that in effect they dictate the way Britain is run at the expense of elected politicians. The counter argument is that in the last decade the explosion in promotional group activity, particularly among radical organisations, indicates a reawakening in the arid grass-roots of democracy, which is offsetting domination by central government and powerful economic interests of business and finance. Some truth attaches to both these arguments. The question is whether the purpose of pressure groups is to participate in the machinery of government, to secure the best deal for the interests they represent, or whether it is to remain outside government, to retain their links with the sections of the community from which they spring and so protest more effectively on their behalf.

In modern Britain it appears that the first function is the one that has attained the highest level of development. Compared with the United States for example, interest groups are more thoroughly organised and representative of their particular groups and they have cultivated closer, more effective contacts with government departments. In the United States, however, individual Congressmen are more susceptible to the rival demands of pressure groups than the British Member of Parliament who is protected by a more tightly drawn party organisation and the traditions of parliamentary privilege. The greater influence of British interests at the centre of national affairs applies not only to business and the professions but also to the trade union movement. Besides the industrial power that it has at its disposal, its special role derives from its relationship with the Labour Party (the unions provide seven-eighths of its members and three-quarters of its income), and its function in solidifying the collective aspirations of a substantial strata of society. Alone among interest groups, the trade union movement is a measurable economic, political and social force.

The growth of close working relationships between government and sectional interests is a product, firstly of the increasing part played by central authority in the regulation of economic and social affairs, and secondly, of the greater technical complexity of those affairs, which calls for expertise often to be found in specialised interest groups. In the creation of a welfare state and the expansion of its provisions, and in the nationalisation of large sectors of industry, government departments are called upon to administer more and more laws. To do this they need the co-operation of employers, professions, trade unions, and academics, and to have it on committees, commissions, tribunals and working groups.

Promotional groups however, especially radical ones, would prefer to consider themselves immune from incorporation into a scheme in which bureaucracy and technocracy work hand in hand. But there are signs that their causes, too, lead to further growth in the government machine. The demands for sexual equality, vigorously pursued by the pressure groups of women's liberation, contributed to the passing of an act which set up the Equal Opportunities Commission; protest and pressure had resulted in the creation of another agency

19

of government. This institutionalisation of protest involves also the establishment by government, with public funds, of organisations intended to become pressure groups against it. Grants are also given to community action groups to enable them to carry on in situations where there is no spontaneous or indigenous demand for a group from the community itself. One of the effects of artificially inspired pressure groups at the local level is to detract from the mainstream of political life, by drawing people away from party branches in favour of possible short-term gains through pressure group action. Over a prolonged period such a tendency would weaken basic political institutions and strengthen bureaucratic control over fragmented sectional groups that lack a coherent view of policy and which are at the mercy of government funds. Sectional interests of any kind speak only for themselves and it is the duty of political parties to take a wider perspective on questions of social and economic priorities.

The traditional strength of British pressure groups has been that they have spoken for genuine interests and sincere causes, that they have not sought power for their own narrow ends and have retained a substantial degree of independence from government control. Today, the power wielded by the big battalions of industry — multi-national companies and the trade unions — augurs the growth of a corporate state that would undermine the parliamentary system. And at the other end of the scale, numerous, fragmented promotional groups are contributing — albeit unintentionally — to the debility of national political life. Pressure groups may be an integral part of a democracy, but interests that become too powerful or divisive signify an unhealthy rather than a healthy state of public affairs.

IV – NOTES ON THE SURVEY AND THE DIRECTORY

The questionnaire

The researchers compiled a list of potential entrants from publications such as *Whitaker's Almanac* and the *Directory of British Associations*, newspapers, including *The Guardian* and *The Times*, and telephone directories.

The information requested on the questionnaire was as follows:

Name and organisation and initials
Address
Telephone, telex and cables number

Aims
Status (e.g. charity, limited company)
Principal officers
Prominent members/member organisations
Number of full-time staff
Current membership
Membership fees
Membership qualification or restrictions
Officers for PR, press, advertising
Representatives in parliament and on official bodies
Publications
Regional/branch offices
Links with other organisations
Brief history
Recent activities and future plans

Completed returns were received from approximately half of the organisations to whom questionnaires were sent. On a sample of returns the researchers looked for any significant factors relating to the age of groups, publications, membership, the location of the group's headquarters, and the number of full-time staff.

Of 184 organisations whose date of formation was noted, exactly half, i.e. 92, had been founded in the 1960s or 1970s (55 and 37 in each decade respectively). The rest were fairly evenly spread with 14 organisations formed in the 1900s, 15 in the 1940s and 18 in the 1950s. This certainly seems to bear out the argument that there has been something of an explosion in recent years although of course the most recently established ones are the most likely to be active today.

21

The membership figures of 191 organisations were gathered, with the following result:

Not a membership organisation	33
Not stated	15
Under 1,000	43
1,000 to 2,500	25
2,500 to 5,000	26
5,000 to 10,000	13
10,000 to 25,000	14
25,000 to 50,000	10
Over 50,000	12

Those who were not membership organisations included charities, umbrella organisations for other groups, and some promotional campaigns. The under 1,000 membership category was overwhelmingly dominated by newer promotional groups and political fringe organisations.

As regards publications, out of 164 groups taken as a sample, 35 said they had no regular publications. Of the 129 remaining, 20 had two publications, giving the following result:

More than once monthly	6
Monthly	41
Bi-monthly	29
Quarterly	35
Other/not stated	38

Of these journals, magazines, newspapers and bulletins, 43 were issued to members only, all but one of which were free of charge.

On the location of the principal office of a sample of 199 groups, nearly two-thirds had addresses in Greater London. This was to be expected, since the survey was concerned with national organisations, who would wish to deal with Parliament, Whitehall and the national media, as well as other pressure groups. The overall figures were:

Central London	87
Outer London	38
Southern England	31
Midlands	8
North of England	19
Wales	4
Scotland	8
Northern Ireland	4

A total of 197 groups were studied to see how many full-time staff were employed and this figure related to the size of the organisation.

Number of members	Organisations with staff	Total organisations in category
Under 1,000	18	43
1,000 to 5,000	24	51
5,000 to 10,000	11	13
10,000 to 25,000	7	14
25,000 to 50,000	9	10
Over 50,000	11	12

Of the remaining organisations 33 had no membership but did have staff, and the rest did not give the relevant information. As might have been expected, the larger the group the more likely it was to have staff. Only twelve organisations had more than 100 full-time staff, whereas 69 had less than ten full-time workers.

On samples of these sizes, the information gathered can only suggest some general features.

The arrangement of the Directory

For ease of reference the Directory is divided into twelve subject categories:

1 *Political:* includes the main parties, subsidiaries, pressure groups and factions within parties, other organisations on their fringes, organisations of the ultra-left and right, and bodies concerned with the electoral or constitutional procedures of the political system.

2 *Employers', industrial and professional organisations*

3 *Trade Unions*

4 *Consumer group and miscellaneous economic interests and campaigns:* includes organisations that are active on financial or economic issues but do not represent any of the major interests in categories 2 or 3.

5 *International:* includes British branches of international organisations and groups concerned mainly with some aspect of international affairs, including the EEC.

6   *Social:* the broadest category, including organisations which represent particular sections of the community and minority groups; and organisations concerned with the welfare of sections of society or which seek social reforms.

7   *Women's organisations*

8   *Health and medical:* besides professional interests includes groups campaigning for reforms in health services or in medical practice.

9   *Educational, scientific and cultural:* including academic and research bodies for specialised subjects.

10 *Religious and ethical:* includes churches, associated bodies and organisations whose main concerns are for man's spiritual or moral well-being.

11 *Environmental:* includes those organisations concerned with the conservation of historic buildings, natural resources, ecology, and the effects of technological development and pollution on the environment.

12 *Animal welfare and protection:* an area of concern traditionally associated with pressure group activity in Britain.

Abbreviations in the Directory

Publications

a	=	annual
bi-a	=	bi-annual
bi-m	=	bi-monthly
d	=	daily
f	=	fortnightly
m	=	monthly
q	=	quarterly
w	=	weekly

A section number given in brackets after an organisation is mentioned under 'Connections' means that the main reference to that organisation will be found in that section.

DIRECTORY

ALLIANCE PARTY OF NORTHERN IRELAND
6 Cromwell Road, Belfast BT7 1JW
Telephone: Belfast 24274/5, 28724

Aims	To support the constitutional position of Northern Ireland as part of the UK; to heal the bitter divisions in the community by equality in all spheres of life and the rooting out of all discriminations and injustice, and participation by all in political, economic and public life.

Officers		
	Chairman	Denis Loretto
	Vice Chairman	Dr Jack Smith
	General Secretary	John Cushnahan
	Party Organiser	Robin Glendenning
	Party Leader	Oliver Napier
	Deputy Leader	Bob Cooper

Staff 5

Membership 15,000   **Fees:** 50p p.a.

Branches 34 through Northern Ireland.

Publications *Alliance* (m)

History Formed in 1970 to attract support of moderates both Catholic and Protestant. When Stormont was prorogued in March 1972, the Party had three sitting members. It took part with Faulkner Unionists (1) and SDLP in the power sharing executive – Oliver Napier was Minister for Law Reform and Bob Cooper was Minister of Manpower Services.

ANARCHIST WORKERS ASSOCIATION
13 Coltman Street, Hull, Yorkshire

Aims To aid the preparation of the working class for their seizure of power, and the establishment of an anarchist society.

Officers *National Secretary*   N Heath

Membership Do not wish to disclose.

Publications *Libertarian Struggle* (m); *Libertarian Communist Review* (q)

History Emerged from now defunct Anarchist Federation of Britain. Formed March 1971 and known as Organisation of Revolutionary Anarchists until January 1975.

27

BOW GROUP
240 High Holborn, London WC1V 7TD
Telephone: 01-405 0878

Aims	To cater for younger Conservatives with active interest in political and social problems.
Membership	1,000
Publications	*Crossbow* (q)
History	Founded 1951.

BRITISH AND IRISH COMMUNIST ORGANISATION
10 Athol Street, Belfast BT 12 4GX
Telephone: Belfast 0232-25851

Aims	To build a Communist Party of Britain and Ireland capable of giving effective leadership to the working class in its struggle against the capitalist class and the capitalist system of production through class exploitation, and for a system of production for use based on the collective ownership of the means of production in a society in which the working class has made itself the ruling class.	
Officers	*Secretary*	Angela Clifford
Membership	Not stated	Fees: None
Regional Offices	Two	
Publications	*The Communist* (m); *The Irish Communist* (m); *Problems of Communism* (q); *Comment* (f); numerous pamphlets on British, Irish and international politics	
Connections	Affiliated to Institute for Workers Control (1); Workers Association for the Democratic Settlement of the National Conflict in Ireland; Communists for Europe (5).	
History	Formed September 1965.	

BRITISH WITHDRAWAL FROM NORTHERN IRELAND CAMPAIGN (BWNIC)
c/o 5 Caledonian Road, London N1

Aims The ending of the union between Northern Ireland and Great Britain; the withdrawal of troops from Northern Ireland.

Publications *BWNIC Bulletin* (occasional)

Connections War Resisters International, Brussels; Love, Peace and Justice, Dublin.

History Formed June 1973, it repudiates the official and Provisional IRA and protestant para-military groups. Fourteen of its members members were acquitted in 1975 on charges under the Incitement to Disaffection Act 1934.

COMMITTEE FOR DEMOCRATIC REGIONAL GOVERNMENT IN THE NORTH OF ENGLAND
c/o Wood Cottage, Ewood Lane, Todmorden, Lancashire OL14 7DF
Telephone: 070681 2510

Aims Promotion of democratic over existing regional administration; transfer of effective political and economic powers from the central government in London to one (or more) regional governments in the North of England, accountable to a democratically elected assembly(ies) or parliament(s).

Officers *Chairman* Michael Steed
Honorary Secretary Paul Temperton

Publications *Northern Democrat* (at least 8 issues p.a.).

History Formed in late 1974. Activities include presentation of specific proposals to MPs from North of England (area covered by North, North West and Yorkshire/Humberside Standard Regions) for extension to the region of any legislation for devolution.

COMMUNIST LEAGUE
26 Cambridge Road, Ilford, Essex
Telephone: 01-509 9977

Aims	The building of a Marxist-Leninist Party free of all revisionist trends.

Officers	*Chairman*	William Bland
	Secretary	Bernard Charnley

Membership	Not published.	Fees: 2½% of income.

Publications	*COMbat* (3 times p.a.); *COMpass* (twice p.a.); *InterCOM* (twice p.a.)

History	Formed as Marxist-Leninist Organisation of Britain at conference in 1967. Became Communist League in 1975.

COMMUNIST PARTY OF GREAT BRITAIN
16 King Street, London WC2 8HY
Telephone: 01-836 2151   Cables: Communal Rand London

Aims	To achieve a socialist Britain in which the means of production distribution and exchange will be socially-owned and used in a planned way for the benefit of all. This necessitates a revolutionary transformation of society, ending the existing capitalist system with its exploitation of man by man, and replacing it by a socialist society in which each will contribute according to his ability and receive according to his work. Socialist society creates the conditions for advance to a fully communist system of society in which each will receive according to his needs.

Officers	*General Secretary*	Gordon McLennan
	Chairman	Mick McGahey
	Industrial Organiser	Bert Ramelson

Prominent Members	John Gollan, Ken Gill, Kevin Halpin

Membership	28,000	Fees: 25p per month; pensioners 5p.

Staff	28

Publications	*Morning Star* (d); *Comment* (f); *Marxism Today* (m).

Regional Offices	Overstrand, Norfolk; Emsworth, Hants; Chatham; London; Birmingham; Nottingham; Oxford; Luton; Newcastle; Manchester; Liverpool; Glasgow; Ilford; Colliers Wood; Brighton; Cardiff; Bristol; Southall; Leeds; Sheffield.

History	Formed in 1920.

30

CONSERVATIVE ACTION FOR ELECTORAL REFORM (CAER)
6 Queen Street, Mayfair, London W1
Telephone: 01-629 2791

Aims	To promote electoral reform and persuade the Conservative Party that this would benefit both the country and the party.	
Officers	*Director*	Anthony Wigram
	Assistant Director	Candida Cooper
Staff	3	
Membership	None	
Publications	*Additional Seats Electoral System; Odd Man Out* (an outline of 17 parliamentary democracies); *Five Points for Freedom.*	
Connections	Conservative Party	
History	Formed June 1974 by Anthony Wigram. Activities include research, preparation and dissemination of information.	

See also National Union of Conservative and Unionist Associations — Page 44.

ELECTORAL REFORM SOCIETY OF GREAT BRITAIN AND IRELAND
(Company limited by guarantee)
6 Chancel Street, Southwark, London SE1 0UX
Telephone: 01-928 9407

Aims	The principal object is to secure the adoption of the single transferable vote (preferential voting with quota counting) in multi-member constituencies, for elections in the British Isles and elsewhere, for parliaments, for provincial, regional and local authorities, and for other public and semi-public bodies; also recommends the use of STV to other organisations for all their elections.	
Officers	*President*	Sir Dingle Foot
	Chairman	R A Newland
	Director	Miss E Lakeman
	Controller of Ballot Services	Major F S Britton
Prominent Members	Dame Margery Corbett-Ashby, Lord Avebury, Lord Gladwyn, J B Priestley, Lord Rea.	
Staff	8	
Membership	800	**Fees:** Minimum £1.25 p.a. (£1 by Bankers Order).
Publications	*Representation* (q); other occasional publications.	

History Founded as Proportional Representation Society in 1884 and reconstituted 1905. Became Electoral Reform Society in 1959. Incorporated 1969. Plans include campaigning for PR/STV to be used in Scottish and Welsh Assemblies, regional, county and district elections in GB, and European Parliament. The society through its ballot services department acts as independent returning officers for a number of trade unions, professional and other organisations.

ENGLISH NATIONAL PARTY
76 Lock Chase, Blackheath, London SE3 0HA
Telephone: 01-852 0627/6728

Aims To become 'the voice and spirit of England — Freedom; Justice; Vision. Independence for England'. Seeks the restoration of individual freedom in place of corporate state; restoration of English parliament; abolition of income tax; end to local authority housing; building of 16-lane immersed Thames Tunnel to link existing London motorways; a spiritual rebirth of faith and religion.

Officers *Chairman* Dr Frank Hansford-Miller
Hon Secretary Mrs Fiona Saffery
Hon Treasurer Mrs Phyllis Hansford-Miller
PRO Bob Brown
Northern Area Robin Atkinson

Prominent Member John Stonehouse MP

Membership 1,000. Members must have love of England and concern for England's future.

Fees £2 p.a. (reduction for OAPs and others in need).

Branches Banbury; Barnstaple; Maxborough; Manchester.

Publications *ENP: Save England Crusade.*

Connections Fraternal with Scottish National Party and Plaid Cymru.

History Founded in 1966 as John Hampden New Freedom Party. Fought both 1974 General Elections and four elections for local government. Holds meetings of parliaments in Birmingham, Bristol and Leeds, and a St George's Day rally in Trafalgar Square and provincial cities.

FABIAN SOCIETY
11 Dartmouth Street, London SW1H 9BN
Telephone: 01-930 3077

Aims	The establishment of a society in which equality of opportunity will be assured and the economic power and privileges of individuals and classes abolished through the collective ownership and democratic control of the economic resources of the community; to secure these aims by the methods of political democracy; the implementation of the Charter of the UN and the Universal Declaration of Human Rights; the creation of effective international institutions to uphold and enforce world peace.

Officers		
	Chairman	Nicholas Bosanquet
	Vice-Chairman	Colin Crouch
	Treasurer	Giles Radice MP
	General Secretary	Tom Ponsonby

Prominent Members	110 Labour MPs including Sir Harold Wilson, Denis Healey, Tony Benn, Shirley Williams, Antony Crosland, Barbara Castle, Jim Callaghan, Roy Jenkins.
Staff	9
Membership	5,500 **Fees:** £3–£9 depending on publications required
Regions and Branches	Regional Committees in Oldham; Newcastle; Dunfermline; Bristol. 107 Local branches.
Publications	*Fabian News* (m) members newsletter; *Third World* (every month); many pamphlets and tracts.
Connections	Affiliated to Labour Party (1).
History	Formed 1884. Prominent members have included Sidney and Beatrice Webb, George Bernard Shaw, Clem Attlee and Hugh Gaitskell.

INDEPENDENT LABOUR PUBLICATIONS
49 Top Moor Side, Leeds LS11 9LW
Telephone: 0542 30613

Aims	An association of socialists committed to the establishment of a socialist society, it seeks to maintain and strengthen the influence of socialist ideas, and to contribute towards the development, through its publications, of analysis, perspective and policy within the labour movement.

Independent Labour Publications (continued)

Officers	*Chairman*	Stan Iveson
	Treasurer	Don Bateman
	Secretary	Barry Winter

Membership Not stated. **Fees: £1.80 p.a.**

Publications *Socialist Leader* (m); *Square One Pamphlets* published by New Leader Ltd.

Connections Affiliated to Liberation; Institute for Workers Control (1); International Association of Labour History Institutions.

History Founded 1893, the Independent Labour Party acted as progenitor of the Labour Party. Organised the opposition to the first world war and was instrumental in developing within the Labour Party the constituency propaganda activity which resulted in the first minority Labour Government of 1924. Supported 1926 General Strike. Disaffiliated from Labour Party in 1932. Active in support of anti-fascist forces in Spanish Civil War. Opposed development of nuclear deterrent. Changed name in 1975, and pledged support to Labour Party and Trade Union movement. Conducted anti-common market campaign.

INSTITUTE FOR WORKERS' CONTROL
Bertrand Russell House, Gamble Street, Nottingham NG7 4ET
Telephone: 0602 74504

Aims To assist in the formation of workers' control groups dedicated to the development of democratic consciousness, to win support for workers' control in all the existing organisations of labour; to challenge undemocratic actions and to extend democratic control over industry and the economy itself by assisting the unification of workers' control groups into a national force in the socialist movement.

Officers	*Chairman*	Bill Jones
	Vice-Chairmen	Brian Nicholson, Audrey Wise MP
	Secretary	Ken Fleet
	Treasurer	Harry Newton
	Editors	Steve Bodington, Chris Farley

Prominent Members Tony Benn MP, Eric Heffer MP, Michael Meacher MP, Stan Orme MP, Jack Jones, Ernie Roberts, Walt Greendale, Arthur Palmer MP, Michael Barratt Brown, Ken Coates, Tony Topham.

Parliamentary Representatives (unpaid): Stan Newens, Neil Kinnock,
Jo Richardson, Harry Selby, Tom Litterick, Ron Thomas.

Membership   Not stated.   **Fees:** £3 p.a.

Publications   *Workers' Control Bulletin* (m); *Pamphlet Series* (6–12 p.a.);
various books and pamphlets.

History   Founded 1968 at Nottingham conference of 500 trade union
delegates addressed by Hugh Scanlon, Ian Mikardo MP and
others. The Sheffield Conference 1969 attracted 1,000 delegates;
the figure rose to 1,200 delegates at Newcastle in 1972 on work-
ins, sit-ins and the problems of unemployment. Numerous special
industry seminars are held every year and it has supported a
number of work-ins and experiments in workers' co-operatives.

INTERNATIONAL MARXIST GROUP
182 Pentonville Road, London N1
Telephone: 01-837 6954

Aims   To bring about international socialist revolution in which the
working class will take power.

Prominent   Tariq Ali, Robin Blackburn, Fred Halliday, Pat Jordan.
Members

Membership   (estimated) 1,000 – 1,500

Publications   *Red Weekly* (formerly *Red Mole*); *International; Socialist Woman;*
numerous books and pamphlets.

Connections   With groups in over 20 countries through the Trotskyist Fourth
International of which it has been the British section since 1969.

History   Founded in 1965. A founder member of the Vietnam Solidarity
Campaign (1966) and the Revolutionary Socialist Students
Federation (1968). It has been associated with many single-issue
campaigns and demonstrations.

INTERNATIONAL SOCIALISTS
6 Cottons Gardens, London E2 8DN
Telephone: 01-739 1878

Aims	The overthrow of capitalism by revolution and not reformism; the establishment of socialism which can only be achieved by independent action of the working class; a workers' state based on councils of work place delegates; the abandonment of all nuclear weapons and military alliances such as the Warsaw and NATO Pacts; unconditional support for all genuine liberation movements.
Prominent Members	Paul Foot, Tony Cliff, Duncan Hallas.
Membership	3,000
Publications	*Socialist Worker* (w); *International Socialism* (m), 25p; also pamphlets, books, leaflets etc.
Connections	National Rank and File Movement; Pluto Press.
History	Formed in 1950 as a breakaway from Trotskyism.

LABOUR ACTION FOR PEACE
81 Orchard Avenue, Croydon CR0 7NF
Telephone: 01-654 5811

Aims	To influence Labour Party foreign and defence policies; to expose the critical and vulnerable situation of Britain caused by provocative nuclear missile bases located on land and in British waters; to expose the potential economic breakdown of Britain caused by excessive and crippling defence expenditure; opposition to arms export sales, especially to the Third World.	
Officers	*Chairman*	Frank Allaun MP
	Vice-Chairman	Lord Brockway, John Mendelson MP, Albert Booth MP, Renee Short MP, Stanley Newens MP, Arthur Latham MP
	Honorary Secretary	Harry W Robertson
	Editor and PR	R W Huzzard
Prominent Members	Lord Soper, Hugh Scanlon, Gordon Schaffer, Lord Taylor of Mansfield; about 70 Labour MPs mainly from Tribune Group including Jo Richardson, Robin Cook.	
Membership	460 **Fees:** individual £1 p.a.; affiliated organisation £2.	
Qualifications	Must be member of Labour Party or of an organisation eligible for affiliation.	

Publications   *Labour Peace Newsletter* (5–6 times p.a.); occasional broad-sheets.

Connections   Affiliated to CND (5); International Peace Bureau (Geneva); Campaign Against Arms Trade; Anti-Apartheid Movement (5) and others. 81 constituency Labour Parties are affiliated to LAP.

History   Formed in 1940 as Labour Peace Fellowship. Changed to Labour Action for Peace in 1970. Lobbies at Labour Party annual conference. Periodic deputations to Ministry of Defence and Foreign and Commonwealth Office. Public meetings at House of Commons and elsewhere. Plans to stimulate action in and out of parliament towards dismantlement of NATO and Warsaw Pact and the creation of a new All-European Security Pact.

LABOUR PARTY
Transport House, Smith Square, London SW1P 3JA
Telephone: 01-834 0434   Cables: Labrepcom Sowest

Aims   'To organise and maintain in Parliament and in the country a Political Labour Party; to secure for the workers by hand or by brain the full fruits of their industry and the most equitable distribution thereof that may be possible upon the basis of the common ownership of the means of production, distribution, and exchange, and the best obtainable system of popular administration and control of each industry or service. Generally, to promote the Political, Social and Economic Emancipation of the People and more particularly of those who depend directly upon their own exertions by hand or by brain for the means of life. Internationally to co-operate with other labour and socialist organisations overseas and to support the UN and other international agencies for peace, human rights and social and economic advancement of the people of the world' (from Clause 4 of the Party Constitution).

Officers
Chairman	Frederick Mulley
Honorary Treasurer	James Callaghan MP
General Secretary	R G Hayward
National Agent	H R Underhill
Secretary, Parliamentary Labour Party	F Barlow
Director of Publicity	Percy Clark

37

Staff	235
Membership	Individuals 665,379; affiliate organisations 5,407,817.
Fees	Individuals £1.20 p.a.; affiliates 17p per member for 1975.
Offices	Regions: Glasgow; Cardiff; Gateshead; Leeds; Salford; Nottingham; Birmingham; Ipswich; Esher; Bristol; London. There are 623 constituency Labour Parties in GB, some with full-time agents.
Publications	*Labour Weekly* (every Friday); *Labour Councillor* (10 issues p.a.); many pamphlets, reports.
Connections	Links with Socialist and Social Democrat parties throughout world through Socialist Internationals. With TUC and Co-operative Union comprises National Council of Labour. TUC—Labour Party Liaison Committee set up 1972.
History	On 27 February 1900 the Independent Labour Party, trade unions, Fabian Society and others met in London to find ways of increasing working class representation in parliament and Labour Representation Committee set up. Six months later two MPs elected and by 1906 (name changed to Labour Party) there were 29 Labour MPs.

First Labour Government took office in 1924 with Ramsay MacDonald as Prime Minister. Party was again successful at 1929 General Election. Joined the coalition during second world war. Won an overwhelming victory in 1945 under Clem Attlee. Held office till 1951 and carried legislation such as the setting up of the National Health Service, nationalisation of the coal industry, railways etc. Hugh Gaitskell became leader in 1955 and when he died in 1963 was replaced by Harold Wilson.

After 13 years in opposition the Labour Party won the 1964 and 1966 General Elections but was defeated in 1970. In February 1974, the Conservative Government was defeated and an overall majority achieved in October 1974.

Other recent activities have included organisation restructuring to fit in with the changes in local government boundaries. Plans include increased representation in parliament and local government; efforts will also be made to improve the party's financial position.

LIBERAL PARTY ORGANISATION
7 Exchange Court, Strand, London WC2 0PR
Telephone: London 01-240 0701

Aims   'To build a liberal society in which every citizen shall possess liberty, property, and security and none shall be enslaved by poverty, ignorance or conformity. Its chief care is for the rights and opportunities of the individual, and in all spheres it sets freedom first' (from the preamble to the Party Constitution).

Officers

Party Leader	Rt Hon Jo Grimond MP *(Interim, May 1976)*	
President	Mrs Margaret Wingfield	
Chairman	Kenneth Vaus	
Leader in the House of Lords	Rt Hon Lord Byers	
Chief Whip	Alan Beith	
Treasurer	Philip Watkins	
Public Relations	David Deeley	

Staff   20 (at headquarters)

Membership   Not stated.   **Fees:** £1 p.a.

Parliamentary Representatives: in the House of Commons 13 MPs and in the House of Lords 40 members take the Liberal Whip.

Regional Offices: 2 in London and in 10 other cities in England.

Other Units of the Organisation: Association of Liberal Councillors; Association of Liberal Trade Unionists; Liberal Agents Association; Liberal Party Organisation Staff Association; National League of Young Liberals (1); The Union of Liberal Students (1); Women's Liberal Federation (7).

Connections   Scottish Liberal Party; Welsh Liberal Party; Ulster Liberal Party; Liberal International; Liberal Social Council.

Publications   *Liberal News* (w); frequent pamphlets etc published by the Liberal Publication Department.

History   A National Liberal Federation was formed in 1877 in Birmingham. The name change to the Liberal Party Organisation did not occur until 1936. It plans in 1977 to hold a number of events to commemorate the centenary of the foundation of the NLF.

MEBYON KERNOW (Sons of Cornwall)
Trewolsta, Trewirgie Hill, Redruth, Cornwall TR15 2TB
Telephone: Rednill 6796

Aims	To maintain the Celtic character of Cornwall and its right to self-government in domestic affairs; to remedy any local conditions prejudicial to the best interests of Cornwall by the creation of informed public opinion and in co-operation with other groups; to press for preference in employment for Cornish people; to foster the study and teaching of the Cornish language, literature, culture, sport and history.

Officers   *Chairman*   R G Jenkins
                Secretary and PR   L H Truran
                Press   D R Rawe

Prominent Members	John Pardoe MP, David Mudd MP, A L Rowse.
Membership	4,000
Fees	50p p.a., Life £10; OAPs and students 25p p.a. Cornish applicants full membership; others associate membership.
Branches	Throughout Cornwall; in London; Plymouth; Bristol; Scotland.
Publications	*Cornish Nation* (q); various booklets.
Connections	Liaison group in Scotland. Member of Federal Union of European Nationalities.
History	Formed 1951 at Redruth following a meeting of a dozen interested people who had been connected with a previous cultural organisation called Tyr ha Tavas (Land and Tongue). Fought its first parliamentary campaign in 1970 at Falmouth—Camborne. Submitted reports to parliamentary committees, including Kilbrandon Commission on the Constitution. Has conducted campaigns for a Cornish postage stamp. Fought last two parliamentary elections for Truro. Future aims are for self-government for Cornwall by constitutional means including parliamentary representation.

MONDAY CLUB
51 Victoria Street, London SW1
Telephone: 01-799 5220   Cables: Mondayclub London

Aims	'An organisation within the Conservative Party dedicated to holding that Party to its basic principles — patriotism and a national cohesion based on fairness; stands for the defence of Britain, her constitution, interests and civilisation; against aggression, subversion and moral corrosion; and upholds the liberty of the individual, the sanctity of the family and the freedom of enterprise. Specifically: freedom of speech, religion and economic activity; compassion in welfare allied to a general acceptance of self-help; role of the State in economic affairs should be drastically reduced; repeal of 1968 Race Relations Act, ending of immigration from new commonwealth and subsidised (voluntary) repatriation; end to Rhodesia sanctions; a return to standards of decency in the media; education to be based on parental choice, encouragement of the independent sector and higher education should be firmly selective.'

Officers	*President*	The Marquess of Salisbury
	Chairman	Sir Victor Raikes
	Director	Cedric Gunnery

Prominent Members	(all MPs) Julian Amery, Alan Clark, Anthony Fell, Mrs Jill Knight, Ivan Lawrence, James Molyneaux, Jasper More, Peter Rost, John Stokes, Edward Taylor, Robert Taylor, Patrick Wall.
Staff	2
Membership	2,000. Must be members of the Conservative and Unionist Party.
Fees	Full £5 p.a.
Branches	20 throughout British Isles.
Publications	*Monday News* (2-monthly); members' newsletter; *Monday World* (q); various pamphlets.
Connections	Conservative Party
History	Founded in 1961 by a group of younger members of the Conservative Party under the patronage of the late Marquess of Salisbury.

NATIONAL FRONT
50 Pawsons Road, Croydon, Surrey CR0 2QF
Telephone: 01-684 3730/4130

Aims	To secure majority representation in parliament and local government to implement policies; to restore to Britain, her parliament and people full national sovereignty in every field; the formation of special trading links with the old Commonwealth; to free Britain from domination by international monopoly capitalism; industrial unionism with workers' participation and profit sharing; to halt all further coloured immigration and to arrange for phased and humane repatriation; to re-establish law and order, freedom of choice and equality in education; to support the Loyalist population in Northern Ireland to remain part of UK; to oppose communism worldwide; to get Britain out of the EEC, UN and all other internationalist and pro-world government agencies.

Officers

Chairman	John Tyndall
Deputy Chairman	Andrew Fountaine
Publicity	Martin Webster
Industrial and TU	Walter Barton

Staff 6

Membership Not disclosed.   **Fees:** Full £2 p.a.; associate £1 p.a.

Qualifications Closed to supporters of fascist, national socialist and communist organisations; open to people of British stock or European stock if naturalised, and to citizens of Commonwealth (or ex-Commonwealth) countries if of wholly British or European stock.

Branches Ilford; London; Croydon; Hayes; Rochester; Crawley; Leicestershire; Wolverhampton; Manchester; Harrogate.

Publications *NF Members Bulletin* (bi-m); *Britain First* (m); *Britain First Press; Spearhead* (m); *Albion Press.*

History Formed on 7 February 1967 from merger of British National Party and League of Empire Loyalists; later expanded after disbandment or lapsing of other organisations such as Greater Britain Movement and National Democratic Party. Regular meetings, demonstrations, marches, etc, caused expansion from London-based pressure group to full national organisation.

(continued)

Ten candidates stood at 1970 General Election, 54 in February 1974 and 90 in October 1974. Best result at a general election 9.5% at Hackney South, October 1974; at a by-election 16.2% at West Bromwich, May 1973; in local elections, it regularly polls 20% of the vote in Leicester.

Holds regular Remembrance Day parades in London; started 1968 with 150 attending, now 6,000–8,000. Campaigned against decision to admit Ugandan Asians. Plans to purchase larger Head Office building with print shop and social facilities nearer central London; open more regional offices and appoint full-time agents; put up hundreds of candidates at future general elections; intensify anti-immigration campaign. Divisions in the organisation in 1975–76 led to a National Party being formed by a group of members.

NATIONAL LEAGUE OF YOUNG LIBERALS
69 Blackfriars Road, London SE1
Telephone: London 01-928 2883

Aims — To further the cause of Liberalism; to stimulate activity by young people in government and public affairs; to represent young people's views and aspirations at all levels within the Liberal Party.

Officers

Chairman	Ruth Addison
Political Vice-Chairman	Iain Brodie-Browne
Organising Vice-Chairman	Rob Renold

Staff 2

Membership 8,000; age limit of 30. Automatically members of Liberal Party.

Fees 50p p.a. Each branch is expected to pay £10 annual quota.

Offices YL Northern Office: 1st Floor, 121 Princes Street, Manchester M1 7AG. Telephone: 061-236 0011.

Publications *Liberator* (m); many leaflets, booklets, manifestos, etc.

Connections Shares offices with Union of Liberal Students (1). Affiliated to Anti-Apartheid Movement (5); NCCL (6); British Youth Council. Member of World Federation of Liberal and Radical Youth and European Federation of Liberal and Radical Youth.

History   Formed about 1904. Throughout its history it has been on the left or radical wing of the Liberal Party. Consistently opposed to electoral pacts including National Government of 1931. In late 1960s known as the 'Red Guards' and espoused direct action tactics. In particular, actions included campaigns against South African sports tours and opposition to census. Mainly responsible for developing and practising the Liberal idea of community politics. Activities recently have included campaigns on disablement, OAPs and hypothermia; against British Lions rugby tour of South Africa; on homosexual equality; women's rights etc; campaigning for radical liberal ideas for remaining in EEC. Plans include moving of HQ and probable closing of Northern Office.

NATIONAL UNION OF CONSERVATIVE AND UNIONIST ASSOCIATIONS
32 Smith Square, London SW1P 3HH
Telephone: 01-222 9000   Cables: Constitute London

Aims   To support and encourage the development of the principles and aims of the Conservative Party; to secure the election of Conservative candidates to councils and to parliament; to form and develop Conservative Associations in every constituency; to form a centre of united action and to act as a link between the leader of the party and all sections of the party; to work closely in co-ordination with the Conservative Central Office.

Officers

President	The Lord Hewlett
Chairman	Miss Shelagh Roberts
Chairman of Executive Committee	Sir John Taylor
Vice-Chairmen	David Sells, Sir Herbert Redfearn, Clive Landa
Secretary	Alan Smith

Membership   Each affiliated association maintains its own individual membership and decides upon its own minimum annual subscription.

Branches   552 constituency associations in England and Wales and 11 area organisations.

Publications   *Conservative Monthly News*

History   Formed in 1867 as The National Union of Conservative Constitutional Associations.

NATIONAL UNION OF LIBERAL CLUBS
22 Carr Manor Mount, Leeds LS17 5DG
Telephone: 0532 682277

Aims	To promote social and political intercourse of members of the amalgamated clubs; to assist in the advancement of Liberal principles especially among members; to spread the influence of Liberalism and social conscience.	
Officers	*President*	Kenneth Forbes
	Chairman	Leslie Anderson
	Secretaryand PR	Kevan Riley
	Vice-President	Jeremy Thorpe MP
	Prominent members	include Richard Wainwright MP, Cyril Smith MP
Membership	2,200 clubs	**Fees:** annual sub. 2p per member
Connections	Directly represented on Liberal Party Executive; Liberal Party Council; also links at local Liberal Party level.	
History	Formed at Gladstone Liberal Club, Nottingham, 9 November 1907. At its height in July 1934 it had 11 county and 19 district federations with 510 clubs and 104,000 members.	

SCOTTISH NATIONAL PARTY (SNP)
14A Manor Place, Edinburgh EH3 7ES
Telephone: 031-226 3661

Aims	'Self-government for Scotland — that is the restoration of Scottish National Sovereignty by the establishment of a democratic Scottish Parliament within the Commonwealth, freely elected by the Scottish people, whose authority be limited only by such agreements as may be freely entered into by it with other nations or states or international organizations for the purpose of furthering international co-operation and world peace; the further-ance of all Scottish interests.'	
Officers	*President*	Dr Robert McIntyre
	Chairman	William Wolfe
	National Secretary	Mrs Rosemary Hall
	Senior Vice-Chairman	Mrs Margo MacDonald
	PR etc.	Stephen Maxwell

Prominent Members	(All MPs): Mrs Winifred Ewing, Mrs Margaret Bain, Douglas Henderson, Hamish Watt, George Reid, Iain MacCormick, George Wilson, Douglas Crawford, Andrew Welsh, George Thompson, Donald Stewart.
Staff	8
Membership	Not currently available.
Fees	(Branch) £1 p.a.; (Headquarters) £2.50 p.a. Members of other political parties excluded.
Publications	Various, including pamphlets, manifestos, and research bulletins.
History	Various groups including Scots National League and Home Rule Association formed the National Party of Scotland in 1928. Became Scottish National Party in 1934 with further amalgamations. Dr Robert McIntyre won Motherwell by-election in April 1945. Winifred Ewing won Hamilton in November 1967 by-election. 1970 General Election, Western Isles won by Donald Stewart and Govan won at November 1973 by-election. Seven MPs returned February 1974. Eleven MPs October 1974. Plans to get 36 MPs elected and a mandate for self-government from the people of Scotland.

SELSDON GROUP
14 South Parade, York YO2 2BA

Aims		To persuade the Conservative Party to adopt policies leading to the reduction of government intervention, and return to the market economy on the grounds that political freedom is not possible without economic freedom; to press for a balanced budget on the grounds that government deficit spending is the principal cause of the inflation now threatening the survival of a free society; it believes that the role of government should be to concentrate on maintaining the framework, notably of law and sound money, within which individuals can express choices about their lives by the way they spend their money.
Officers	*Patron*	Lord Coleraine
	President	Sir Frederick Corfield
	Vice-Presidents	Ronald Bell MP, Richard Body MP, Jock Bruce-Gardyne MP, Nicholas Ridley MP, Professor Alan Walters

Chairman	David Alexander
Deputy Chairman	Richard Henderson
Honorary Secretary	Stephen Eyres
Honorary Treasurer	Hugh Simmonds

Membership 200. Members must belong to the Conservative Party.

Fees Minimum subscription £5 p.a.

Publications Members' newsletter; *Step by Step against Inflation; Killing the Goose; Taxes on Capital are Taxes on Capitalism.*

Connections Seeks links accorded to other Conservative Party groups.

History Formed early 1973 after disillusion with Conservative government's failure to implement policies associated with shadow cabinet conference at Selsdon Park in January 1970. Holds regular meetings, provides speakers etc and has a regular publications and research programme.

SOCIAL CREDIT PARTY
BCM/Socred, London WC1V 6XX

Aims The establishment of a government in the UK which shall put into effect a national monetary policy and such other related measures as are necessary to achieve a genuine economic democracy. Economic democracy is defined as absolute economic security for the citizen with progressive release from economic compulsion; specifically the reform of the banking-credit system and the establishment of a national credit account which would reflect in financial terms the physical facts of the nation's economic situation; the introduction of a further type of consumer credit by a new and scientific system of retail price compensation.

Officers	*President*	R S J Rands
	Vice-President	Miss Irene Rathbone
	Chairman	F A Hatton
	Hon Secretary and PRO	J W Leslie, 108 Holmefield House, Hazelwood Crescent, London W10 5DP Telephone: 01-960 2087

Membership 50 plus **Subscription:** £1.50 p.a.

Publications Bulletin (m)

Connections Social Credit Centre.

History Founded October 30th 1965. Future plans include parliamentary candidature.

SOCIAL DEMOCRATIC ALLIANCE
5/20 Shepherds Hill, Highgate, London N6

Aims   'Our aim is a classless society and to this end the Labour Party should be a practical, humanitarian and reformist party which recognises the essential unity and interdependence of all groups. We see the Labour Party as not inspired by Marxist, Maoist or Castroist traditions. Its roots lie in radicalism, free co-operation, nonconformity and Christian socialism.'

Officers

Chairman	Peter Stephenson
Vice-Chairmen	Bob Cochrane, John O'Grady
Hon Secretaries	Stephen Haseler, David Carlton
Hon Treasurer	Douglas Eden

Membership   Initially 100. Must be a member of the Labour Party.

History   Formed June 1975 to counteract the dominance of the Labour Party by an unrepresentative minority and to represent the interests of the centre of the party. Plans include a series of meetings to boost support and the possible publication of a newsletter.

SOCIALIST EDUCATION ASSOCIATION
(See Section 9)

SOCIALIST MEDICAL ASSOCIATION
(See Section 8)

SOCIALIST PARTY OF GREAT BRITAIN
52 Clapham High Street, London SW4 7UN
Telephone: 01-622 3811

Aims   The establishment of a system of society based upon the common ownership and democratic control of the means and instruments for producing and distributing wealth by, and in the interest of, the whole community.

Membership   800. Applicants must accept party's analysis of society and oppose all other views in public giving view of party; contrary views permitted only at party meetings. All members of equal status.

48

Fees   25p per calendar month. No obligation to pay dues for OAPs.

Branches   Bolton; Birmingham; Edinburgh; Glasgow; Manchester; Swansea; Stevenage; Welwyn Garden City; plus 7 in London. Groups in Merseyside; Oxford; Sunderland; Woking.

Publications *Socialist Standard*

Connections   Only abroad with Socialist Parties of Australia, Canada and New Zealand; World Socialist Parties of US and Ireland; Bund Democratscher Sozialisten (Austria).

History   Founded 12 June 1904 under present name, principles and object. *Socialist Standard* began publication in September 1904, is controlled by membership at annual conference and other meetings, and the executive committee administers between conferences. 1914 opposed World War I. 1917 asserted that socialism had not been established in Russia, and in 1931 forecast that capitalism would not collapse. 1939 re-asserted case against 'capitalist war'.

SOCIETY FOR INDIVIDUAL FREEDOM
55 Park Lane, London W1Y 4LB
Telephone: 01-499 6476

Aims   To promote by all possible constitutional means the liberty, importance and personal responsibility of the individual; the sovereignty of parliament and its effective control over the executive; the rule of law and the independence of the judicature; free enterprise: the case for state intervention must at all times be clearly established.

Officers   *Chairman*   Sir Ian Mactaggart
                  Treasurer   Mrs H Eyles Monk

Staff   1

Membership   500. Includes 25 MPs   **Fees: £10 p.a.**

History   Formed in 1942 by the amalgamation of the Society of Individualists (formed by Sir Ernest Benn) and the National League for Freedom (formed by Lord Lyle).

SOCIETY OF LABOUR LAWYERS
9 King's Bench Walk, Temple, London EC4
Telephone: 01-353 0478

Aims	Law reform.	
Officers	*Chairman*	Bruce Douglas-Mann MP
	Secretary	Conrad Ascher
	Assistant Secretary	Daphne Wickham
	Treasurer	David de A Saxe

Membership 500. Must be connected with or members of the legal profession and also a member of the Labour Party.

Fees London members £3 p.a.; provincial members £1; students 50p.

Connections Affiliated to the Labour Party (1).

History Founded in 1948. It has followed a policy of advocating law reform and has issued various publications through the Fabian Society and prepared evidence for submission to many government enquiries.

TROOPS OUT MOVEMENT
103 Hammersmith Road, West Kensington, London W14
Telephone: 01-602 1899

Aims To build a mass movement in Britain, based primarily on the Labour and Trade Union movements, campaigning for the immediate withdrawal of the British Army from Ireland, on the basis of self-determination for the Irish people as a whole.

Officers	*Co-ordinator*	Alistair Renwick
	Treasurer	Bill Freeman
	Press Officer	Alan Hayling
	Prominent members	include Joan Maynard MP, Hackney Trades Council

Membership 750 plus 10,000 through affiliated organisations.

Fees £1 p.a.

Publications *TOM-TOM* (q); *Alternative White Paper on Ireland;* Internal newsletter (members only).

Branches 20 throughout Great Britain.

Connections British Peace Council.

History   Formed November 1973 with 30 members in west London. Spread throughout Great Britain following national conference in May 1974. First national demonstration on 27 October 1974 in London attended by over 7,000 including six Labour MPs. Plans include a further national demonstration and trade union conference.

ULSTER DEMOCRATIC UNIONIST PARTY (DUP)
1a Ava Avenue, Ormeau Road, Belfast, BT7 3BN
Telephone: Belfast 691021/2

Aims   To uphold and maintain the Constitution of Northern Ireland as an integral part of the United Kingdom as at present constituted; to impose and maintain the rule of law in all areas of Northern Ireland so that all citizens are not only equal under the law but are equally subject to it; to devise and urge a policy of social betterment and equal opportunity for all sections of the community in the economic, educational and social welfare spheres.

Officers

Leader	Rev Dr Ian Paisley MP
Chairman	Rev W J Beattie
Secretary/Press Officer	Peter Robinson
Treasurer	D S Herron
Vice-Chairman	Cllr D N Calvert

Staff   3

Membership   Not available.   **Fees:** £1 p.a.

Publications   *Year Book* (a); various occasional political commentaries.

Connections   Forms part of the United Ulster Unionist Coalition at Westminster and in the Northern Ireland Convention.

History   Formed in 1971 out of the Protestant Unionist Party set up two years previously in opposition to the policies of the then Prime Minister Capt O'Neill. The DUP had eight representatives in the Northern Ireland Assembly elected in 1973 and had 12 in the Convention of 1975—76. The party also has many representatives on local councils throughout Northern Ireland.

ULSTER UNIONIST COUNCIL
3 Glengall Street, Belfast BT12 5AE
Telephone: 0232 24601/3   Cables: Council Belfast

Aims	To maintain N Ireland under the Crown as an integral part of the UK and to uphold democratic institutions of Government for N Ireland; to safeguard the British citizenship of the people of N Ireland; to act as a further link between Ulster Unionists and their parliamentary representatives to settle in consultation with them the parliamentary policy and to be the medium of expressing Ulster Unionist opinion as current events develop and generally to advance and defend the interests of Ulster Unionism.

Officers	*Patron*	Lady Brookeborough
	President	Col James G Cunningham
	Leader	H W West
	Honorary Secretaries (& PR)	M H Armstrong, Josiah Cunningham Dr James Laird, Miss N A Cooper
	Honorary Treasurer	John D Laird
	Vice-Presidents	Capt Sir George A Clark, Lt Col G E Liddle, James Molyneaux MP, Rev Martin Smyth
	Secretary	J O Bailie
	Assistant Secretary/ Organiser	Norman Hutton

Members of Parliament	John Carson, James Kilfedder, Harold McCusker, James Molyneaux, William Ross, Enoch Powell.
Staff	10
Membership	Approximately 500,000.
Fees	At discretion of Constituency Association. Must not be a member of any other political party or support candidature of anyone in opposition to Ulster Unionist candidates.
Offices	Regional HQ in each UK constituency — North Belfast; East Belfast; South Belfast; West Belfast; North Antrim; South Antrim; Armagh; North Down; South Down; Fermanagh and S Tyrone; Londonderry; Mid Ulster.
Publications	*UUC Year Book; Century Newspapers; Annual Report; Northern Whig;* plus irregular pamphlets.

Connections County Grand Lodges of the Loyal Grange Institution;
Apprentice Boys of Derry; Queen's University Conservative
and Unionist Association.

History UUC formed 1905. Sir Edward Carson became Ulster's Leader
and Chairman of Irish Unionist Party in 1910. Ulster Covenant
signed by over 471,000 people — 1912. Government of Ireland
Act passed 1920. Sir James Craig became Prime Minister of
N Ireland — 1921. Achievements include seven Ulster Unionists
elected to House of Commons February 1974 and six in October
1974. (Joined with other pro-union members to form coalition
of 10). Plans to obtain, on same basis as Scotland, full representation for N Ireland at Westminster; restoration of an elected
legislative body and administration; normal democratic local
government as in the rest of the UK.

UNION OF LIBERAL STUDENTS
69 Blackfriars Road, London, SE1
Telephone: 01-928 2883

Aims To represent the interests of all Liberal students both within
and outside the Liberal Party and to co-ordinate activities.

Officers *Chairman* Barry Birch

Membership 3,000. Must be students at time of joining.

Fees 10p p.a.

Connections Co-operate closely with National League of Young Liberals.

History Developed out of Union of University Liberal Students. Formed
after 2nd World War to represent all Liberal Students. Plans to
fight NUS elections and try to combat the stranglehold of the
'broad left'.

UNIONIST PARTY OF NORTHERN IRELAND
Kinnaird Building, 15 Chichester Street, Belfast BT1 4ND
Telephone : Belfast 32301

Aims To maintain Northern Ireland as an integral part of the United
Kingdom; to work towards the restoration of a devolved
Northern Ireland government supported by all sections of the
community; to restore respect for law and order in all sections
of Northern Ireland.

Officers	*President*	Sir John Andrews
	Chairman	F C Tughan
	Leader	Rt Hon Brian Faulkner
	Treasurer	G Swann

Prominent Members in Northern Ireland Convention: Rt Hon Brian Faulkner, Mrs Ann Dickson, Mr Joss Cardwell, Lord Brookeborough, Mr Lloyd Hall-Thompson.

Staff 3

Membership Not disclosed. **Fees:** minimum of 50p p.a.

Publications *Union and Partnership* (Party manifesto 1975).

History Formed in September 1974 as a separate political party, UPNI was previously known as the Pro-Assembly Unionist Group and was part of the Ulster Unionist Council.

WOMEN'S LIBERAL FEDERATION
7 Exchange Court, Strand, London WC2R 0PR
Telephone: 01-240 0513/0701

Aims To promote the adoption, development and diffusion of Liberal principles and their application in the government of the country; to advance political education; to form Women's Liberal Associations in every constituency and to campaign for equal rights for women.

Officers	*President*	Lady Seear
	Treasurer	Lady Banks
	Secretary	Mrs Morag Barlow
	PR etc.	Mrs Hilda Bainbridge

Prominent Members Lady Seear, Lady Robson, Mrs Margaret Wingfield JP (President, Liberal Party).

Staff 2

Membership 1,000 **Fee:** minimum 50p p.a.

Publications *News and Views* (10 issues p.a., members only).

History Founded May 1886. Activities include permanent campaigning for equality for women; evidence submitted to parliamentary committees, etc; liaison with other women's organizations; political education; fund raising. Annual council meeting open to all women Liberals.

WORKERS' REVOLUTIONARY PARTY
186a Clapham High Street, London SW4 7UG
Telephone: 01-622 7029

Aims	Trotskyist revolution, involving the overthrow of capitalism and the establishment of a socialist state based on the nationalisation of industry under workers' control.
Officers	*General Secretary* — Gerry Healy
	Prominent members — include Vanessa Redgrave
Publications	*Fourth International* (occasional); *Newsline.*
Connections	All Trades Union Alliance, the party's industrial wing and the Young Socialists, its youth section.
History	Formed in November 1973 from the Socialist Labour League that had existed from 1959. Its supporters took control of the Labour Party Young Socialists in the early 1960s but were expelled in 1964, after which they formed a separate organisation. Its newspaper *Workers' Press* — the first Trotskyist daily paper in the world — ceased publication in 1976 after nearly six and a half years existence. The paper's journalists combined to launch a new paper, *Newsline,* to support the WRP, appearing for the first time on 1 May 1976.

YOUNG FABIAN GROUP
11 Dartmouth Street, London SW1H 9BN
Telephone: 01-930 3077

Aims	See Fabian Society.	
Officers	*Chairman*	Ian Wilson
	Secretary and Treasurer	Hilary Barnard
	Vice-Chairman	Chris Smith
Membership	2,000. Same as Fabian Society but must be under 30.	
Publications	Various pamphlets from 15—30p.	
Connections	Sub-group of Fabian Society (1).	
History	Founded 1960, does not take a collective view on issues. Its aim is to provide a forum for the ideas of members. Activities include meetings, weekend and summer schools and research activities.	

ADVERTISING STANDARDS AUTHORITY LTD
15/17 Rigmount Street, London WC1E 7AW
Telephone: 01-580 0801/6

Aims	The supervision of the British Advertising Industry's system of self-regulation and the attainment thereby of advertising that is legal, decent, honest and truthful.
Officers	*Chairman* Lord Drumalbyn *Director and Secretary* Peter Thomson *Agency for Advertising* Roe Humphreys Ltd.
Staff	25/30
Membership	The authority's only members are those on the governing council.
Publications	Annual Report; Case reports (every two months, free); *British Code of Advertising Practice* (5th edition).
History	Established 1962. Recent activities include initiation of a substantial expansion plan with budget increased seven-fold; launching of national advertising campaign; recruitment of large staff to undertake additional monitoring, advice and investigation work.

ASSOCIATION OF BRITISH TRAVEL AGENTS LIMITED
50-57 Newman Street, London W1P 4AH
Telephone: 01-580 8281

Aims	To support the interests of travel agents and tour operators in the United Kingdom; to administer compensation funds and organise bonding of members.
History	Formed 1950.

ASSOCIATION OF PROFESSIONAL FORESTERS
Brokerswood House, Brokerswood, Nr Westbury, Wiltshire, BA13 4EH
Telephone: Westbury 2238

Aims	To provide a central organisation for all individuals and bodies who earn their livelihood through private commercial forestry, to elevate the status and advance the interests of the profession; to improve technical and general knowledge.
Officers	*Chairman* E M Liddon *Secretary and PR* A G Phillips *President* Duke of Richmond and Gordon
Staff	2
Membership	Represents 75% of those engaged in private sector forestry. Members must be aged 25 or over and have been in practice for 5 years.
Fees	Depend on membership category.
Publications	*APF Newsletter* (q); to members and all forestry bodies.
Connections	Full members of the European organisation for foresters. Liaison with Institute of Foresters; Forestry Commission; Timber Growers. Representatives on Forestry Training Council; Tree Council; Arboricultural Association; Forestry Safety Council.
History	Formed in 1959. Activities include development of European links. Intended to broaden scope of membership following introduction of capital transfer tax. Has become watchdog of those involved in private sector and hopes to encourage development of forestry and draw attention to the fact that this will reduce balance of payments bill for timber imports.

BRITISH ASSOCIATION OF SOCIAL WORKERS
(See Section 6)

BRITISH INSTITUTE OF MANAGEMENT LTD (A Charity)
Management House, Parker Street, London WC2B 5PT
Telephone: 01-405 3456   Cables: Brinsman London

Aims   To promote the art and science of management and to advance public education therein.

Officers   *Chairman*   Sir Frederick Catherwood
                Executive Director and
                General Manager   Philip J S Churchill
                Executive Director and
                Secretary   Michael Kirk
                Press and PR   John Richards

Other official and Council members: include Viscount Watkinson, John Bolton, Sir Basil Smallpeice, Sir Derek Ezra, Professor R J Ball.

Staff   150

Membership Companies 13,500; individuals 47,000. Individual members join specific grades according to experience etc. Fellows are elected.

Fees   Entrance £10; affiliate £7.50 p.a.; Fellow £11 p.a.; Member £11 p.a.; Associate member £8.50 p.a.
                Companies' fees related to number of employees.

Regional Offices   Glasgow; Manchester; Leeds; Warley; Bangor (Co Down); Bristol.

Publications *Management Today* (m); *Management Review and Digest* (q).

Connections Representation on many bodies including Conseil International pour l'Organisation Scientifique; European Foundation for Management Development; Council for National Academic Awards; Manchester Business School.

History   Formed in 1947. Autonomous and self-financing. It has become the national source of management information and has made a major contribution to the rapid development of management education. Plans include the establishment of special working parties to study and make recommendations on issues of major importance to management; increasingly to offer impartial opinions to management with a view to becoming the recognised voice of management; to improve its knowledge of international practices, particularly in relation to Western Europe.

59

BRITISH MEDICAL ASSOCIATION
BMA House, Tavistock Square, London WC1H 9JP
Telephone: 01-387 4499   Telex: 265929   Cables: Medisecra London

Aims	To promote the medical and allied sciences and to maintain the honour and interests of the medical profession; to promote research and to publish.

Officers

Patron	HM The Queen
President	Sir Ronald Tunbridge
Chairman of Representative Body	Dr J S Noble
Chairman of Council	Walpole Lewin
Treasurer	Dr J E Miller
Press Information Officer	R A F Thistlethwaite
Advertising Manager	M B Cozens
Editor, BMA Journal	Dr M Ware

Membership	68,000. Full membership restricted to registered medical practitioners. Also associates, temporary and honorary members.
Fees	£30 p.a. maximum, concessionary rates for certain classes of member.
Regional Offices	Leeds; London; Liverpool; Birmingham; Sheffield; Newcastle; Manchester; Bristol; Middlesbrough; Cardiff; Edinburgh; Glasgow; Belfast.
Publications	*British Medical Journal* (w); *BMA News* (6–12 times p.a.); *BMA Calendar* (a); other specialist journals and publications.
Connections	Member of World Medical Association; Commonwealth Medical Association; Standing Committee of Doctors of the EEC. Affiliated with medical associations of 23 Commonwealth and ex-Commonwealth countries.
History	Formed 1832 as Provincial Medical and Surgical Association.

BRITISH RESORTS ASSOCIATION
c/o Secretary, 23 Midhurst Avenue, Westcliff-on-Sea, Essex SS0 0NP
Telephone: Southend 40563

Aims	To consider matters affecting mutual interests of resorts and tourist centres and regions, to take such action as may be necessary or advisable to protect and promote those interests and, wherever possible, provide information of value to its members.	
Officers	*Chairman*	N M Haskins
	Secretary	S W G Last
Prominent Members	include B Godman Irvine MP.	
Membership	83 resorts.	**Fees:** 35p per 1,000 population.
Connections	Institute of Municipal Entertainment; Association of British Tourist Officers.	

BRITISH STANDARDS INSTITUTION (BSI)
2 Park Street, London W1A 2BS
Telephone: 01-629 9000

Aims	(As set out in its Royal Charter): to coordinate the efforts of producers and users for the improvement, standardization and simplification of engineering and industrial materials so as to simplify production and distribution, and to eliminate the national waste of time and material involved in the production of an unnecessary variety of patterns and sizes of articles for one and the same purpose; to set up standards of quality and dimensions, and prepare and promote the general adoption of British Standards and from time to time revise and amend such specifications as experience and circumstances may require.	
Officers	*President*	Baroness Seear
	Chairman of Executive Board	Professor Sir Frederick Warner
	Director General	G B R Fielden CBE FRS
	Head of Public Relations	Miss M A Allen
	Press Officers	Mrs J Petts; Mr T I Hammond
	Information Officer (Consumer Affairs Department)	Mrs J Horrocks
Staff	917	

Membership   16,000 subscribers plus 28,000 represented on BSI Committees.

Fees   Minimum of £25, calculated according to remuneration and turnover.

Regional Offices   Hemel Hempstead (technical help to exporters, quality assurance); Manchester (textiles and clothing); sales counters at the Birmingham, Glasgow, Liverpool and Norwich Chambers of Commerce and at the Wire Industry Research Association, Leeds.

Publications   *BSI News* (m); *Annual Report; BSI Yearbook; Sale Bulletins; British Standards.*

Connections   With Department of Prices and Consumer Protection which administers a government grant to BSI, and with chambers of commerce. Is a founder member body of the following inter-national standards bodies: International Organization for Standardization (ISO); International Electrotechnical Commission (IEC); European Committee for Standardization (CEN); European Committee for Electrotechnical Standariza-tion (CENELEC). Is involved in the work of a number of other European organizations e.g. International Commission on Rules for the Approval of Electrical Equipment (CEE). BSI also maintains close links with standards bodies overseas.

History   Its ancestor was the Engineering Standards Committee set up by the Institution of Civil Engineers in 1901. In 1929 it was granted a Royal Charter and in 1931 with a supplemental Charter changed its name to the British Standards Institution. Its present day major activities include the operation of certification schemes to standards and the Technical Help to Exporters (THE) service which provides the exporter with information on overseas legislation, regulations and standards. Consumer Standards Advisory Committee (CSAC), formerly the Women's Advisory Committee, represents the views of all important consumer interests on BSI technical committees.

CHEMICAL INDUSTRIES ASSOCIATION LTD
Alembic House, 93 Albert Embankment, London SE1 7TU
Telephone: 01-735 3001

Aims   Trade association.

Officers   *Director General*   Martin E Trowbridge

Membership   340 firms.

History   Founded 1966.

CONFEDERATION OF BRITISH INDUSTRY
21 Tothill Street, London SW1H 9LP
Telephone: 01-930 6711   Telex: 21332   Cables: Cobustry London

Aims	'The acknowledged representative of the management element of industry and commerce for the UK. It exists to promote and safeguard the interests of British business at Westminster, Whitehall, the regions, Brussels or wherever decisions are taken likely to affect the business community. Policy priorities are to uphold the market system and profit motive that sustains it; to oppose further encroachment on the private sector wherever this is inconsistent with the market system; to work for the development of an economy (in conjunction with governments and trade unions) in which high real incomes result from a high level of profitable investment, increased productivity and soundly based growth; to secure a framework in which industry can best discharge its responsibilities to shareholders, employees, creditors, consumers and the public.'

Officers

President	Ralph Bateman
Director-General	John Methven
Director of Information	Richard Dixon

Staff   Approximately 400.

Membership   12,000 firms and 200 employers' associations and trade associations.

Fees   Sliding scale partly based on turnover.

Offices   11 in UK. EEC liaison office in Brussels.

Publications   *Members Bulletin (f); Review (q);* many regular reports and books.

Connections   Most important is its role as member of National Economic Development Council. Links with many other national and international government and other bodies.

History   Founded July 1965 by the fusion of the British Employers' Confederation, Federation of British Industries, National Association of British Manufacturers and Industrial Association of Wales. Among CBI's best know activities is the quarterly Industrial Trends Survey, first started in 1958, which gives the most up-to-date picture of prevailing business conditions and sentiment in UK.

63

DAIRY TRADE FEDERATION
20 Eastbourne Terrace, London W2 6LE
Telephone: 01-262 6722   Telex 262027

Aims	To make representations to government, Ministry of Agriculture, Fisheries and Food, Milk Marketing Board and European Commission on behalf of members on all dairy matters; to keep members informed on all current legislation and policy matters being decided by these bodies; to provide and build strong links with consumer interests and the public.

Officers
Director General	J R Owens
Director/Secretary	Miss Elizabeth Gadsby
Public Relations	J Vosper
Press Officer	W Duxbury

Staff	27
Membership	No direct membership; individuals or companies must be members of one of the four organisations that make up the DTF: the Amalgamated Master Dairymen; Creamery Proprietors' Association; Co-operative Milk Trade Association and the National Diarymen's Association.
Publications	*The Milk Industry* (m).
Connections	Ministry of Agriculture, Fisheries and Food, Milk Marketing Board; Milk Powder Association; Food and Drink Industries Council; Food, Drink and Tobacco Industries Training Board; Irish and Scottish Milk Marketing Boards; Irish Dairy Board; Scottish Milk Trade Association; Northern Ireland Milk Alliance; EEC bodies.
History	Founded in 1933 as the Central Milk Distributive Council.

ENGINEERING EMPLOYERS' FEDERATION (EEF)
Broadway House, Tothill Street, London SW1H 9NQ
Telephone: 01-930 6314

Aims	To develop and promote sound industrial relations practices within the engineering industry; to make the views of the engineering industry known to government and to the public.

Officers
Director General	A F Frodsham
PR and Press	N de Jongh

Staff	90

Membership	More than 5,000 engineering companies employing over 2 million people.
Fees	Related to amount of payroll.
Branch Offices	20 associations throughout the UK.
Publications	*EEF News; Annual Review; Guides to Legislation* (primarily for members only).
Connections	Member of CBI (2); represented on NEDO.
History	Formed in 1896 as the Employers' Federation of Engineering Associations, it took its present name in 1961.

FARMERS' UNION OF WALES
Llys Amaeth, Queen's Square, Aberystwyth, Dyfed SY23 2EA
Telephone: 0970 2755

Aims	To provide Welsh farmers with an independent producer organisation offering a comprehensive service to members; to safeguard and further the interests of farmers and land-owners in Wales and to promote a sympathetic understanding of their problems; to represent Welsh farmers in all matters appertaining to their interests and to make their views known to all bodies and organisations interested in Welsh agriculture.

Officers	*President*	Te Myrddin Evans
	General Secretary	Evan Lewis
	Executive Officer	Ma Fitter
	Press and PR	G L Thomas

Staff	57
Membership	12,000
Fees	£8 basic plus 7p per acre. Open to farmers and landowners in Wales.
Branches	County Secretaries at Anglesey; Brecon and Radnor; Caernarvon; Cardigan; Carmarthen; Denbigh and Flint; Glamorgan; Merioneth; Monmouth; Montgomery; Pembroke.
Publications	*Y Tir; Welsh Farmer* (alternate months).
History	Established in 1955. Activities include continual representation on matters of import to Welsh farmers, for example its successful opposition to the establishment of the Cambrian Mountains National Park.

INSTITUTE OF DIRECTORS
10 Belgrave Square, London SW1X 8PW
Telephone: 01-235 3601   Cables: Boardroom London

Aims	To advance the interests of members as Directors or holders of other equivalent office in bodies corporate; to provide facilities and services; to organise and support conferences, etc. of interest or benefit to members; to collate, collect, publish; to support in law as appropriate; to campaign and research in the interests of the Institute.

Officers

President	Earl of Drogheda
Chairman of Council	Lord Erroll
Leader of Parliamentary Panel	Cecil E Parkinson MP
Director-General	Jan Hildreth
Assistant Director-General	Roger D F Marlow
Secretary	J Whitfield
European Liaison Officer	Bryce Cousens
Editor, The Director	George Bull

Staff	170
Membership	44,000. Fellows must hold directorship in body corporate. Associate membership non-directors.
Fees	£30; overseas £20; retired £10.
Branches	27 throughout UK, Commonwealth and South Africa.
Publications	*The Director* (m)
Connections	Institute of Directors in Australia.
History	Founded in 1903. Granted Royal Charter in 1906.

INTERNATIONAL TANKER OWNERS' POLLUTION FEDERATION LTD
41/43 Mincing Lane, London EC3R 7AE
Telephone: 01-623 9487   Telex: 887514   Cables: Tovalop

Aims	To administer the Tanker Owners Voluntary Agreement concerning Liability for Oil Pollution (TOVALOP) and to provide as required, technical services in connection with the prevention of, minimising of and cleaning up of oil pollution.

International Tanker Owners' Pollution Federation (continued)

Officers	*Chairman*	A B Kurz
	Managing Director	A S M Hetherington
	Press and PR (Assistant to Managing Director)	D B A Ockenden

Staff 10

Membership 4,000; includes almost all tanker owners.

Fees Calculated according to tonnage of tankers.

Publications *Members and Ships* (a); *TOVALOP* (the agreement, reprinted when amendments become effective).

Connections Strong links with other anti-pollution bodies, oil companies and insurers. Close relationship with IMCO, Chamber of Shipping and governments.

History Incorporated 24 December 1968. TOVALOP agreement became effective 6 October 1969 when over 50% of world tanker tonnage was registered with Federation. Within a year this rose to 80%. Present gross registered tonnage is over 154 million or 99% of world's tonnage. Has assisted in the satisfactory settlement of most major oil spills that have occurred. Has drawn up contingency plans for oil spills should they occur in several critical areas. In process of developing computer programme on oil spills which it is hoped will be helpful in providing data which will assist in prevention of spills.

LAW SOCIETY OF SCOTLAND
Law Society's Hall, 26 Drumsheugh Gardens, Edinburgh EH3 7YR
Telephone: 031-226 7411   Telex: 72436 Lawscot Edinburgh
Cables: Lex Edinburgh

Aims The promotion of the interests of the profession of solicitor in Scotland and the interests of the public in relation to that profession; and the doing of all such things as are incidental or conducive to the exercise of the said powers and duties and the attainment of the said objectives.

Officers	*President*	J D Wheelans
	Vice-President	I R Kirkwood
	Secretary	R B Laurie
	Press and PR	Miss Joan Clark

Staff 120

Law Society of Scotland (continued)

Membership	3,500; restricted to solicitors.
Fees	£55 p.a.
Branch Office	Glasgow
Publications	*Journal of the Law Society of Scotland* (m).
Connections	Close consultation with the Law Society in England and Wales.
History	Incorporated by statute on 30 July 1949.

LOCAL RADIO ASSOCIATION
A Limited Company
35 Connaught Square, London W2 2HL
Telephone: 01-262 5988

Aims	To represent the interest of consortia, radio producers in negotiations with the government and the Independent Broadcasting Authority.	
Officers	*Chairman*	Wyndham Lewis
	Vice-Chairman	Joe Scott-Clark
	Secretary	Mark Elwes
Staff	2	
Membership	75 companies or consortia; 15 radio production companies; 3 consultancy/service companies; 20 individuals.	
Fees	Individuals £10; companies £30—£100.	
Qualifications	Interest or involvement in commercial radio.	
Publications	Newsletters, minutes and occasional papers for members only.	
History	Formed in 1963 as a campaign for the introduction of independent radio.	

LONDON BOROUGHS ASSOCIATION
Westminster City Hall, Victoria Street, London SW1E 6QW

Aims	To provide a forum in which the London Boroughs can discuss common problems, machinery through which they can co-ordinate their activities, and a means through which they can deal jointly with the government and the GLC.	
Officers	*Honorary Secretary*	Sir Alan Dawtry
Membership	32 London Boroughs and City of London.	

Publications   *LBA Handbook* (every 2 years, free).

Connections   With Association of Metropolitan Authorities including arrangements to avoid duplication of activities.

History   Formed in 1964 as London Boroughs Committee. Present name adopted in September 1966.

MOTOR AGENTS ASSOCIATION
201 Great Portland Street, London W1
Telephone: London 01-580 9122

Aims   An industrial association for agents and dealers in the motor trade.

Officers   *Director General*   F E Higham

Membership   18,000 firms.

Publications   *Motor Trade Executive* (m).

History   Founded 1912.

NATIONAL CHAMBER OF TRADE LTD
Enterprise House, Henley-on-Thames, Oxon RG9 1TU
Telephone: Henley 6161

Aims   To create an efficient, independent, commercial community in every town and/or district in the UK so that local and national authorities may obtain an intelligent and carefully considered viewpoint from the traders and other business people of the community concerned; to provide an advisory service to the distributive industries and generally to business; to promote, support or oppose legislation affecting trade and business generally.

Officers   *National President*   K L Smith
Director General   L E S Seeney
Chairman of the
Board of Management   Miss Mildred Head
Admin Secretary   Miss Brenda Povey

Hon Vice-Presidents   Earl of Derby, Viscount Watkinson, Lord Barnby, Lord Chelmer, Lord Coleraine, Lord Fraser, Lord Palmer, Lord St Helens, Lord Wade, Lord Duncan-Sandys

MPs	John Biggs-Davison, A P Costain, Sir John Eden, R W Elliott, Sir Raymond Gower, A G F Hall-Davis, Sir Keith Joseph, Sir Stephen McAdden, Maurice Macmillan, R Graham Page, Michael N Shaw, Richard F Wood
Staff	15 plus 10 part-time provincial officers.
Membership	Ordinary (individuals) 2,000; affiliated Chambers of Commerce and Trade 835 representing 100,000 traders and companies; affiliated national trade associations 33 representing 2½ million traders. Members must be persons or firms engaged in trade or profession associated or Chamber of Trade.
Fees	(under review) Individual £3.40 p.a.; firms £5.10 p.a.; national association £70 p.a.; chamber of trade or commerce 75p per local member.
Publications	*Intercom* (m); *The Distributor* (q).
Branches	Fleetwood; Bradford; Swansea; Stourbridge; Leicester; Norwich; Torquay; Sherborne; Enfield; Tunbridge Wells; Belfast; Glasgow.
Connections	One of four founder members of Retail Consortium.
History	Founded in 1897 on initiative of Hull Chamber of Trade who ran HQ. Moved to London in 1930s and to Henley in 1972. Recent achievement was to persuade the government to refund purchase tax when VAT was introduced. It plans to complete the nationwide pattern of Chambers of Trade affiliated to the national body.

NATIONAL FARMERS' UNION OF SCOTLAND
17 Grosvenor Crescent, Edinburgh EH10 5QS
Telephone: 031-337 4333/6

Aims	To represent the interests of Scottish agriculture in negotiation with government and other authorities on prices, legislation and structure; to maintain a stewardship for the industry.
Officers	*Director and General Secretary* Harry G Munro
Staff	64 (18 in HQ).
Membership	21,300; full membership only to those with active participation in farming, horticulture.

Fees   Range from £2.70–£109.50.

Publications   *Scottish Farming Leader* (m).

Connections   Recognised as the official voice of Scottish agriculture and
                   represented on all major Scottish and UK bodies concerned
                   with agriculture.

History   Formed 1913. Amalgamated with Chamber of Agriculture in
                   1928.

NATIONAL FOOD AND DRINK FEDERATION
Federation House, 17 Farnborough Street, Farnborough, Hants
Telephone: Farnborough 515001/2

Aims   To represent the independent food retailers of the United
                   Kingdom and to uphold their interests with the government.

Officers   *Chief Executive*   L E Reeves-Smith
                   National President   J W P Hall
                   Treasurer   R G Wiltshire

Staff   10

Membership   10,000   Fees: Members £12; Fellows £15.

Qualifications Limited to operators of retail food stores or off licences,
                   manufacturers supplying them or other organisations connected
                   with the trade.

Publications   *News and Views* (m, members only); *Grocery Trade Hand-
                   book* (a).

Connections   Founder member of the Retail Food Confederation in 1972.
                   Represented on more than 20 national and international trade
                   or official bodies; extensive contacts with government depart-
                   ments; is represented by several MPs whose identity it prefers
                   not to disclose.

History   Formed in 1974 on a merger between the National Off-
                   Licence Federation and the National Grocers Federation,
                   which had existed since 1891. Its present activities include
                   lobbying the government, parliamentary representation,
                   liaison with retailers and manufacturers, and training courses
                   for retailers. It has succeeded in gaining some concessions from
                   government in connection with the operation of the prices
                   code and profit margins. During the winter of 1975/76 it held
                   76 seminars throughout the country.

ROAD HAULAGE ASSOCIATION LTD.
Roadway House, 22 Upper Woburn Place, London WC1H 0ES
Telephone: 01-387 9711

Aims	To protect the interests of road haulage operators and to provide them with advice and services.

Officers		
	Director General	G K Newman
	Secretary	E W Russell
	Press and PR	F R Lyon
	Advertising	E J Barber

Staff	134
Membership	17,500
Qualifications	Members must be engaged in road haulage.
Fees	From £14 to £500 p.a. according to the number of goods vehicles operated.
Area Offices	In 15 cities throughout the UK.
Connections	With CBI (2), British Road Federation and the International Road Transport Federation.
Publications	*Road Way* (m); *Haulage Manual* (a).
History	Incorporated in 1944 as a result of a merger between several national and local associations of hauliers. In the first ten years after the war its membership fluctuated in reaction to the policies of successive governments. Its activities have included securing a number of important modifications to legislation.

ROYAL COLLEGE OF NURSING
(See Section 8)

ROYAL TOWN PLANNING INSTITUTE (A Charity)
26 Portland Place, London W1N 4BE
Telephone: 01-636 9107; 01-580 2436

Aims	To advance the science and art of town planning in all its aspects (including local, regional and national planning) for the benefit of the public; it is the recognised organisation representing the town planning profession.

Officers		
	Secretary	Philip Rathbone
	Press and PR	Margaret Cox (Information Officer/ Editor)

Hon Members	Paul Cadbury, Dame Sylvia Crane, Lord Duncan-Sandys, Lewis Mumford, Sir Frederick Osborn, Professor Steen Rasmussen, Lady Evelyn Sharp, Lord Wolfenden
Membership	11,000
Fees	Fellows £21.50 p.a.; members £17.50 p.a.; students £4.50 p.a.
Qualifications	Minimum age 23, passes in the RTPI examinations and two years practical experience.
Offices	9 regional offices covering UK; overseas branches in Malaysia; Central Africa; Hong Kong; Singapore.
Publications	*The Planner* (10 p.a.); *RTPI News* (distributed with *The Planner* to members only); other books and pamphlets including *Britain's Planning Heritage.*
Connections	Associated organisations include Society of Town Planners; Student Planners Association; overseas affiliates in Australia, South Africa, New Zealand, India.
History	Founded in 1914. Distinguished presidents include Sir Raymond Unwin (1915–16), Sir Patrick Abercrombie (1925–6), Sir William Holford (1953–4). Gold Medal winners include Professor Sir Colin Buchanan and Lord Silkin. Incorporated by Royal Charter 1959. Charitable status 1971. First woman president was Miss Sylvia Law (1974–75). Its last conference in June 1975 was on 'Cities in Crisis – The Environment'.

SCOTTISH LANDOWNERS FEDERATION
26 Rutland Square, Edinburgh EH1 2BT
Telephone: 031-229 8202

Aims	To represent the interests of all persons connected with the land; to defend their interests with all relevant authorities and to further the most efficient system of management of land under private enterprise.	
Officers	*President*	The Viscount Arbuthnott
	Convenor	Capt P L Mackie-Campbell
	Secretary	A F Roney-Dougal
	Presss and PR	Major D F Callandar
Staff	12	
Membership	4,000; must own four or more hectares of rural land in Scotland.	
Fees	According to land holding.	

Branches	Highland; Central; North East; South East; South West.
Publications	*Landowning in Scotland* (q); members only.
Connections	Close liaison with Country Landowners Association on all matters and with others such as National Trust for Scotland and the Countryside Commission.
History	Formed in 1906 as Scottish Land and Property Federation.

SMALL INDUSTRIES COUNCIL FOR RURAL AREAS OF SCOTLAND
27 Walker Street, Edinburgh EH3 7HZ
Telephone: 031-225 2846/7

Aims	To promote the economic development of Scotland by co-ordinating the development of industries for the benefit of rural areas; to assist, identify and stimulate small companies to develop towards their maximum potential and to encourage opportunities for employment, particularly in those parts of the country where rural depopulation presents economic and social problems.	
Officers	*Chairman*	Alan R Devereux
	General Manager	David A Ogilvie
	Secretary	Thomas I Geddes
	PR	Miss O H Savage
Staff	56	
Membership	Not a membership organisation.	
Offices	Elgin; Montrose; Castle Douglas; Houston; Edinburgh.	
Publications	*Craftwork Magazine* (q); Annual Reports.	
History	Established 1936 as Scottish Country Industries Development Trust. Re-constituted as a limited company under present title in 1969 as an agency of the Development Commission. Plans include the possible extension of services beyond the rural areas.	

SOCIETY OF CHEMICAL INDUSTRY
(See Section 9)

SOCIETY OF MOTOR MANUFACTURERS AND TRADERS LTD.
Forbes House, Halkin Street, London SW1X 7DS
Telephone: 01-235 7000   Telex: 21628   Cables: Movendum London

Aims	To encourage and promote in the UK and abroad the interests of the whole motor industry; to formulate and influence general policy in regard to industrial, economic, fiscal, commercial and technical questions and to act as a national point of reference for those seeking the industry's views; to develop the contribution of the motor industry to the national economy; to watch over and encourage efficiency and competitive power and to provide advice, information and services to that end. (Labour relations, working conditions and wage negotiations are outside the society's terms of reference.)

Officers

Director	J Beswick
Deputy Director	J D W Gent
Secretary	M G Feather
Press and PR	J R Weinthal

Staff	110
Membership	1,550 organisations. 4 classes of membership: honorary, ordinary, associate and retailer.
Fees	Minimum £50 p.a. based on motor industry turnover.
Publications	Mainly consists of information booklets such as regulations, statistics, buyers' guides etc.
Connections	With a large number of other organisations both national and international concerned with the motor industry.
History	Formed 15 July 1902.

UNITED ASSOCIATION FOR THE PROTECTION OF TRADE LTD.
145/149 London Road, Croydon CR0 2RG
Telephone: 01-686 5644

Aims	To promote and protect the industry and trade of the UK by the provision of credit rating and accounts collection services.

Officers

President	W Norman Peet
Director General	C McNeil Greig

Staff	582
History	Founded in 1842 as the London Association for the Protection of Trade.

CLAIMANTS AND UNEMPLOYMENT WORKERS UNION
120 Standhill Crescent, Barnsley, South Yorks S71 1SP
Telephone: Barnsley 87776

Aims	To help all claimants without distinction to secure their full social security entitlements; to educate, organise and agitate, not only to secure those basic rights, but to lift standards to a level that affords a decent and respectable life without the need for begging for additional grants; to educate claimants to become their own advocates; to bring an end to all means tested benefits, the wages stop, the co-habitation laws and an end to the disqualification of benefits before the hearing at an appeal tribunal.
Press & PR	Pat Wilkins, 11B Regent Street, Barnsley, S Yorks Telephone: Barnsley 89000
Membership	20,000
Fees	Full 50p p.a. (Full members must be in receipt of social security, unemployment benefits etc or pensions, hardship allowances); Associates £2 p.a.
Branches	5 regional; 124 local.
Publications	*Roundabout* (q); many advice pamphlets and reports.
Connections	Loose links with National Council of Social Service; Child Poverty Action Group (6); EEC Action Against Poverty.
History	Formed May 1969 – previously Study Group on Welfare Rights. Organises study groups to assist claimants in making claims including writing letters etc. Represents members in applications, appeals or Commissioners hearings. Has won thousands of pounds in extra benefits. Also runs courses on strike benefits for trade unionists. Aims to build regional co-ordination centres.

CONFEDERATION OF HEALTH SERVICE EMPLOYEES (COHSE)
Glen House, High Street, Banstead, Surrey
Telephone: Banstead 53322

Aims	To obtain and maintain reasonable hours of employment and a fair remuneration for Health and Welfare Service employees; to consider any matters relating to the general administration and efficiency of the Health and Welfare Services; to promote good relations between employers and employees; to establish a local Joint Staff Consultative Committee for each hospital or establishment; to secure settlement of disputes by negotiation or other lawful means; to provide legal assistance for members in approved cases in matters arising out of and in the course of their employment, or during the course of travel to or from such employment; to assist members in approved cases when out of employment by reason of a dispute between employers and employees; to provide benefits for members in accordance with the Rules; to promote legislation for the benefit of members and to maintain a political fund for the furtherance of this object; to circulate among members an official journal, monthly or otherwise; to assist other unions, societies, bodies or individuals catering for the welfare of workers and the community, subject to the discretion of the National Executive Committee; to secure generally, the complete organisation of all persons directly employed in the Health and Welfare Services and to improve the status and promote the welfare of all members of the union.

Officers	*General Secretary*	Albert Spanswick
	Assistant General Secretary	David Williams
	National President	Robert Vickerstaff
	Public Relations	Nick Grant

Prominent Members	(Parliamentary Representatives:) John Cronin, Bill Molloy, Michael Meacher, Alec Jones, Willie Hamilton.

Staff	95	
Membership	180,000	**Fees:** Joining 5p; 21p p.w.
Regional Offices	In 9 cities, throughout the UK.	
Publications	*Health Services* (m).	
Connections	Affiliated to the Trades Union Congress (3) and the Labour Party (1).	

History Dates from the National Asylum Works' Union in 1910; became the Mental Health and Institutional Workers' Union in 1930 and in 1946 merged with the Hospital and Welfare Services Union to become the present day COHSE. It now has representatives on more National Health Services negotiating committees than any other organisation. In 1974 COHSE organised the first ever national strike by nurses and increased its membership by 18.4%, the largest recorded growth in a single year of TUC affiliated unions. It aims to establish a single union for the health service and has a membership target of 200,000 by the end of 1976.

ELECTRICAL POWER ENGINEERS ASSOCIATION
Station House, Fox Lane North, Chertsey, Surrey KT16 9HW
Telephone: Chertsey 64131/4

Aims To act as a protective organisation and obtain for members the best possible conditions of employment and remuneration.

Officers
President	J R Acklan
General Secretary	J Lyons
Prominent members	include A Palmer MP

Staff 64

Membership 34,000

Fees £1.05 on joining. £12–18 p.a. according to salary.

Publications *EPE* (m)

Connections Affiliated to Trades Union Congress (3) and Public Services International.

History Formed in 1913 under the title of Association of Electrical Station Engineers; it took its present name in 1918 when it had approximately 7,000 members.

IRON AND STEEL TRADES CONFEDERATION
Swinton House, 324 Gray's Inn Road, London WC1X 8DD
Telephone: London 01-837 6691

Aims Principally to 'regulate the relations between workmen and employers, and between workmen and workmen and between employers and employers, and to impose restrictive conditions on the conduct of any trade or business and the provision of benefits to members'.

Officers	*General Secretary*	W Sirs
	Assistant General Secretary	R L Evans
	National Staff Officer	H A Feather
	PRO	R H Clayton

Prominent Members — include D Coleman MP

Membership — 120,000 (open to manual, staff and management workers in the steel and metal industries).

Publications — *Man and Metal* (m)

Connections — Affiliated to the Trades Union Congress (3) and the Labour Party (1).

History — Formed in 1917 as a result of a merger between the chief unions in the steel industry, the main one of which has been the British Steel Smelters. The architect of this amalgamation was Arthur Pugh, its General Secretary and Chairman of the TUC in 1926, at the time of the General Strike. A more recent General Secretary was Sir David Davies, who also served as Chairman of the Labour Party.

NATIONAL ASSOCIATION OF SCHOOLMASTERS/UNION OF WOMEN TEACHERS (NAS/UWT)
Swan Court, Waterhouse, Hemel Hempstead, Herts HPI IDT
Telephone: Hemel Hempstead 2971/4

Aims — To protect and promote the interests of its members; to improve the professional status of teachers; to improve the education service.

Officers	*President*	J Chalk
	Senior Vice-President	L Cooper
	Treasurer	R B Cocking
	General Secretary	Terry Casey

Staff — 44

Membership — 85,000

Fees — £12 p.a. (Qualified teachers recognised by the Department of Education and Science.)

Regional Offices — Birmingham; Liverpool; Washington, Tyne and Wear; Edinburgh; Newtownards, Co. Down.

Publications   *The Schoolmaster and Career Teacher* (9 p.a.).

Connections   Affiliated to the TUC(3); affiliated to National Federation of Professional Workers; represented on Burnham Committee, Schools Council, Open University, National Federation for Educational Research and on all Examining Boards for the Certificate of Secondary Education.

History   NAS formed 1919; it gained representation on the main negotiating body, the Burnham Committee in 1961 and merged with the Union of Women Teachers at the beginning of 1976, increasing its membership from 65,000 to 85,000. The new organisations plan to campaign for the setting up of a general teaching council.

NATIONAL SOCIETY OF OPERATIVE PRINTERS, GRAPHICAL AND MEDIA PERSONNEL (NATSOPA)
Caxton House, 13–16 Borough Road, London, SE1 0AL
Telephone: 01-928 1481

Aims   To endeavour to improve the conditions and protect the interests of its members; to endeavour to obtain and to maintain reasonable hours of work and fair rates of wages to promote a good understanding between employers and employed, the better regulation of their relations, and the settlement of disputes between them by arbitration or other lawful means; to provide the means of advancing the education standard and technical qualifications of its members, and to provide recreational facilities for its members and to appoint and employ where necessary technical and expert advisers in carrying out the intentions of these objects; to provide specified benefits.

Officers   *General Secretary*   Owen O'Brien

Staff   100

Membership   55,000   **Fees:** 35p p.w.

Regional Offices   2 in London; Sheffield; Manchester; Bristol; Glasgow.

Connections   Affiliated to the Trades Union Congress (3) and the Labour Party (1).

History   Established in 1889.

NATIONAL UNION OF AGRICULTURAL WORKERS

Headland House, 308 Gray's Inn Road, London WC1X 8DS
Telephone: 01-278 7801

Aims	To improve the pay and conditions of agricultural workers and to provide its members with benefits and services.

Officers

President	B Hazell
General Secretary	R N Bottini
Editor and Information Officer	S J Haywood

Membership	(approximately) 100,000.
Fees	Joining 10p; 95p per month.
District Offices	31 locations throughout England and Wales.
Branches	(approximately) 2,900.

Parliamentary Representative: Miss Joan Maynard MP

Publications *Land Worker* (m)

Connections Affiliated to the Trades Union Congress (3) and the Labour Party (1). The union has extensive contact with official and semi-official bodies, nationally and internationally, such as: the Agricultural Wages Board; the Agricultural Training Board; the Forestry Commission Industrial and Trades Council; the Forestry Workers Advisory Committee; the Farm Safety Steering Group of the Ministry of Agriculture; the Agriculture Safety Committee of the Royal Society for the Prevention of Accidents; the Economic Development Committee for Agriculture; the European Advisory Committee of the International Federation of Plantation, Agricultural and Allied Workers. Other connections include the Technical Committee of the British Standards Institution (2); British Agro-Chemical Association; British Occupational Hygiene Society; Socialist Medical Association (8) and the International Labour Organisation.

History Founded in 1906. It has had only six General Secretaries during its life. It took its present name in 1966. The union's current activities include securing wages and conditions equal to those in industry; pressing for the abolition of the tied cottage system; improving health safety and amenities of agricultural workers; opposing Britain's membership of the EEC and pressing for land nationalisation.

NATIONAL UNION OF BANK EMPLOYEES
Queen's House, 2 Holly Road, Twickenham, Middlesex TW1 4EL
Telephone: 01-891 9011/7

Aims	To improve the condition of service of bank employees; to provide services for its members; to negotiate on their behalf at national, institutional and office level.	
Officers	*General Secretary*	Lief Mills
	Deputy General Secretary	G G Hogg
	Research Officer	Jon Robinson
	Publicity Officer (and Editor NUBE News)	Bill Vose
Staff	80	
Membership	105,000	Fees: £12 p.a.
Regional Offices	In London and seven cities; 12 area organisers and branches nationwide.	
Publications	*NUBE News* (m)	
History	The seventh largest white-collar union in Britain, its membership is extending among insurance companies, finance houses and building societies. It is independent of employers' organisations and political parties alike.	

NATIONAL UNION OF JOURNALISTS
Acorn House, 314 Gray's Inn Road, London WC1X 8DP
Telephone: 01-278 7916

Aims	A trade union representing journalists working editorially in newspaper, magazine or book production, in radio, television and in public relations; to represent such members on conditions of employment etc and defend the professional interests of members.	
Officers	*General Secretary*	Kenneth Morgan
	Assistant Secretary	Ronald Hallett
Staff	19	
Membership	29,000	
Fees	Vary from £4 to £24 depending on membership category.	
Publications	*The Journalist* (m).	

Connections	Trades Union Congress (3); Scottish TUC; Press Council; Federation of Broadcasting Unions; British Copyright Council.
History	Formed 1907. Affiliated to TUC 1921; disaffiliated 1923; reaffiliated 1940. It has attempted amalgamation with Institute of Journalists on numerous occasions.

NATIONAL UNION OF MINEWORKERS
222 Euston Road, London NW1 2BX
Telephone: 01-387 7631

Aims	To protect and further the interests of its members.	
Officers	*President*	Joe Gormley
	Vice-President	Mick McGahey
	Secretary	Lawrence Daly

Prominent Members P Heathfield, J Collins, S Vincent, L Clarke, J Whelan W McLean, D Francis, E Williams, O Briscoe, P Tait, A Scargill, F Smith.

Parliamentary Representation: T Swain (NE Derbyshire), E G Varley (Chesterfield), D Skinner (Bolsover), R E Wolf (Blaydon), M T McGuire (Ince), E A Fitch (Wigan), G Grant (Morpett), J D Concannon (Mansfield), A Eadie (Midlothian and Pebbles), A Hunter (Dunfermline Burghs), A Wilson (Hamilton), A Woodall (Hemsworth), R Mason (Barnsley), E Wainwright (Dearne Valley), A Roberts (Normerton), J Harper (Pontefract), R Kelly (Don Valley), E Ogden (Liverpool, West Derby).

Membership	267,000
Fees	Vary according to area; each area pays the national union 20½p per member.
Regional Organisation	14 area secretaries and eight specialist groups (e.g. Power Group, Scottish Engineers, Northumberland Mechanics).
Publications	*The Miner* (m)
Connections	Affiliated to Trades Union Congress (3); Labour Party (1); Miners' International Federation.
History	Formed in 1945 as the successor to the Miners' Federation of Great Britain. Demonstrated its industrial power in the national strikes of 1972 and 1974 which led to the eclipse of Mr Heath's government.

NATIONAL UNION OF PUBLIC EMPLOYEES
Civic House, Aberdeen Terrace, London SE3
Telephone: 01-852 2842

Aims	To represent the interests of its members and to provide them with services.
Officers	*General Secretary* Alan Fisher
Prominent Members	(Parliamentary Representatives) A Bottomley, K Lomas, E Leadbitter, P Hardy, R Moyle, T Pendry.
Staff	120 officers and 300 clerical.
Membership	550,000
Fees	20p per week (full time employment); 14p (part time).
Regional Offices	25 offices throughout the UK. 1,800 branches.
Publications	*Public Employees* (m); *EC Report* (a); *Conference Report* (bi-a).
Connections	Affiliated to TUC (3); Scottish and Welsh TUCs; Irish Congress of Trade Unions; Public Services; International; National Council for Civil Liberties (6); Labour Research Department.
History	Formed in 1888 as the London County Council Employees Protection Society and took its present title in 1927.

NATIONAL UNION OF STUDENTS OF THE UK
3 Endsleigh Street, London WC1H 0DU
Telephone: 01-387 1277   Telex: 25951   Cables: Undergrad London

Aims	To represent the students of the UK locally, nationally and internationally; to promote and maintain the educational, social and general interests of students.
Officers	*President* Charles Clarke
Staff	NUS 70; owned service companies 400.
Membership	700,000. Membership is by block affiliation of students unions in universities and colleges.

Fees	Fixed percentage of membership fees to individual unions.
Publications	*Yearbook* (a), contains directory of all student organisations; *Grants Handbooks* (every 2 years); many other publications on student welfare and campaigns.
Connections	Member International Student Travel Conference; Council for Educational Advance; National Council for Civil Liberties (6); represented on most national bodies concerned with student affairs. Regular contact with Department of Education and Science.
History	Founded 1922 with membership restricted to universities. Technical and training colleges admitted 1940. Merged with Scottish Union in 1971. Governed by delegate conference which meets twice a year to determine policy and elect national executive. Independent National Union of School Students formed 1972. Recent activities have included campaigns against apartheid, cuts in education spending and for homosexual rights. It has plans in hand for re-development of HQ, improved welfare services for students and development of field staff to service student unions.

NATIONAL UNION OF TAILORS AND GARMENT WORKERS
Radlett House, West Hill, Aspley Guise, Milton Keynes
Telephone: 0908 583099

Aims	To protect and further the interests of its members; to improve the conditions of employment in the whole clothing industry; the moral and social elevation of its members; to regulate the relation between workmen and employers and between member and member; to eliminate all exploitation of labour by capital and to struggle to replace the present capitalist system by a socialist co-operative commonwealth.
Officers	*General Secretary* Jack Macgougan
	Assistant General Secretary Alex Smith
Staff	120
Membership	110,000 Fees: 16—22p per week.

Regional Divisions	London and South; Leeds and Yorkshire; Scotland; Ireland; North West; Western; East Midlands; North East.
Publications	*The Garment Workers* (m)
Connections	TUC (3); Labour Party (1); Amnesty International (5); Clothing Economic Development Board; Clothing Industry Training Board; International Textile, Garment and Leather Workers' Federation (Brussels).
History	Records go back as far as 1417, but a union started functioning in the clothing industry in 1710. From then, through a series of amalgamations, a line of descent leads to the present day union, the largest in the industry.

NATIONAL UNION OF TEACHERS
Hamilton House, Mabledon Place, London WC1H 9BD
Telephone: 01-387 2442
Cables: Curriculum London

Aims	To advance the status and conditions of the teaching profession; to advance the education system in the interests of the children.
Officers	*General Secretary* Fred Jarvis *Organising Secretary* Noel Jones *Press and PR* Henry Clother
Staff	200
Membership	250,00. Open to all qualified teachers.
Fees	£9 p.a. (£4 first year, £6 second year).
Publications	Annual Report; Members Handbook; many books and pamphlets.
History	Founded 1870 as National Union of Elementary Teachers; present name adopted 1873. Performs normal negotiating functions of a trade union. Plans to campaign for reduction in class size to 25 for reception classes and 30 for others. Membership increased by 15,000 in 1974 and 30 members were elected MPs in the October 1974 General Election.

PROFESSIONAL FOOTBALLERS' ASSOCIATION (PFA)
124 Corn Exchange Buildings, Hanging Ditch, Manchester M4 3BN
Telephone: 061-834 7554   Cables: Defensive Manchester

Aims	To represent its members as a trade union.	
Officers	*Chairman*	A D Dougan
	Secretary	C Lloyd
Staff	4	
Membership	Open to registered professional footballers in England and Wales.	
Connections	Affiliated to Ratio and Television Safeguards Committee; Federation of International Professional Footballers.	
History	Formed December 1907.	

TRADES UNION CONGRESS (TUC)
Congress House, Great Russell Street, London WC1B 3CS
Telephone: 01-636 4030   Cables: Tradunic

Aims	To do anything to promote the interests of all or any of its affiliated organisations or anything beneficial to the interests of past and present individual members of such organisations. Generally to improve the economic or social conditions of workers in all parts of the world and to render them assistance whether or not such workers are employed or have ceased to be employed; to affiliate to or subscribe to or to assist any other organisation having objects similar to those of the Congress; to assist in the complete organisation of all workers eligible for membership of its affiliated organisations and to settle disputes between the members of such organisations and their employers or between such organisations and their members, or between the organisation themselves.	
Officers	*Chairman*	Cyril Plant
	Vice-Chairman	Mrs Marie Patterson
	General Secretary	Len Murray
	Head of Information	Brian Murphy

General Council	D Basnett, R Birch, R N Bottini CBE, L W Buck, R W Buckton, F J Chapple, L Daly, A M Donnet, G A Drain, F Dyson, J F Eccles, L F Edmondson, A W Fisher, K Gill, J Gormley OBE, C D Grieve, T Jackson, F F Jarvis, C Jenkins, J L Jones MBE, W H Keyes, G Lloyd, D McGarvey CBE, J Macgougan, J T Morton, T Parry OBE, S Pemberton, Miss A M Prime, A L Sapper, H Scanlon, W Sirs, J H Slater, G F Smith CBE, C H Urwin, S Weighell
Staff	110–120
Membership	(approximately): 10,000,000 (in affiliated trade unions).
Fees	15p per member per annum.
Regional Offices	Include 9 Regional Councils and 54 County Associations and Trades Councils.
Publications	*Labour* (information broadsheet); *Annual Report; Economic Review* (a).
Connections	Six TUC members serve on the National Economic Development Council, also on the National Council of Labour (representing the TUC, Labour Party and Co-operative Union), and on the Economic and Social Committee of the European Community; European Trade Union Confederation; International Labour Organisation; TUC–Labour Party Liaison Committee.
History	Formed in 1868 and has since had a continuous existence as an association of trades unions; it is the accepted voice of organised labour. Between annual congresses its part in the continuing process of consultation between government, management and unions is supported not only by the contributions of the individual unions which are affiliated to the TUC but by the work of the specialist committees on which members of the general council serve at the 'back room' departments of the TUC; these include organisation, education, international, research, production, social insurance and industrial welfare, finance, press and publications. Representatives or nominees of the TUC, thus equipped, may serve on over 100 official or semi-official committees, boards, councils and commissions at any one time.

TRANSPORT AND GENERAL WORKERS' UNION (TGWU)
Transport House, Smith Square, London W1P 3JB
Telephone: 01-928 7788   Cables: Transunion London

Aims	To obtain, maintain and improve the wages and working conditions of members; generally, to promote the welfare of members; to provide certain cash benefits, legal advice and assistance; to further political objects.

Officers		
	General Secretary	Jack Jones
	Deputy General Secretary	Harry Urwin
	Press and PR Officer	R Harrison

Parliamentary Representatives: the TGWU sponsor 22 Members of Parliament.

Staff	1,200
Membership	1,850,000
Fees	Entrance 5p; 18p or 26p per week.
Regional Offices	11 throughout the UK, plus 160 District offices.
Connections	Affiliated to the Trades Union Congress (3), Scottish, Irish and Welsh TUCs and the Labour Party (1); it is affiliated also to international federations representing workers in transport, metal, commercial, clerical, technical, public service, chemical and industrial organisations; through the TUC it is closely associated with the International Congress of Trade Unions, at the International Labour Organisation; its members serve on numerous official bodies including National Economic Development Council; Advisory, Conciliation and Arbitration Service; European Communities Economic and Social Committee; National Ports Council; British Overseas Trade Board; National Enterprise Board; Industrial Development Advisory Board; Manpower Services Commission; Industrial and Safety Advisory Council of the Department of Employment.
Publications	*The Record* (m); *The Highway* (bi-m); numerous pamphlets and educational booklets for members' use.

History   On the initiative of Ernest Bevin in 1922 fourteen trade unions
amalgamated to form the TGWU. The total that has amalgamated
now stands at over 80, and the union, Britain's largest, is divided
into eleven trade groups embracing the many industries in which
it has members. Its future campaigns include the continuing
demand for the end of low pay and for a higher state retirement
pension.

TRANSPORT SALARIED STAFF ASSOCIATION
Walkden House, 10 Melton Street, London NW1 2EJ
Telephone: 01-387 2101   Cables: Foreshadow London

Aims   To represent and receive into membership clerical, technical,
supervisory, administrative and professional employees of
British Railways Board; London Transport; British Transport
Docks Board; British Waterways Board; National Freight
Corporation; Coras Iompair Eireann and the Ulster Transport
Authority and, at discretion of the Executive Committee, any
other transport undertakings in Great Britain and Northern
Ireland.

Officers   *President*   Tom Bradley MP
General Secretary   D A Mackenzie
Treasurer   W H Johnson MP
Press Officer   P H Wyatt

Prominent   *(Parliamentary representatives)* Tom Bradley MP,
Members   W H Johnson MP, S Cohen MP

Staff   84

Membership 73,000   **Fees:** 25p per week

Regional   York; Glasgow.
Offices

Publications *TSS Journal* (m, members only)

Connections Affiliated to the Trades Union Congress (3), the Labour Party (1)
and the National Federation of Professional Workers.

History   Formed in 1897 as the National Association of Railway Clerks.
It acquired its present name in 1952.

UNION OF CONSTRUCTION, ALLIED TRADES AND TECHNICIANS
UCATT House, 17 Abbeville Road, London SW4 9RL
Telephone: 01-622 2442

Aims	To advance and protect the working condition of all those employed in the construction industry of using construction skills in other industries.
Officers	*Chairman of*
	Executive Council H L Wilkinson
	General Secretary G F Smith
Prominent Members	(Parliamentary Representatives) E S Heffer MP, T W Urwin MP, R E Bean MP
Staff	300
Membership	270,000 **Fees:** 32p per week.
Regional Offices	In twelve centres.
Publications	*Viewpoint* (m)
Connections	Affiliated to the Trades Union Congress (3) and the Labour Party (1); represented on the National Joint Council for the Building Industry.
History	Formed in 1971 as the result of a merger between the Amalgamated Society of Woodworkers, the Amalgamated Society of Painters and Decorators, the Amalgamated Union of Building Trade Workers, and the Association of Building Technicians.

UNION OF POST OFFICE WORKERS
UPW House, Crescent Lane, Clapham, London SW4 9RN
Telephone: 01-622 9977   Cables: Postact London

Aims	To protect and promote the interests of members; to obtain improved pay, hours, leave, superannuation, and other general conditions of service; to pursue joint consultation with management at all levels of the service in order to secure the greatest possible measure of effective participation by the Union in all decisions affecting the working lives of its members; to encourage the amalgamation of organisations catering for Post Office workers into one industrial union.

Union of Post Office Workers (continued)

Officers	*General Secretary*	Tom Jackson
	Deputy General	
	Secretary	Norman Stagg
	Treasurer	F W Moss
	Editor	H Burnett

Prominent Members   (Parliamentary Representatives) H Ewing MP and C R Morris MP.

Staff   121

Membership   190,000

Fees   Full-time workers 21 and over 32p per week; under 21 or part-time 17p per week.

Qualifications Members must work in the postal, telegraph, telephone radio and communications industries.

Branches   1,200 throughout the UK.

Publications   *The Post* (f); *The Branch Officials Bulletin* (w, restricted circulation).

Connections   Affiliated to Trades Union Congress (3); Scottish TUC; Irish Congress of Trade Unions; Labour Party (1); Northern Ireland Labour Party; Council of Post Office Unions; Postal Telegraph and Telephone International.

History   Formed in 1920 by the amalgamation of 10 separate unions. Its withdrawal from the TUC and Labour Party was precipitated by the Trades Disputes Act in 1927, but the Act's repeal in 1946 enabled the Union to re-affiliate.

AIMS FOR FREEDOM AND ENTERPRISE
5 Plough Place, Fetter Lane, London EC4A 1AN
Telephone: 01-353 0621

Aims	To defend free enterprise and promote free market economy.	
Officers	*Chairman*	Sir John Reiss
	Director	Michael Ivens
	Secretary	E C L Hulbert-Powell
Staff	20	
Membership	4,000	
Fees	Variable; to corporate members only.	
Publications	*Government, Parliament and Industry* (newsletter, m), numerous booklets, briefings for MPs etc.	
Connections	With similar organisations abroad.	
History	Founded 1942. Has fought many campaigns for free enterprise including Mr Cube against nationalisation of sugar refining. Recently it has campaigned against more nationalisation and state control; against extremists; and against direct labour building by local authorities. Plans include campaign to promote understanding of role of free enterprise. Known as Aims of Industry until 1975 when a 'Free Enterprise Week' was held in July and the organisation renamed.	

AIR LEAGUE (Company limited by guarantee)
142 Sloane Street, London SW1X 9BJ
Telephone: 01-730 9285

Aims	To create greater awareness in official circles of the key contributions made by successful air activity to Britain's overall trade, communications and defence; to press for a strong Royal Air Force with effective air arms for the Royal Navy and the Army; strong air transport where airlines, business aviation and general aviation all make a full contribution; strong research and development; and strong teaching at all levels.

Officers	*Chairman*	Dr K G Bergin
	Director	John Motum
	Organising Secretary	Lily R Stewart
	Vice-Chairmen	Air Marshal Sir Harry Burton
		Rear Admiral H C N Goodhart
		Rex A Smith, Earl of Kinnoull
		Michael McNair-Wilson MP

Staff   2

Membership   Below 1,000

Fees   Patrons £5 p.a.; Ordinary membership under review.

Publications   *Notes* (intermittent); other occasional publications.

Connections   Strong links with Royal Aeronautical Society and friendly links with sectional interests.

History   Formed in 1909. Activities have included submissions to ministers and government departments on a continuing basis. Also, recent public forums on British Aviation in the EEC and Focus on Air Safety. Continued support for Concorde and Harrier and other supersonic or vertical take-off aircraft.

AIR SAFETY GROUP
5 Chalfont House, Chesham Street, London SW1
Telephone: 01-235 1850

Aims   To promote safety in civil air operations on an international basis with particular reference to those matters being given insufficient attention by statutory authorities and the aviation industry, emphasising the provision of a service to the air traveller.

Officers	*Chairman*	A F Taylor
	Honorary Secretary	Anna MacKenzie
	President	Dr K G Bergin
	Vice-Presidents	Lord Avebury, B W Townshend
	Deputy Chairmen	N B Tebbit MP, Lt Cdr C J Howe

Membership   35   **Fees:** £2 p.a.

Publications   *Cabin Staff and Air Safety; A Review of the Aviation Fuel Controversy.*

History   Founded 1964.

ANTI DEAR FOOD CAMPAIGN
Neville House, Wendens Ambo, Saffron Walden, Essex CB11 4LB
Telephone: Saffron Walden 40023

Aims	To work for policies that permit British consumers to purchase good food at the cheapest possible prices; to protest about and oppose vigorously all actions of Government which have the effect of making food more expensive to the ultimate consumer than would otherwise be the case; to organise opposition to the Government's acceptance of deliberate dear food policies under the European Community's Common Agricultural Policy.

Officers		
	Chairman	Oliver Smedley
	Honorary Secretary	R E Banks
	Honorary Treasurer	S W Alexander
	Public Relations	Miss Liz Brewer, Flat 1, Blenheim House, 180 Kings Road, London SW3.
	Vice-Presidents	Lord Briginshaw, Mrs M Johnstone, Christopher Frere-Smith, Sir Ian MacTaggart, C Gordon Tether

Prominent Members	Include Rev Richard Acworth, P Clavell Blount, Lady Demitriadi, Douglas Jay MP, Lady Alexandra Studd
Staff	1
Membership	1,500
Fees	Ordinary, minimum £1 p.a.; Benefactor £10 p.a.; OAP 50p; Associated Organisations under 100 members £2, over 100 £5 p.a.
Publications	*Anti Dear Food Campaigner* (irregular)
Connections	With all anti Common Market groups (5).
History	Formed March 1973 from members of Free Trade League and Cobden Club. Is successor of the Cheap Food League of the 1950s and Anti Corn Law League of 1940s. Activities have included demonstrations outside the office of the Intervention Board, National Farmers Union, the Treasury and the House of Commons. Has distributed over ½ million leaflets. In the referendum of 1975 it supported the Get Britain Out Campaign and has since continued with cheap food campaigning.

AUTOMOBILE ASSOCIATION
Fanum House, Basingstoke, Hampshire, RG21 2EA
Telephone: Basingstoke 20123

Aims	To conduct an association of members interested in all or any means of travel or transportation; to provide services and benefits for members; to promote safety on the roads.

Officers	*Chairman*	Lord Erroll
	Treasurer	Professor Esmond Wright
	Director General	A C Durie
	Secretary	W Lynch
	Public Relations	
	Manager	R S Campbell

Staff 6,500

Membership 5,222,700 **Fees:** Joining £2.50; £7.50 p.a.

Offices 5 regional HQs — Teddington; Bristol; Halesowen; Cheadle Hulme; Erskine. 150 branch offices and service centres throughout UK and Eire.

Publications *Drive* (bi-m); *Members Handbook,* (every two years); many other books, pamphlets etc., covering motoring, travel and leisure.

Connections Founder member of Alliance Internationale de Tourisme. With RAC (4) and Royal Scottish RAC forms standing committee to formulate policy on matters affecting all motorists. Member of British Roads Federation, and part-owner of Thomas Cook. Regular liaison with many bodies including GLC; Home Office; DoE; Metropolitan Police and Motor Agents Association (2).

History Formed in 1905 to protect interests of motorists being persecuted by the Police. From this it soon became a service organisation and later introduced sign-posting, hotel classification, touring facilities and free legal defence. It has pioneered many new services and now provides world's most comprehensive service. Recent activities include introduction of new services such as relay under which members suffering severe breakdown can have a car, luggage etc. transported anywhere in GB for a small fee. Published first detailed study of state of used cars following examination of 50,000 vehicles. Has also expanded consumer protection services (including Seal of Approval). Has continued to represent motorists views on issues such as taxation, legislation, environment, road construction etc.

BRITISH MEASURES GROUP
(A Charity)
6 Park Road, Teddington, Middlesex

Aims	Conservation of imperial measures; opposition to metrification.
Officers	*Chairman* Christopher Brunel
	Honorary Secretary Antony Insoll
Membership	No formal membership. Support welcomed from sympathisers.
Publications	*Bulletin* (occasional, restricted circulation); also free leaflets.
History	Formed June 1973 by merger of Anti-Decimal Group and the British Measures Group.

BRITISH STANDARDS INSTITUTION
(See Section 2)

CAMPAIGN FOR INDEPENDENT BROADCASTING
13 Ashwood House, London NW4
Telephone: 01-203 0861   Telex: 263236

Aims	To promote and maintain the introduction of licensed independent radio, with the aim of as many stations as technically feasible and commercially viable.
Officers	*Hon General*
	Secretary J W Wyndham-Kay
	Hon Press/PR Martin Rosen
Membership	500 **Fees:** 50p p.a.
Publications	Newsletter (q, to members only)
History	Formed in 1968 as National Commercial Radio Movement. Its name was changed in 1970. It is submitting a report to the Committee on the Future of Broadcasting. The organisation represents listeners and carries out discussions with the independent local radio stations.

99

CONSUMERS ASSOCIATION
14 Buckingham Street, London WC2N 6DS
Telephone: 01-839 1222   Telex: 918197

Aims	To offer an impartial comparative testing of consumer goods and service.	
Officers	*Chairman of Council*	Christopher Zealley
	President	Dr Michael Young
	Director	Peter Goldman
	Assistant Director	Alistair Macgeorge
	Deputy Directors	Miss Eirlys Roberts, Robin Woolf
	Secretary	David Tench
	Press Officer	Linda Millington
	Hon Vice-Presidents	include Dame Elizabeth Ackroyd, Mark Bonham Carter, Lord Boyle, Lord Feather, Baroness Gaitskell, Sir Geoffrey Howe MP, Sir Julian Huxley
	Members of Council	include Professor Gordon Borrie, Professor Alan Day, Philip Goodhart MP

Staff 432

Membership 700,000   **Fees:** Subscription to *Which?* – £3.75 p.a.

Publications *Which?* (m); also other *Which* magazines on Motoring, Money, Handyman, Holidays (each q); *Drug and Therapeutics Bulletin* (f); *Good Food Guide* (a); other booklets.

Connections Provides annual grant for National Federation of Consumer Groups (4). Miss Eirlys Roberts is Director of BEUC (European Consumers Bureau) and Peter Goldman is President of International Organisation of Consumer Unions.

History Formed 1957. Started with *Which?* and subscriptions grew rapidly. Other magazines introduced over the years. CA is independent of trade and government and neither accepts advertisements nor allows findings to be used in any form of advertisement or promotion. Apart from publishing, CA aims to improve the climate for the shopper in general by pressing for improvements in law and encouraging the government at home and in Europe to consult consumer opinion in the same way it consults trade, industry and trade unions. Recent legislation for which CA has lobbied has included the Consumer Credit Act, and the Unsolicited Goods Act.

CO-OPERATIVE UNION OF GREAT BRITAIN AND IRELAND LTD
Holyoake House, Hanover Street, Manchester M60 0AS
Telephone: 061-834 0975   Cables: Congress Manchester

Aims The national federation of the consumer co-operative movement in England, Wales, Scotland and Ireland, it acts as the co-ordinator, adviser and spokesman of the British co-operative movement; represents, with the exception of agricultural co-operatives, all branches and organisations of co-operative activity.

Officers

Chairman	B T Parry
Vice-Chairman	J H Perrow
General Secretary	D L Wilkinson
Deputy General Secretary	R Bluer
Manager, Publications and Information Dept	K Hulse

Staff 200

Membership 300 member societies **Fees:** Related to societies turnover

Regions (Sectional offices) Glasgow; Newcastle; Leeds; Manchester; Birmingham; London; Bristol; Belfast

Publications *Co-operative Review* (m); *Co-operative Gazette* (produced as required only to members)

Connections Retail Consortium; International Co-op Alliance; National Council of Labour; European Community of Consumer Co-operatives. Members include Co-op Wholesale Society; Co-op Insurance Society; Co-op Press.

History The Co-operative Union was established in 1869 to organise co-operative societies and diffuse knowledge of principles of co-operation. Now that movement is well established, Union's primary function is to co-ordinate, inform and advise Britain's retail societies and act as their national spokesman. Over the past 106 years has organised annual national congresses of the movement to decide on national policy and make pronouncements on political, social and economic affairs. The movement has its own political party which sponsors Labour Party candidates. Recent activity has involved the reorganisation of the structure of the movement. Regional Plan 2 envisages the reduction of the present 240 consumer societies into 26 large, powerful regional societies covering all Great Britain.

DUODECIMAL SOCIETY OF GREAT BRITAIN
69 Scotby Road, Scotby, Carlisle, CA4 8BG
Telephone: Scotby 430

Aims	To provide a constructive alternative to the metric system; to demonstrate the superiority of measures and currency based on dozenal arithmetic (12) to any based on decimal; to demonstrate that naturally developed methods, largely based upon divisible groups of twelve are superior to those restricted to an inflexible decimal progression; to afford a channel of informed resistance against any proposal intended to restrict our thinking to inept and outmoded methods.

Officers	*President*	Sir Iain Moncreiffe of that Ilk
	Secretary	Shaun Ferguson
	Information Secretary	
	and PR	F Whillock
	Chairman	Robert B Carnaghan

Membership 70   **Fees:** £1.20 p.a.

Offices   Information Secretary: 29 Underhill, Moulsford, Berks.

Publications   *Duodecimal Review*, (1 or 2 p.a.).

Connections   Two sister organisations: Duodecimal Society of America and Association Dozenalista de Sao Paulo, Brazil. Also corresponds with other anti-decimal groups.

History   Formed in 1958 by B R Bishop, Secretary to 1967. Joined by Duodecimal Association in 1966. International Duodecimal Conference held at LaHerpiniere, Beaumontel, Eure, France in 1960. Plans include continuing resistance to metrication; development of alternatives including provision of a metric (dozenal) system superior to either imperial or metric.

HOUSEOWNERS' ASSOCIATION
181 Queen Victoria Street, London EC4
Telephone: 01-248 3457/8

Aims	To provide advice and assistance on all aspects of buying and selling and financing houses and flats.

Membership   1,000

Publications   *Where to live in London* (bi-a); *The Houseowner* (q)

History   Founded 1970.

INCOME TAX PAYERS SOCIETY
1st Floor, 5 Plough Place, Fetter Lane, London EC4A 1XN
Telephone: 01-583 8181

Aims	To give advice on direct tax problems to members and making representations on tax anomalies to the Chancellor and in Parliament; to campaign for lower tax rates and to fight for fair taxation.

Officers		
	Chairman	W G Clark MP
	Honorary Treasurer	H P R Hoare
	Director	E C L Hulbert-Powell

Prominent Members	John Biffen MP, Bernard Vinson, Sir Ian Mactaggart Bt, Michael Ivens
Staff	2 (part-time)
Membership	Not disclosed.
Fees	Personal £3.30 p.a. Overseas: £4.40; Business/Professional £7.70.
History	Formed 1921, it has succeeded in getting some Budget suggestions adopted.

INSTITUTE OF ADVANCED MOTORISTS LTD
(A Charity)
Empire House, Chiswick, London W4 5TJ
Telephone: 01-994 4403

Aims	To improve the standard of driving and for the advancement of road safety; to establish an Advanced Driving Test.

Officers		
	President	Duke of Gloucester
	Vice-President	R K Munday
	Chairman	Major General E H G Lonsdale
	Vice-Chairman	F A Welch
	Treasurer	J M Robotham
	Chief Executive and Secretary	R B Peters
	Chief Examiner	W F Spinks
	Council Members	include Sir Harwood Harrison MP, Lord Somers, Lord Strathcawan

Staff	45		
Membership	65,000	Fees:	Test £6; Membership £3 p.a.
Qualifications	Members must pass the Advanced Driving Test.		

Publications   *Milestones* (q)

Connections   BMA (2); Royal Society for the Prevention of Accidents; Motor Schools Associations; Magistrates' Associations; AA (4).

History   Formed 1956.

LONDON PASSENGER ACTION CONFEDERATION
c/o 43 King Edward Mews
Telephone: 01-340 1547

Aims   To represent the views of the public transport users of the Greater London area; to campaign for the improvement of public transport facilities; to campaign against the further deterioration in facilities; to campaign for concessionary fares for old age pensioners and the disabled.

Officers
Chairman	A J Blackburn
Secretary	Dr M D Ashton
Treasurer	D H Henderson
President	Mrs Joyce Butler MP
Vice-President	John Page MP

Membership   21 transport, consumer, residents and other associations.

Fees   £2 per organisation.

Publications   *Fare Free and Frequent, Running Late,* criticism of GLC/LT policy.

History   Formed March 1970 by group of public transport users associations, it has helped achieve improvements including London Transport Passengers Committee and Public Transport Users Organisation, the introduction of minibus service C11, new trains on Northern Line and unions' acceptance of women drivers; supplemental licensing and bus-only routes for inner London now being campaigned against. Officers have appeared on BBC, ITV, Capital Radio, LBC and Radio London programmes to give their viewpoint.

LOW PAY UNIT
(Seeking charitable status)
9 Poland Street, London W1V 3DG
Telephone: 01-437 1780

Aims	To draw attention to the extent of law pay and its concentration in the wages council sector; to propose measures to tackle low earnings and act as a watchdog on Government, employers and trade unions to see how their actions affect the well-being of the low paid.
Officers	*Director* Frank Field *Advisory Committee:* *Chairman* B Philip Rowntree, Prof A B Atkinson, Hon D Layton, Roy Moore
Staff	4
Membership	No membership.
Publications	*Low Pay Bulletin* (bi-m); Low Pay Pamphlets, (approximately ten per year).
History	Formed in mid-1974, the unit has submitted its comments on relevant Government White Papers, discussion documents and proposed wage settlements. Plans include studies of low pay in catering, agriculture, and clothing and retail distribution. Circulation of *Low Pay Bulletin* to Wages Council members to stimulate a more informed debate on the problem of low pay.

NATIONAL ASSOCIATION OF RATEPAYERS' ASSOCIATIONS (NARA)
47 Victoria Street, London SW1H 0EQ
Telephone: 01-222 6220/01-886 8114

Aims	To provide a non-party-political platform for the protection and furtherance of the interests of ratepayers and residents individually and collectively, and for the discussion of common problems; to encourage and stimulate public interest and participation in local government and to secure an efficient and economical local government system of high integrity; to conduct campaigns in the interest of ratepayers and residents on such issues as may be agreed; to give a united voice to the ratepayers movement and enhance its influence and maintain public recognition of NARA as the representative organisation of ratepayers and residents throughout the country.

Officers	*President*	Lord Ellenborough
	Chairman and	
	PR Officer	Major Henry Haydon
	Honorary General	
	Secretary	Mrs M M Hobbs
	Honorary Treasurer	W L Stiles Cox

Membership 450–500 affiliated Federations and Associations; 200 individual members.

Fees £2 p.a. per 100 members to a maximum of £20. Constitutions must be completely non-party-political.

Publications *Information Bulletin* (q); Proposals for Rating Reform, evidence submitted to Layfield Committee 1974; also various leaflets.

History Founded in 1921. In past two years it has organised mass movement in favour of rating reform and has support of many MPs of all parties, and associations not in NARA. Submitted written evidence to Layfield Committee on Local Government Finance in 1974 and oral evidence in January 1975. Plans to continue for reform to eliminate the existing inequitable system of local taxation by rates and pending implementation of any proposals arising from Layfield, to urge the government and parliament to introduce interim measures to alleviate the rates burden. As a result of the massive rate increases, membership in both categories increased faster than any other comparative time, during 1974–75.

NATIONAL CAMPAIGN AGAINST INFLATION
59 Sherwood Avenue, Parkstone, Poole, Dorset, BH14 8DG
Telephone: Parkstone 744556

Aims To end inflation.

Officers	*Chairman*	John Mitchell
	Honorary General	
	Secretary	C Howard Jones

Membership Members not sought, it operates on basis of unregistered supporters.

Publications Reports (approximate m)

History Formed September 1973.

NATIONAL CONSUMER PROTECTION COUNCIL
London NW4 4NY
Telephone: 01-202 5787/6303/0212

Aims	To help the individual consumer with their individual consumer problems on a personal basis and to campaign for any action which might be against the consumers' interest; to help inform all consumers.

Officers

Patron	Dame Elizabeth Ackroyd
Honorary President	Cllr Mrs Rosa Freedman
National Organiser	Mrs R Dollas
Honorary Treasurer	Mrs C Klinger
Honorary Secretary	Miss Q Haimes
Parliamentary Advisers	(MPs) Geoffrey Finsberg, Dr Maurice Miller

Membership None. Finance comes from satisfied consumers.

Publications *Watch* (q, when finances permit).

History Founded in 1971 it has established close contact with official bodies and is represented on various committees.

NATIONAL FEDERATION OF CONSUMER GROUPS
61 Valentine Road, Birmingham, B14 7AJ
Telephone: 021-444 6010

Aims	To increase the awareness of consumers; to identify and promote the proper interests of consumers and the means of their protection; to provide a channel for consumer opinion and representation.

Officers

Secretary	Mrs Janet Upward
Vice-Presidents	Dame Elizabeth Ackroyd, Dr Michael Young, Mrs Jennifer Jenkins, Mrs Alma Williams, Mrs Mary Adams, Miss Elizabetl Gundrey, Michael Possener
Press Officer	Ken Bell

Membership 60 member groups with 11,000 members.

Fees Group £5 plus 7% subscription income; Associates £30 p.a.; Individual membership to groups usually £1 p.a.

Publications Monthly newsletter, to federated groups and associates only; *Index of Consumer Group Reports* (q); most groups produce their own literature.

Connections   Represented on Consumer Standards Advisory Committee; Consumer Complaints Panel Radio and TV Retailers Association; EEC Co-ordinating Group.

History   1961 Conference of Consumers' Association (4) decided to set up local groups to provide information at local level. Consumer Group formed at Oxford. 1963 32 local groups formed National Federation and national office set up. In 1972 the office moved to Birmingham and run with part-time helpers from secretary's home. Activities include active campaigns on one or two specific items each year. Recent campaigns include 'standard packaging', the banning of exclusion clauses in service contracts, better publicity for planning applications, and the setting up of small claims courts.

THE NATIONAL FEDERATION OF OWNER OCCUPIERS AND OWNER RESIDENTS ASSOCIATIONS LTD
c/o Paulian, 29 Norview Drive, East Didsbury, Manchester M20 0QF
Telephone: 061-445 6567

Aims   To promote the aims of owner occupiers' associations in matters of concern at Government level with regard to rating, town and country planning legislation, house building legislation and mortgage interest rates.

Officers

President	R C Blues
Chairman	M S Fisher
Secretary	J W Clark
Treasurer	I A Walton
Press and PR	J Galvin

Membership   10,000

Fees   5p p.a. through local association; open to all owner occupiers.

Regional Offices   Manchester; Barrow in Furness; Stafford.

Connections   Official delegates on National House Building Council, delegates on Clean Air Council and local delegates on Transport Authorities. Co-member of British Owner Occupier Council; liaises with National Union of Ratepayers Representatives.

History   Formed 1938. Recent activities include memorandum to inquiry into local government finance. Plans include campaigns on the abolition of present rating system and reduction of mortgage interest rate.

NATIONAL FEDERATION OF SELF EMPLOYED
Yorkshire Bank Chambers, The Square, Lytham St Annes, Lancashire
Telephone: St Annes 727075, 720911/2

Aims	To provide a national non-political-party voice and platform for its members and to take such steps as may be necessary to improve the lot of its members and to protect the interests of its members against all conflicting interests.

Officers	*President*	Norman C Small
	Chief Executive Officer	Keith M Shouls
	Public Relations	Russell Greer and Associates

Staff	32
Membership	30,000. Open to any person who is self-employed or directs or controls a small business.
Fees	£12 p.a.
Branches	Throughout country.
Publications	*First Voice.*
History	Formed September 1974 after a public meeting at a Blac. ~ol hotel.

NATIONAL HOUSE OWNERS' SOCIETY
19 Sheepcote Road, Harrow, Middlesex
Telephone: 01-427 6218

Aims	To remove the solicitors' monopoly in conveyancing; to modernise the British conveyancing system, possibly by title insurance as in the USA; to represent and protect the interests of owner occupiers.

Officers	*President*	Ken Weetch
	Chairman	Basil Blower
	Secretary	S G Carter

Staff	20
Membership	25,000
Fees	£1 p.a. for 7 years; £5 for life membership.
Offices	Teesside; South London; East London; Portsmouth; Essex; Hampshire; Exeter.

Connections   The House Owners Co-operative Limited.

History   Formed 1963 as Harrow Owners' Society. Achievements have included abolition of fixed scales for solicitors in conveyancing and changes in Land Registry forms indicating that solicitors have no monopoly of approach to Land Registry.

PERSONAL RIGHTS ASSOCIATION
31 Parkside Gardens, London SW19 5ET
Telephone: 01-946 0950

Aims   The Establishment of free enterprise.

Officers   *Honorary Secretary and Editor*   Henry Meulen

Prominent Members   Prof D R Myddelton, George K Young, Senator O P Hopwood (Minister of Indian Affairs, S Africa)

Staff   2

Membership   150   Fees: £3 p.a.

Publications   *The Individualist* (bi-m)

History   The Association was founded in 1871 by Professor J H Levy of London University. The last Honorary Secretary and Editor was the late Arnold Lupton MP who was succeeded by Henry Meulen in 1937. Plans include campaigning for end to government interference in currency exchange and gold price rates. The Association believe that the cause of boom and slump economy is state control of money supply. Floating price of gold should be introduced, and a 'clean' floating price for foreign currencies; freedom of note issue should be restored to commercial banks and state note issues abolished. This would enable many new banks to get started. The resultant growth of competition between banks would cause a cheapening of credit in an economy which, being unchecked by periodic 'stop—go' would develop freely. This would enable men of ability to start their own businesses and compete with the present uneconomic giant mergers. Industrial monopoly would thus be ended by a policy of greater individual freedom.

ROYAL AUTOMOBILE CLUB
83–85 Pall Mall, London SW1Y 5HW
Telephone: 01-930 4343   Telex: 23340   Cables: Raclubian

Aims	To provide services for motorists including roadside and breakdown, touring assistance, legal aid, publications; to improve road safety through training, films; control motor sport in GB and parts of the Commonwealth; to protect the interests of the motorists by propaganda and representations to central and local government and other bodies.

Officers

Chairman	Andrew G Polson
Secretary-General	Nelson Mills Baldwin
Home Services	Eric Charles
Motor Sport	Dean Delamont
Press and PR	Phil Drackett
Public Policy	A J A Lee
Touring Services	Eric Strologo

Staff	Approximately 3,000.
Membership	1,500,000
Fees	Joining £2; family £5.50 p.a. if one car only; other fees for motor sport etc.
Offices	Throughout UK.
Publications	*RAC World* (bi-m, free); *RAC Guide and Handbook* (a); many guides and publications.
Connections	With other motoring organisations in Standing Joint Committee; member of Federation International de l'Automobile; British Road Federation; Commonwealth Conference; close links with many other bodies and government departments.
History	Founded in 1897 as Automobile Club of Great Britain and Northern Ireland; granted Royal prefix in 1907. It was the first body to instruct and examine driving instructors, 1902; carry out observed trials on cars, 1900; train motor-cyclists, 1947; and introduce driving classes. Events organised include L Driver of the Year; International Rally of GB; London–Brighton Run; British Grand Prix etc. Recent activities have included prevention of closing of Albert Bridge to traffic; encouragement to a number of towns to adopt parking disc

schemes instead of parking meters. It plans to fight GLC in particular, which supports road-pricing and reduction of car parking space; to press government for reduction in motoring taxes and to accelerate the road construction programme, and to expand RAC Road Safety Office.

TELEPHONE USERS ASSOCIATION
35 Connaught Square, London W2 2HL
Telephone: 01-262 5988

Aims	To campaign for an improved telephone service; to provide an information service; to pursue particular personal problems with the Post Office on behalf of members.
Officers	*Chairman* Mrs Mary Adams *General Secretary* Mark Elwes
Prominent Members	include John Gorst MP
Staff	2
Membership	300 companies, 250 individuals who must be telephone subscribers.
Fees	Companies, £52.50 (with issued capital of more than £10 million or £10.50 p.a.; individuals £2 p.a.
Publications	Newsletter (bi-m)
History	Founded May 1965.

WIDER SHARE OWNERSHIP COUNCIL
22 Wormwood Street, London EC2
Telephone: 01-550 5617

Aims	To encourage a wider interest in investment.
History	Founded 1958.

AMNESTY INTERNATIONAL
53 Theobalds Road, London WC1X 8SP
Telephone: 01-404 5831   Telex: 28502   Cables: Amnesty London

Aims	To secure the release of prisoners of conscience: men and women imprisoned anywhere for their beliefs, colour, ethnic origin or religion, provided they have neither used nor advocated violence, and to provide them and their families with assistance where necessary; to oppose torture and capital punishment in all cases and without reservation; to secure fair and speedy trials for all political prisoners; to seek observance throughout the world of the UN Universal Declaration of Human Rights and of the UN Standard Minimum Rules for the Treatment of Prisoners.

Officers

Chairman	Dirk Börner
Vice-Chairman	Thomas Hammerberg
Secretary-General	Martin Ennals
Head of Information and Publications	Mark Grantham

Prominent Members
: The Archbishop of Canterbury, Sean MacBride, Roger Baldwin, Prof. Eric Fromm, Yehudi Menuhin, Prof. Gunnar Myrdal

Staff
: 70

Membership
: 40,000 in 60 countries. **Fees:** Vary by country.

Offices
: National sections in 32 countries plus one adoption group in the Soviet Union.

Publications
: *AI Newsletter* (m); individual reports.

Connections
: With UN bodies in New York and Geneva. Consultative status with ECOSOC, Council of Europe, recognised by UNESCO and OAU etc.

History
: Began as a one-year campaign called Appeal for Amnesty 1961. Campaign grew rapidly and an international meeting was held in Luxembourg by five European countries. Name changed in 1962, and an International Secretariat and Research Bureau set up in London 1963. Consultative status granted in 1964 at UN and Council of Europe. In 1972 evidence of growth of systematic torture by governments led to launch of campaign for the

Abolition of Torture. Major conference held in Paris in December 1973 and AI set up a special department to work full-time for the abolition of torture. By 1974, AI had 3,600 prisoners under adoption or investigation. During 1973/4, more than £100,000 was dispensed in relief to prisoners and their families and 27 missions and observers sent to 27 countries.

AMNESTY INTERNATIONAL (British Section)
55 Theobalds Road, London WC1X 8SP
Telephone: 01-242 1871/3

Aims	To campaign for Amnesty International in Britain including fund-raising; to start and maintain local groups which adopt and work for the release of prisoners of conscience, in any country except Britain.	
Officers	*Chairman*	The Rev. Paul Oestreicher
	Director	David Simpson
Staff	4	
Membership	2,500	**Fees:** £3 p.a.
Publications	*British Amnesty* (bi-m)	
History	See Amnesty International. Plans to double membership in UK and increase awareness of AI by wide range of national and local publicity drives.	

ANARCHIST BLACK CROSS
83a Haverstock Hill, London NW3
Telephone: 01-722 1604

Aims	Aid to all suffering from oppression but specifically political prisoners and as a beginning libertarian political prisoners in both 'East' and 'West' countries, help to international class struggle and active solidarity to victims.	
Officers	*Chairman*	Albert Meltzer
	Secretary	Stuart Christie
	International Secretary	Miguel Garcia
Membership	Restricted	
Publications	*Black Flag* (m)	

Connections   International Black Cross; work with other anarchist organisations in the country.

History   Originally, Anarchist Red Cross which helped political prisoners in Tsarist Russia and later Bolshevik Russia. Also general help in Italy and Spain until overwhelmed by repression and fascism. Revived by Scottish anarchist Stuart Christie after leaving Spanish prison, linking with Meltzer's Aid for Chinese Prisoners.

Since 1968, active throughout the world 'despite heavy secret police persecution', and it supports resistance in several totalitarian countries. Aids libertarian prisoners especially in Spain, and is building an international anarchist contact system. Italian and German secretaries died in police custody. Plans include greater involvement industrially in local affairs.

ANGLO-ARAB ASSOCIATION
33 Cavendish Square, London W1M 0AA
Telephone: 01-629 9405

Aims   To further Anglo-Arab friendship, on social, cultural, non-political planes.

Officers

Chairman	Sir Charles Duke
Vice-Chairman	D R Llewellyn
Hon Treasurer	G H Keast
Hon Secretary	M H Raath
Admin Secretary and Public Relations	Miss T M Rowe
Advertising	M Metcalfe

Staff   1

Membership   1500. New members must be introduced by an existing member.

Fees   £3 p.a.

Publications   *The Arab World* (q)

History   Present structure formed in 1961 after amalgamation with Anglo-Iraq Society. Activities include lectures, film shows, dinners, parties etc.

ANGLO CHILEAN SOCIETY (A Charity)
12 Devonshire Street, London W1N 2DS
Telephone: 01-580 1271

Aims	To advance the education of the people of the UK about Chile, its people, history, language and literature, its institutions, folklore, culture and economic life.	
Officers	*President*	The Chilean Ambassador, Rear Admiral Kaare Olsen
	Chairman	Dr Harold Blakemore
	Vice-Chairman	Sir Frederick Mason
	Hon Treasurer	Ralph D Young
	Secretary and PR	W R Smithson
Staff	2 — part-time	
Membership	450	
Fees	£3 p.a; £4.50 per married couple; £30 Life membership per person; £45 Life membership per married couple; £1.50 Junior and retired members	
Publications	*Chilean News* (2/3 times p.a.)	
Connections	A sister society in Santiago, Chile, with which there is close co-operation.	
History	Founded 1944. Supplies general information regarding Chile to colleges, schools etc, and has filmstrips, literature concerning Chile for lending free of charge. Also holds social events and lectures and talks on Chile.	

ANGLO-RHODESIAN SOCIETY
Calder House, 1 Dover Street, London W1X 4EH
Telephone: 01-493 4328   Cables: Angrohod, London

Aims	To provide a channel for the maintenance and expansion of understanding, friendship, contacts and goodwill between the United Kingdom and Rhodesia.	
Officers	*President*	Colonel Lord Forester
	Vice-President	The Marquess of Salisbury
	Chairman	T D Lardner-Burke
	General Secretary	T P Lawler
Prominent Members	R M Bell MP, Stephen Hastings MP, Harold Soref	
Staff	4	

Membership	500		**Fees:** £3 p.a.

Publications   *Rhodesian Report* (6 issues p.a.)

History   Formed as Friends of Rhodesia Association in February 1964. Re-formed as Anglo-Rhodesian Society in July 1965.

ANTI-APARTHEID MOVEMENT
89 Charlotte Street, London W1P 2DQ
Telephone: 01-580 5311

Aims   To end all British collaboration with the racist regimes of Southern Africa and to gain support for the struggle for freedom in Zimbabwe, Namibia and South Africa.

Officers

Chairman	John Ennals
Hon Secretary	Abdul Minty
Executive Secretary	Basil Manning
Treasurer	A P O'Dowd
Hon President	Rev. Ambrose Reeves
Vice-Presidents	Jack Jones, Bishop Trevor Huddleston Joan Lestor MP, Jeremy Thorpe MP

Sponsors   include Lord Brockway, Reg Prentice MP, David Steel MP

Staff   6

Membership   3,500

Fees   £2.00 p.a.; other rates for institutions, pensioners etc

Branches   40 local groups organising campaigns etc; also many student groups

Publications   *Anti-Apartheid News* (ten p.a.), fact sheets, reports and pamphlets

Connections   Consultative status with UN Economic and Social Council; many organisations affiliated to AAM including 40 represented on the national committee.

History   Formed 1959 following call of Chief Albert Lutuli for international boycott of apartheid South Africa. Previously known as Boycott Movement. Activities include meetings, campaigns, demonstrations, lobbying etc.

ANTI-COMMON MARKET LEAGUE
52 Fulham High Street, London SW6
Telephone: 01-736 7393

Aims	Opposition to British membership of the EEC under the Treaty of Rome.	
Officers	*Chairman*	Sir Robin Williams
	Treasurer	T N Neate
	Secretary	Mrs M Coneybeare
	President	Victor Montagu
Staff	1	
Membership	6,000	**Fees:** None fixed
Branches	50 throughout Britain	

Publications Newsletters, leaflets including *What the Treaty of Rome means* (1967), *Britain not Europe* (1962)

Connections Shares office and aims with Common Market Safeguards Campaign.

History Formed 1961 to oppose application of Macmillan Government to join EEC. Mounted active campaign and distributed over one million leaflets. Similar campaign in 1970/72. Formed National Referendum Campaign with other 'anti' groups in 1975. Actively campaigned to mobilise votes during the referendum.

ANTI-SLAVERY SOCIETY FOR THE PROTECTION OF HUMAN RIGHTS
(A Charity)
60 Weymouth Street, London W1N 4DX
Telephone: 01-935 6498

Aims The eradication of slavery and forced labour in all their forms. The protection and advancement of aboriginal people; the defence of human rights in accordance with the Universal Declaration of Human Rights 1948.

Officers	*Chairman*	Jeremy Swift
	Hon Treasurer	E H Brooks
	Secretary	Colonel J R P Montgomery

Presidents, Vice-Presidents and Committee: include Dr Nnamdi Azikiwe, Lord Wilberforce, Dr Hastings Banda, Lord Butler, Dame Margery Perham, Peter Archer MP, Sir Robert Grant-Ferris MP, Tom Iremonger, James Johnson MP, Dame Joan Vickers, Baroness White

Staff	2
Membership	1,000
Fees	Ordinary £2 p.a.; Associate 50p p.a.; Life £50
Publications	Annual Report; *Anti-Slavery Reporter and Aborigines' Friend* (irregular)
Connections	Consultative status at UN Economic and Social Council; on ILO Special List.
History	The Aborigines Protection Society founded 1838 and the British and Foreign Anti-Slavery Society founded 1839, merged in 1909 to form present society. It is the sole source of published material on contemporary slavery throughout the world. Aims to provide governments with verified information for investigation and proceeds by discreet diplomacy, submission to the UN or publication whichever is the most appropriate. The society prepared the first drafts of the Slavery Conventions of 1926 and 1956. The latter has been ratified by 79 states. Recent activities have included effective enforcement of anti-slavery law in Cameroun (1969), report on opium growing by serf labour in Afghanistan in 1971 which led to two official Afghan government committees in 1972, and visits to Iran and Brazil to assess measures taken to enforce the law. Society representatives have spoken in UN ten times in past decade.

ASSEMBLY OF CAPTIVE EUROPEAN NATIONS
8 Alma Terrace, London W8 6QY
Telephone: 01-937 1797

Aims	Joint political action for the self-determination of peoples of Albania, Bulgaria, Czechoslovakia, Estonia, Hungary, Latvia, Lithuania, Poland, Rumania.
Publications	*ACEN News*
History	Founded in 1954

BERTRAND RUSSELL PEACE FOUNDATION LTD
Bertrand Russell House, Gamble Street, Nottingham NG7 4ET
Telephone: 0602 74504   Cables: Russfound

Aims	To oppose institutionalised violence and cruelty, to identify the obstacles to world community and campaign against them, and to further the cause of peace with freedom and justice; to promote research into problems of disarmament, wars and imperial domination and to publish the results.
Officers	*Directors* Ken Coates, Chris Farley *Secretary* Ken Fleet
Staff	8
Offices	In Brisbane, Australia; France; Nagasaki, Japan; Ljubljana, Yugoslavia
Publications	*The Spokesman* (bi-a); Spokesman pamphlet series (10 p.a.); many books and pamphlets
Connections	Close working relationship including shared offices with International War Crimes Tribunal; Russell II Tribunal on Repression in Latin America; Institute for Workers Control (1); Russell Press. Close links with Amnesty International (5); NCCL (6); British Indonesia Committee etc.
History	Founded 1963 and incorporated 1966. Founded International War Crimes Tribunal 1966. Established Bertrand Russell House. Activities have included continuing campaigns in support of Cambodia and Sihanouk Government; in support of Allende Government in Chile and against post-coup repression; world university campaign against repression of dissidents and academic freedom in Eastern Europe. Constant work on behalf of political prisoners in many countries. Plans to develop work of Russell II Tribunal.

BRITISH CAMPAIGN FOR PEACE IN VIETNAM
313/5 Caledonian Road, London N1 1DR
Telephone: 01-607 0465

Aims	To promote peace in Indo-China
Officers	*President* Lord Brockway *Chairman* Alfred Lomas *Vice-Chairman* Dick Nettleton *Joint Secretaries* Florence Croasdell and Jack Askins *Treasurer* A H Macdonald

Membership 200

Fees Individuals £1.50 p.a.
Organisations: National £5 p.a; Regional £3 p.a; Local £2 p.a.

Branches Kent Council, Rochester; North West Council, Middleton, Lancs.

Publications Pamphlets published at intervals

Connections Stockholm Conference on Vietnam, International Liaison Committee; National Peace Council (5); All-Britain Peace Liaison Group.

History Formed as British Council for Peace in Vietnam in 1965. Consistently campaigned for peace and protested against US bombing. Campaigned for peace agreement and British government recognition of Provisional Revolutionary government of the Republic of South Vietnam.

CAMPAIGN FOR NUCLEAR DISARMAMENT
Eastbourne House, Bullard's Place, London E2 0PT
Telephone: 01-980 0937
Scottish CND: 420 Sauchiehall Street, Glasgow

Aims The unilateral abandonment by this country of nuclear weapons, bases and alliances as a prerequisite for a British foreign policy which has the abandonment of nuclear, chemical and biological weapons as its prime objective; opposed to the manufacture, stockpiling, testing, use and threatened use of such weapons by any countries; believes this stance is not consistent with support for any of the power blocs and will oppose the policies of any country which — in the view of the Campaign — make a nuclear holocaust more likely or hinder the achievement of a world without nuclear, chemical or biological weapons.

Officers
Chairman	John Cox
Vice-Chairmen	Olive Gibbs, Dick Nettleton and Jo Richardson MP
Treasurer	Alistair Macdonald
General Secretary	Dan Smith

Sponsors Include 14 MPs, representatives of the arts, sport, church, trade unions, etc, including Benjamin Britten, Spike Milligan, J B Priestley, Lord Soper, Lord Brockway, Gwynfor Evans MP, Michael Foot MP, Ian Mikardo MP, Clive Jenkins, Jack Jones, Hugh Scanlon, John Arlott, James Cameron, Sir Julian Huxley.

Staff	3
Membership	Full — 3,000; affiliated — 1,200,000
Fees	Adult £4; joint £6; student £2; youth/OAP £1; affiliation on application
Publications	*Sanity* (every two months); *Briefing* (q)
Connections	National Peace Council (5); United Nations Association; International Conference for Disarmament and Peace. Affiliated bodies include many unions including NUPE (3), ASLEF, SOGAT.
History	Formed January 1958. First public meeting February 1958 and first Aldermaston March Easter 1958.

CHILE COMMITTEE FOR HUMAN RIGHTS
64 Millbank, London SW1

Aims	To bring relief to those suffering as a result of the events in Chile, September 11th 1973.	
Officers	*President*	Joan Jara
	Hon Secretary	Alec Kitson
	Secretary and PR	Wendy Tyndale
	Press	Susan Carstairs
Sponsors	Include Lord Ramsey, Mgr Bruce Kent, Lord Soper, Dame Peggy Ashcroft, Harold Pinter, Norman Buchan MP, Stanley Clinton Davis MP, Judith Hart MP, Eric Heffer MP, Greville Janner MP, Russell Johnston MP, Neil Kinnock MP, Cyril Smith MP, Graham Tope, Lord Gardiner, Irish Murdoch	
Staff	2	
Membership	200	**Fees:** £2 p.a.
Publications	*Chile One Year After the Coup, Life in Chile*	
History	Formed January 1974. Chile Relief Fund registered as charity 1974. Activities have included pressure on government to permit refugees to enter Britain, sending investigating missions to Chile and meetings held to raise funds including £500 sent to Committee for Peace in Chile.	

COMMUNISTS FOR EUROPE
138 Lordship Road, London N16
Telephone: 01-802 6182

Aims	A democratic union of European nations; the transfer of sovereign political power to the European parliament from the EEC's member states; the establishment of a directly elected European parliament; the development of European working class organisations in political parties and a European TUC; greater workers' control in European industries; economic and monetary union of the EEC states.	
Officers	*Chairman*	Alan Jones
	Secretary	Richard Spicer
	Treasurer	John Lloyd
Staff	Nil	
Membership	200	Fees: £1 p.a.
Regional offices	10 Athol Street, Belfast 26 Essex Quay, Dublin	
Publications	*Convention Documents* (a); *International Bulletin* (bi-m — members only); *The Economic Case for the EEC*	
Connections	British and Irish Communist Organisation; attempting to join with other groups of similar beliefs and aims.	
History	Formed early 1975 and actively participated in the referendum campaign independently of the main 'Britain in Europe' organisation which it regarded as devoid of principle by denying the essential importance of political union. Intends to continue activity among socialists in Britain and to develop contacts in Europe.	

ESPERANTO LOBBY
140 Holland Park Avenue, London W11 4UF
Telephone: 01-727 7821   Cables: Esperanto London

Aims	To promote the international language Esperanto; to ensure that the case for Esperanto is known to MPs, governments throughout the world; to promote and aid the promotion of Esperanto in government by groups of Esperantists and non-esperantists.	
Officers	*Chairman*	Ron Coverson
	Secretary	Miss Joan Burton
	Press Officer	Brian Barker

Staff	2
Membership	500. Open only to supporters who have particular skills or knowledge in the promotion of ideas/beliefs/causes to government and are prepared to be active in this field. There is an Esperanto parliamentary group of 43 members.
Fees	None
Publications	*Esperanto Lobby* (8 per year); *Parliamentary Courier* (3 per year, English-speaking MPs world-wide)
Connections	British Esperanto Association; European Esperanto Centre; Universal Esperanto Association
History	Founded by present Chairman in May 1972. Organised parliamentary group, originally with 33 members. Ernle Money MP addressed Universal Congress in Hamburg 1974. Organised nomination by 23 MPs of the Universal Esperanto Association for Nobel Peace Prize 1975. Plans include setting up of group in European parliament, a campaign to secure support in the UN, and to gain acceptance of Esperanto as GCE subject.

EUROPEAN MOVEMENT (BRITISH COUNCIL) LTD
Europe House, 1A Whitehall Place, London SW1A 2HA
Telephone: 01-839 6622

Aims	To promote European unity, including the creation of a full European economic and political union, democratically controlled by a directly elected European parliament.	
Officers	*Chairman*	Lord Harlech
	Deputy Chairman	Sir Geoffrey de Freitas MP
	Vice-Chairmen	Lord Gladwyn and Lord Duncan-Sandys
	Director	Ernest Wistrich
	Prominent members	include 325 MPs (225 Conservative, 87 Labour, 13 Liberal)
Staff	45	
Membership	3,000	**Fees:** £3 p.a.
Branches	50 throughout the United Kingdom	
Publications	*Facts* (m); *New Europe* (q)	

Connections	International European Movement, with its head office in Brussels.
History	Formed 1948 following the first Congress of Europe held in the Hague, May 1948. Continuing work to promote a European Union by 1980.

HASLEMERE GROUP
467 Caledonian Road, London N7 9BE
Telephone: 01-607 3834

Aims	To discuss and draw public attention to the growing social and economic crisis facing the Third World, and the failure of the rich industrialised countries to recognise their responsibilities for this crisis; to engage in research and public education on these issues.	
Officers	*Chairmanship*	Rotates on a three-monthly basis
	Treasurer	Barbara Hughes
	Press and PR	Penny Cloutte
Staff	1	
Membership	Fifty	**Fees:** 50p p.a.
History	Formed 1968 with publication of Haslemere Declaration, which has sold 250,000 copies world-wide.	

INTERNATIONAL LANGUAGE (IDO) SOCIETY OF GREAT BRITAIN
18 Lane Head Rise, Staincross Common, Mapplewell, Barnsley
South Yorks S75 6NQ.   Telephone: Darton 2538

Aims	To study, encourage and spread the use of the international language IDO by individuals, groups and interested organisations; to urge the UN through HM Government to recommend the use of IDO as a second language to be taught in schools in all countries.	
Officers	*President*	Henry Neulen
	Chairman and Acting Secretary	Niklas apGawain
	Treasurer and Editor	Tom Lang
Membership	30	**Fees:** £1.25 p.a. Students 50p

International Language (IDO) Society (continued)

Publications *IDO-Letro* (q, in English and IDO); *Progreso* (q, entirely in
IDO); *Kroniko di IDO (q)* (IDO Society of America);
IDO for All (textbook)

Connections Affiliated to *Uniono por la Linguo Internaciona*, Geneva, which
has consultative status by UNESCO. Friendly relations with
IDO Societies in other countries.

History The British Idistic Society was founded about 1912. Among
early Presidents were Professor Otto Jesperson, Professor
F G Donnan and Dr J L Moore. In recent years active members
have included Henry Jacob, lately Director of Publications,
British Museum and author of several standard works on international language, Dr Siegfried Auerbach and Rev Dr W J Bolt.
From 1930 has published a regular bulletin, now a quarterly
known as *IDO-Letro*. Representatives sent to International IDO
Conference in Cardiff, July 1973. Runs a book service for books
in IDO or dealing with international language in general.

JUSTICE (British Section of the International Commission of Jurists)
12 Crane Court, Fleet Street, London EC4
Telephone: 01-353 9428

Aims An all-party lawyers association to promote the principles of
the rule of law and assist in maintaining the highest standards
of administration of justice.

Membership 1,500

History Founded 1957

MINORITY RIGHTS GROUP (A Charity)
Benjamin Franklin House, 36 Craven Street, London WC2 5NG
Telephone: 01-930 6659

Aims To secure justice for minority or majority groups suffering
discrimination, by investigating their situation and publicising
the facts as widely as possible, to educate and alert public
opinion throughout the world; to help prevent such problems
from developing into dangerous and destructive conflicts; to
foster, by its research findings, international understanding of
the factors which create prejudiced treatment and group
tensions. The aims of MRG are remedial, preventive and
educative.

Officers	*Chairman of Council*	Jo Grimond MP
	Director	Ben Whitaker

Sponsors and Council   Include Lady Butler, Lord Goodman, Sean MacBride, Gunnar Myrdal, Dr Joseph Needham, David Astor, Professor Sir Robert Birley, George W Cadbury, Rev Michael Scott

Staff   2

Publications   Over 20 reports dealing with various ethnic, religious and other groups

Connections   Consultative status with UN (ECOSOC)

History   Formed 1969. Initially funding came from Ford Foundation grant and a few private individuals. It does not have a membership structure and relies on donations. Apart from publishing activities MRG plans meetings, seminars and conferences on minority issues.

NATIONAL PEACE COUNCIL
29 Great James Street, London WC1N 3ES
Telephone: 01-242 3228

Aims   To educate people in the ways of peace and prevention of war, to promote the study of good relations between peoples and of approaches to international co-operation in their religious, economic, scientific, political and social aspects; to consider policies necessary for the settlement of disputes, the maintenance of peace and the prevention of war and to promote these policies at all appropriate levels.

Officers	*Chairman*	Arthur D Hewlett
	Secretary and PR	Albert E Tomlinson

Prominent members   Philip Noel Baker, Frank Allaun MP, Lord Soper, Lord Caradon

Affiliates   Include ASTMS, TGWU (1), USDAW, CND (5)

Staff   1

Membership   700 plus 76 affiliate organisations

Fees   £3 p.a.; £5 for organisations (minimum)

Publications   News Sheet (members only)

Connections   Affiliated to International Peace Bureau

History   Formed in 1908. During 1973, delegation visited the Soviet Union.

OXFAM (Oxford Committee for Famine Relief) (A Charity)
274 Banbury Road, Oxford OX2 7DZ
Telephone: Oxford 56777   Telex: 83610   Cables: Oxfam

Aims	To relieve poverty, distress and suffering in any part of the world and primarily when arising from any public calamity (including famine, earthquake, pestilence, war or civil disturbance) or the immediate and continuing result of want or artificial resources. In particular, to provide food, healing, clothing, shelter, training and education or assist in work to achieve that purpose; to promote research into medical, nutritional and agricultural matters related to the relief and publication of results.
Officers	*Chairman* Michael Rowntree *Director* Brian Walker
Staff	300
Membership	No formal membership
Offices	144 throughout UK
Publications	*Oxfam News* (m); Annual Report; various booklets on population, world food resources etc.
Connections	With Oxfam in US, Canada, Belgium; Community Aid Abroad, Australia; International Committee of Voluntary Agencies; Voluntary Committee on Overseas Aid; Disasters Emergency Committee.
History	Formed 1942 as Oxford Famine Relief Committee and registered as war charity. Became a company limited by guarantee in 1957 and adopted name Oxfam in 1965 by permission of Board of Trade. About 70 % of overseas programme (some £3 million) is used to fund long-term projects designed to encourage self-help and to lessen the effects of disasters and famine. Aid is given without regard to politics, race or sectarian religion to nearly 100 countries. Approaches made to government on matters affecting charities, tax etc and where political settlements rather than violent actions are desirable.

PALESTINE ACTION CAMPAIGN
101/103 Gower Street, London WC1

Aims	To publicise the Palestinian case in Britain and to provide a focus for support for the Palestinians in Britain.
Officers	*President* Andrew Faulds MP
Membership	500
Fees	£2 p.a; students £1; senior citizens 50p
Publications	*The Case of Shawqi Khatib* (1974); Diary of Palestine, and a newsletter to members.
History	Founded 5th June 1972. Holds regular meetings for members in London and organises public meetings several times a year and provides speakers and films for meetings on Palestine. An independent organisation which is not associated with any other in Britain or overseas.

SOCIALIST INTERNATIONAL
88a St John's Wood High Street, London NW8
Telephone: 01-586 1101   Telex: 261735   Cables: Intesocon London

Aims	To strengthen relations between affiliated parties to co-ordinate their political attitudes by consent; to work for association with parties which stand in the democratic socialist tradition but which are not yet formally in membership; to end all forms of exploitation — of man by man and of nation by nation — and to establish social justice within and between nations.	
Officers	*Chairman*	Dr Bruno Pitterman
	Vice-Chairmen	Willy Brandt, Trygve Bratteli, Sicco Mansholt, Golda Meir, Francois Mitterand, Pietro Nenni, Giusseppe Saragat, Sir Harold Wilson
	Secretary	Hans Janitsche
Staff	11	
Membership	56 affiliated parties, 7 organisations and 1 regional organisation	
Fees	Affiliation fees are annual and depend on size and capacity of member party to pay.	

Publications *Socialist Affairs* (bi-m); *Sinews* (a news and feature bulletin)

Connections Associated Organisations of the SI are International Council of Social Democratic Women; International Falcon Movement/ Socialist Educational International; International Federation of the Socialist and Democratic Press; International Union of Social Democratic Teachers; International Union of Socialist Youth; Labour Sports International; Socialist Union of Central-Eastern Europe. Also consultative status with the United Nations and close contacts with International Confederation of Free Trade Unions.

History Dates from First International — International Workingmen's Association 1964—76; Second International 1889—1914; Labour and Socialist International 1923—40; International Socialist Conference 1846—51 and became Socialist International 1951, established by over 100 representatives from 34 parties. Congresses held every three years. Recent activities include bureau meeting in Santiago, Chile 1973, Party Leaders' Conference London, November 1973 and Chequers, June 1974; mission to the Middle East 9—16 March 1974; Party Leaders' Conference, West Berlin, February 1975; Australian Bureau Meeting, May 1975; Congress 1975; mission to the Middle East, 1975.

SOUTH WEST AFRICA PEOPLE'S ORGANISATION (SWAPO)
(London Office) 21—25 Tabernacle Street, London EC2
Telephone: 01-588 1878

Aims Liberation movement of Namibia (South West Africa); fighting for the total withdrawal of South Africa and the independence of Namibia as a unitary state.

Officers *President* Sam Nujoma
Acting Vice-President Mishake Muyongo
National Chairman David Meroro
Representative in the
UK & Western Europe Peter H Katjavivi

Offices Head Office — PO Box 577 Lusaka, Zambia; others in London, Stockholm, New York, Dar es Salaam, Dakar

Publications *Namibia News* (bi-m)

History   Founded in 1958 under the name Ovamboland People's Organisation; soon became national party under present name. In 1966 began armed struggle against South African forces. In 1968, 38 leaders including Herman Toivo, the founder of SWAPO, sentenced to 20 years or life imprisonment on Roben Island. In 1973, recognised by UN as authentic representative of the Namibian people.

WORLD DEVELOPMENT MOVEMENT LIMITED
Bedford Chambers, Covent Garden, London WC2E 8HA
Telephone: 01-836 3672

Aims   The fight against the injustice of poverty: a process of social, economic and political change which will enable all to realise their full human potential; by campaigning in Britain it hopes to close the gap in living standards between the developed countries and the Third World.

Officers

Chairman	Miss Sarah Wells
Hon Secretary	Rupert Pennant Rea
Hon Treasurer	Chris Stockwell

Prominent members   Include His Excellency Gamani Corea, Robert Gardiner, Bishop Trevor Huddleston, Lord Caradon, Anthony Tasker, Rev Colin Morris, Professor Gunnar Myrdal, Lord Brockway

Staff   12

Membership   128 local action groups. Only open at present to action groups though individual and affiliate membership to be opened shortly.

Fees   £40 p.a. minimum

Branches   Rugby, Leeds, Reading

Publications   *Spur* (m); various pamphlets and leaflets

Connections   Works closely with charitable aid agencies and churches; also linked to Third World Publications.

History   Began in 1970 as Action for World Development after a National 'Sign-In' in the churches about world poverty. At first promoted by Oxfam, Christian Aid etc but now independent and democratically controlled by a nationwide grass-roots organisation. Has recently campaigned for more government aid, continued access for Commonwealth sugar producers, the removal of trade barriers against the import of cotton textiles from poorer nations and for fairer relations between the EEC and the Third World. Current activities include campaign about food crisis in Third World. Plans to campaign about UNCTAD IV Conference in Nairobi in 1976 and its work is expanding in the Labour and Liberal parties and trades unions.

AGE CONCERN ENGLAND
(A Charity)
Bernard Sunley House, 60 Pitcairn Road, Mitcham, Surrey, CR4 3LL
Telephone: 01-640 5431

Aims	To promote the welfare of the elderly by assisting with and carrying out investigations and surveys into their needs; arranging exhibitions, meetings, lectures, classes and training courses; by promoting co-operation nationally and locally by bringing together in conference voluntary agencies, statutory authorities and individuals engaged in the care of the elderly.

Officers

Patron	HRH The Duchess of Kent
President	Lord Seebohm
Chairman	Professor J C Bricklehurst
Director	David Hobman
Press and PR	Corinne Pearlman
Advertising	Jack Hayward

Staff	44
Membership	300
Fees	Scheme 1: £8 p.a.; Scheme 2: £2.50 p.a.; Scheme 1 is for those requiring full technical service.
Offices	Well over 1,000 local organisations throughout UK, and corresponding national bodies in Scotland, Wales and N Ireland.
Publications	*Age Concern Today* (q); *Your Rights* (a); many other research reports etc.
Connections	With many other national voluntary organisations.
History	Formed in 1940 as Committee for the Welfare of the Aged. In 1955 became known as National Old People's Welfare Council. Old people's welfare committees were formed in local areas with encouragement of NOPWC. In 1971 adopted the name Age Concern and became Age Concern England in 1973. Has campaigned for higher pensions and the abolition of the earnings rule for several years. Publication in May 1975 of *Manifesto on the Place of the Retired and the Elderly in Modern Society*, the culmination of two years' work with the

contribution of 10,000 people. Age Concern will promote this and campaign on issues arising such as visiting schemes, emergency telephone contact, self-help employment co-operatives, nursing care, housing etc. Many other reports have been carried out on subjects such as shopping, health, transport etc and these have been used as a basis for policy for presentation to government. The national body provides support for the many local bodies which provide a wide range of voluntary help to old people.

AMATEUR ATHLETIC ASSOCIATION (AAA) (A limited company)
70 Brompton Road, London SW3 1EE
Telephone: 01-584 7715

Aims	To co-ordinate and govern amateur athletics in England and Wales.
Officers	*Chairman* R W Goodman *Hon Secretary* B E Willis *Hon Treasurer* R I Stroud *National Administrator* *and PR Officer* F J Martell
Staff	10
Membership	1,000 clubs (who must be amateurs as defined in AAA Rules).
Fees	£3 to £30 p.a.
Regional	Southern Counties: 70 Brompton Road, London SW3 1EE Midland Counties: Devonshire House, High Street, Deritend, Birmingham B12 0LP Northern Counties: Rooms 288–290, Corn Exchange Building, Fennel Street, Manchester M4 3HP Welsh: Hon Secretary, Winterbourne, Greenway Close, Llandough, Penarth, South Glamorgan
Publications	Technical books on organisation and judging.
Connections	On British Amateur Athletics Board; member of Central Council of Physical Recreation (9) and British Olympic Association.
History	Formed in 1880 it is the oldest athletic organisation in the world. In its most successful year to date, it was placed fourth in the 1975 European Cup Final. Among the other activities is an annual proficiency certificate for children, of which more than a million a year are now awarded.

APEX CHARITABLE TRUST
(A Charity)
9 Poland Street, London W1V 3DG
Telephone: 01-734 4658

Aims	To obtain suitable employment for the ex-offender in line with his ability and qualifications; to provide suitable men and women to fill vacancies in an employers' organisation; to undertake research to make the placing services more effective and more professional; to seek to encourage employers to operate a fair employment opportunities policy.	
Officers	*Director and PR*	Freddie Pentney
	Assistant Director	Elizabeth Moffat
	Trustees	Anthony Vicent, Mrs Marna Glyn, Roger Warren-Evans, Robert Gore
	Sponsors	include Sir Campbell Adamson, Lord Brown, Lord Campbell of Eskan, Clive Jenkins, Professor Sir Claus Moser, Sir Richard Powell
Staff	6	
Membership	Not a membership organisation.	
Publications	*Employment and Parole;* annual reports and several other reports and pamphlets.	
Connections	Director is member of Council of National Association for the Care and Resettlement of offenders (6). Informal links with many after-care organisations.	
History	Established in 1965 to provide an employment service for ex-offenders. Project 1 – a research and placing project at Wormwood Scrubs and Pentonville – was completed in 1969 and is subject of the book *The Prisoners Release* by K L Soothill. Since then five other projects set up. It seeks support for work by publicising successes to encourage other employers to employ ex-offenders, and plans to continue work until an effective service for the socially handicapped ex-offender is provided.	

ASSOCIATION OF BRITISH ADOPTION AGENCIES
(A Charity)
4 Southampton Row, London WC1B 4AA
Telephone: 01-242 8951

Aims	To promote high standards of adoption practice by providing services to member agencies and by increasing public and professional understanding of the complex social, legal and psychological issues involved in the adoption of children.
Officers	*Chairman* A Rampton *Director* Miss Jane Rowe *Press and PR* Miss Margaret Kornitzer
Staff	5
Membership	Ordinary 105; Associate 50; Individual 40; open only to organisations and individuals directly or indirectly concerned with adoption.
Fees	Members — based on size/annual expenditure; Associate £7.50–£10; Individual £3.
Branches	Has 3 sub-groups; Scottish, medical, legal.
Publications	*Child Adoption* (q) and pamphlets.
History	Inaugurated May 1970. Grew out of the Standing Conference of Societies Registered for Adoption which had provided a forum for 20 years. Now represents almost all adoption and allied bodies. Has run conferences, training courses etc and represented member agencies on government and other consultative bodies. The findings of research study *Children Who Wait* (1973) led to national concern about large numbers of children in care who need placement in substitute family homes. Plans include assisting member agencies in implementation of Children Bill when it becomes law; expanding services to cover fostering, providing funds become available.

BRITISH ASSOCIATION OF RETIRED PERSONS
14 Frederick Street, Edinburgh EH2 2HB
Telephone: 021-225 7334

Aims	To act as the voice for the retired people in the UK, facing inflation with fixed or nearly fixed small incomes, speaking on their behalf to parliament and government and other authorities; and to publish information on activities and ways in which they may be able to help themselves.

Officers	*Chairman*	Ian Mackenzie
	Hon Secretary	Mrs E Macintyre
	Hon Treasurer	A R McLeod
	Hon President	Lord Erskine
	Hon Vice-Presidents	include Baroness Elliott, Dame Joan Vickers, Dame Irene Ward, Miss Janet Fookes MP, Russell Johnston MP, W G Price MP, Nicholas Winterton MP

Staff 1, plus 3 voluntary unpaid.

Membership 3,000   **Fees:** 50p p.a.; Life £5

Publications Members' bulletins (q)

Connections Unofficial liaison with Age Concern (6); Pre-Retirement Association; National Federation of Old Age Pensioners Associations.

History Formed March 1970. Immediately made representations to Chancellor of the Exchequer and has done so in each subsequent year. Has also made representations to other bodies such as British Rail, Post Office etc. At 1970 and 1974 elections sent 7-point questionnaires to all parties and sent replies to members.

BRITISH ASSOCIATION OF SOCIAL WORKERS
10 Kent Street, Birmingham B5 6RD
Telephone: 021-622 3911

Aims Concerned with the standards of professional practice and training, with the advancement of knowledge and the fostering of public understanding of social work, with the welfare of the community and with the seeking for social workers the working conditions which will enable them to promote these objectives.

Officers	*Chairman*	Miss May Richards
	Vice-Chairmen	Derek Carter, Richard Wolfe
	Honorary Treasurer	Maurice Hawker
	General Secretary	Chris Andrews
	Assistant General Secretary	Joan Baraclough
	Assistant General Secretary and PR	Terry Bamford
	Advertising	Mrs Rita Chaundey

Staff 29

Membership	10,500. Members must have successfully completed an approved educational course. Associate member workers not holding qualifications for membership. Student members must be accepted and studying in an approved course.
Fees	Members £3–£15 depending on salary; associates, students, guest members £3–£14.
Publications	*Social Work Today; British Journal of Social Work; Parliament and Social Work,* (weekly during parliamentary sessions).
Connections	Association of Directors of Social Services; Association of Directors of Social Work (Scotland); British Medical Association (2); Supplementary Benefits Commission.
History	Formed April 1970 by an amalgamation of 7 organisations concerned with various aspects of social work.

BRITISH SOCIETY FOR SOCIAL RESPONSIBILITY IN SCIENCE
(See Section 9)

BRITISH TEMPERANCE LEAGUE YOUTH CONFERENCE CENTRES LTD
(A Charity)
Livesey-Clegg House, 44 Union Street, Sheffield S1 2JP
Telephone: Sheffield 22770

Aims	To hold conferences, summer schools etc., for young people in furtherance of the objects of the British Temperance League – to spread throughout the UK the principle of abstinence from all intoxicating liquors and the removal of the causes and occasions of intemperance.	
Officers	*Chairman*	John Harrison
	Secretary	Miss Muriel Danial
Staff	5	

CAMPAIGN FOR THE HOMELESS AND ROOTLESS (CHAR)
(A Charity)
The Basement, 15 Cleveland Square, London W2
Telephone: 01-723 2749

Aims	To enforce and extend existing rights to housing, social services and employment for Britain's single homeless people and bring together in united action those voluntary bodies who at present care for the homeless and rootless.

Officers	*Chairman*	Frank Field
	Director	M Beacock
	Prominent members	include Jock Stallard MP

Staff   4

Membership   90 voluntary organisations

Fees   National organisations £10; local projects £5 p.a.; individuals £2 p.a.

Branches   Manchester; Merseyside

Publications   *Newsheet* (m); *Campaign Charter,* Annual Report; many reports and pamphlets.

History   Formed in 1972 on joint initiative of several voluntary projects: Christian Action; Child Poverty Action Group (5); Cyrenian; St Mungo's; Outset (6). Activities include work for homeless alcoholics, non-medical needs of homeless and hostel users; co-ordination of voluntary aid to single homeless. It plans to stress housing needs of single homeless, draw attention to employment problems and call for repeal of vagrancy laws.

CAMPAIGN FOR HOMOSEXUAL EQUALITY (CHE)
28 Kennedy Street, Manchester M2 4BG
Telephone: 061-228 1985

Aims   Acceptance of homosexual and bisexual people by society, as fully entitled to lead their lives openly; social and legal equality between all men and women and reform of laws which deny this; eradication of the prejudice and hostility faced by the homosexual; the creation of social meeting places where both homosexual and heterosexual men and women may gather in a congenial atmosphere.

Officers	*President*	Allan Horsfall
	Chairman	Barrie Kenyon
	Vice-Chairman	Glenys Parry
	General Secretary	Alan Clarke
	Asst General Secretary	Chris J Bowden-Smith
	Press and PR	Bernard Greaves

Non-Executive Vice-Presidents: include Sir Alfred Ayer, Lord Beaumont, Professor Anthony Flew, Dr Jonathan Miller, Rev John Robinson, Lord Soper, Dr Michael Winstanley, Humphrey Berkeley, David Hockney, George Melly, Brigid Brophy, Margaret Drabble, Tony Smythe

Staff	3

Membership 6,000   **Fees:** £2.50 p.a. minimum

Branches Over 100 throughout England and Wales — theoretically autonomous — including 15 London branches.
London Information Centre: Basement, 22 Great Windmill Street, London W1X 7PH, Telephone: 01-437 7363.

Publications *CHE Bulletin* (m); local groups also publish newsletters and resell *Gay News;* booklets etc.

Connections Scottish Minorities Group (6); affiliated to National Council for Civil Liberties (6); Friend, CHE's wholly-owned subsidiary counselling and aid service is affiliated to National Association for Mental Health (8).

History Formed in 1963 as North-Western Homosexual Law Reform Committee. Became a national organisation in 1969 as Committee for Homosexual Equality. Renamed 1970. First homosexual political reform movement run by themselves. Started because founders dissatisfied with the 1967 legal reforms. Recent activities include questionnaire to all major party candidates at 1974 General Elections; expansion of welfare and counselling services and establishing links with transvestite and trans-sexual organisations. Plans include introduction of bill to parliament to put homosexual activity on the same footing as heterosexual activity, including lowering of homosexual age of consent to 16, a medical campaign for doctors, and to promote teaching in schools, to reduce the isolation and neuroses suffered by adolescent and teenage homosexuals.

CHILD POVERTY ACTION GROUP (A Charity)
1 Macklin Street, London WC2B 5NH
Telephone: 01-242 3225

Aims Believe that families should have a guaranteed income as of right; many poor families do not claim the range of means-tested help available to them because of lack of information, complexity of claiming and stigma; aims at a reduction in the number of means-tests to help solve some of these problems, with increased national insurance benefits and family allowances as effective ways of helping low income families.

Officers   *Chairman*   Professor Peter Townsend
            Director and PR   Frank Field

Staff 14

Membership 2,500

Fees Minimum £2 p.a.; £5 p.a. entitles member to all publications.

Publications *Poverty* (q); *Welfare Rights Bulletin* (every 6 weeks — social service departments only); many booklets, research pamphlets etc.

Connections Works closely with many organisations concerned with poverty and housing problems. Also links with social service departments.

History Formed 1965 to draw attention to the hundreds of thousands of families living at or below the poverty line. As well as helping thousands of families about the help available, CPAG's efforts are directed to informing the public of the needs of the poor, and also to demand government action. Recent activities have included evidence to committees including select committee on tax credits, Department of Health and Social Security enquiry into the cohabitation rule, Child Health Services Committee. Plans include development work with Trade Union movement to pave the way for reforms of social and economic policy to help low income families.

CITIZENS PROTECTION SOCIETY
611 Collingwood House, Dolphin Square, London SW1V 3N
Telephone: 01-834 0887

Aims To secure the return of capital punishment for terrorists and the gunman, also for premediated murder; stricter penalties for acts of violence against the person.

Officers *President* Rev Percy Grey
Chairman Mrs Charlotte Hurst
Vice-Chairman Mrs Jane Hitchcock
Secretary Mrs Eileen Bond

Membership 10,000 **Fees:** Voluntary

Publications Literature to members.

History Formed January 1970. Activities include sending post cards to 630 MPs, lobbies at House of Commons, press, radio and television publicity.

COMMITTEE ON UNITED KINGDOM CITIZENSHIP
P O Box 138, London WC1B 3RW

Aims	To campaign for the restoration of full rights for United Kingdom citizens in East and Central Africa, India and Pakistan.

Officers		
	Chairman	John Hunt MP
	Vice-Chairman	Lord Foot
	Honorary Secretary	Prafu Patel
	Committee members	include Lord Hunt, David Steel MP, Dame Joan Vickers, Nigel Fisher

Connections	United Kingdom Immigrants Advisory Service.
History	Formed in 1968 it is supported by members of both Houses of Parliament. It takes an active part in questions on immigration and race relations in the United Kingdom.

COUNCIL FOR CHILDREN'S WELFARE
183/189 Finchley Road, London NW3
Telephone: 01-624 8766

Aims	To see that all children are given the opportunity to develop their full potential.
Officers	Mrs I Bertram
Publications	*Our Children*
History	Founded 1953.

FAMILY WELFARE ASSOCIATION
(A Charity)
501 Kingsland Road, London E8
Telephone: 01-254 6251

Aims	To relieve distress, poverty and sickness by promoting family welfare.
Officers	Miss Janet Lacey
Publications	*Charities Digest*
History	Founded 1869.

142

FOOTBALL ASSOCIATION OF WALES LTD
3 Fairy Road, Wrexham, Clwyd, Wales LL13 7PS
Telephone: Wrexham 2425   Cables: Welsoccer Wrexham

Aims	The promotion of Association Football in Wales.
Officers	*President* T H Squire *Vice-Presidents* L Withers and R G Jones *Hon Treasurer* S Jenkins *Secretary* Trevor Morris
Staff	6
Membership	98 football clubs and 6 area associations in *full* membership. Restricted to senior football clubs in Wales.
Fees	£3.24
Publications	*Official Handbook Annual*, 50p
Connections	Affiliated to FIFA, EUFA. Sister organisation to similar bodies in England, Scotland and Ireland.
History	Founded 1876. Controls football throughout Wales and organises international matches and the Welsh Cup competition.

GAY LIBERATION FRONT
c/o 5 Caledonian Road, London N1

Aims	To 'bring out' gay people 'to realise that their gayness is as normal as heterosexuality and to campaign for gay rights for gay people.'
Officers	*Chairman* Martin Corbett *Secretary* Peter Madders *Treasurer* David McLellan
Membership	No membership.
Branches	South London; Leeds; Newcastle; Manchester etc.
Publications	*GLF Manifesto; Come Together* (irregular).
History	Formed 1970. Gay Pride Week coincides with Stonewall Gay Pride Riot (USA) July 1969. Organises gay activities to bring gays together as equals. Address is only an accommodation address.

HOWARD LEAGUE FOR PENAL REFORM
125 Kennington Park Road, London SE11 4JP
Telephone: 01-735 3773

Aims	To ensure the fair, effective and humane treatment of offenders.	
Officers	*President*	Lord Gardiner
	Director	Martin Wright
	Chairman	Louis Blom-Cooper
Prominent members	include Sir Kenneth Younger, Professor T C N Gibbens, Professor Nigel Walker	
Membership	2,000—3,000	**Fees:** £4 p.a.
Publications	*Howard Journal* (a); Annual Report; newsletter (q).	
Connections	Some information work done in conjunction with National Association for the Care and Resettlement of Offenders (6); and co-operation with National Campaign for the Abolition of Capital Punishment; Justice (5).	
History	Founded as Howard Association in 1866, named after John Howard, High Sheriff of Bedfordshire and pioneer in prison reform. First President was Lord Broughton. The Penal Reform League, established in 1907, amalgamated with Association in 1921 to adopt present name. Recent achievements include support for Rehabilitation of Offenders Act (1975).	

HUMAN RIGHTS SOCIETY
27 Walpole Street, London SW3
Telephone: 01-730 5928

Aims	To ensure that the dignity and worth of the human person are respected, by general acceptance of human rights and responsibilities, including upholding of United Nations and European Conventions, to defend in particular the right to life of all, including the sick, the handicapped and the aged, to to uphold and defend the rights of conscience of the medical and nursing professions, to promote discussion of the nature and extent of human rights in contemporary society.	
Officers	*President*	Lord St Helens
	Chairman	Dr Richard Lamerton
	Treasurer	Sir Victor Raikes
	Press and PR	Mrs Phyllis Bowman

144

Prominent Members	Lord Bishop of Bath and Wells, Viscount Barrington, Earl of Cork and Orrery, Earl of Longford, Norman St John-Stevas MP, Gordon Oakes MP, Mrs Jill Knight MP
Membership	500 **Fees:** £1 p.a. or £10 life membership.
Branches	West Yorkshire; Merseyside; Sussex.
Publications	*Bulletin,* (bi-m to members only); various pamphlets on euthanasia and other subjects.
Connections	Mothers Union (10); Let Live; National Council of Women.
History	Established 1969 in response to Voluntary Euthanasia Bill which was seen as part of a much larger erosion of the respect for human life. Conferences have been held in London, Bristol, Hove, Liverpool and Leeds and individual cases of infringement of rights have been taken up and investigated. Plans include branches in every county and the defeat of proposed euthanasia bills and similar legislation.

JOINT COUNCIL FOR THE WELFARE OF IMMIGRANTS
(A Charity)
233 Pentonville Road, London N1 9NJ
Telephone: 01-278 6726/7

Aims	To give assistance to immigrants in connection with immigration control and welfare problems; to secure the removal of all restrictions on United Kingdom passport holders and secure a non-discriminatory immigration policy.	
Officers	*Chairman*	K R Goswami
	Vice-Chairmen	Eric Jay, Dilbagh Chann, Dr D Prem
	Treasurer	Q M Anwar
	General Secretary and PR	Mrs M Dines
	Executive Secretary and PR	V D Sharma
Membership	Not stated but includes 150 organisations.	
Fees	£3 p.a.	
Branch	Rawlpindi, Pakistan.	
Publication	Annual Report	

History   Formed September 1967. Pressure on Government re immigration rules and practices, e.g. the control of East African United Kingdom passport holders. Opposed to National Security Clauses of Immigration Act 1971.

JOSEPHINE BUTLER SOCIETY
49 Hawkshead Lane, North Hatfield, Herts
Telephone: Potters Bar 43150

Aims   To promote a high and equal standard of morality and sexual responsibility for men and women, in public opinion, law and practice; to secure the abolition of state regulation of prostitution, to combat the traffic in persons and to expose and prevent any form of exploitation of prostitution by third parties.

Officers   *Secretary*   Miss Margit Schwarz

Membership About 400.

Publications *Shield*

History   Founded 1870 as Association for Moral and Social Hygiene.

JUSTICE AGAINST IDENTIFICATION LAWS (JAIL)
90 Fawe Park Road, London SW15 2EA
Telephone: 01-874 2420

Aims   To campaign on behalf of victims of mistaken identity and secure reforms in the law and procedure on identification evidence.

Committee   *Chairman*   Lea Ward
            Secretary   Barbara Whitby
            Treasurer   Rose Davis

Prominent members   include Peter Hain, President of the Young Liberals (1)

Membership 200   **Fees:** nil

History   First formed in late summer 1975 and formally launched on 1 December 1975, following on the widespread publicity over the George Davis and Peter Hain cases.

146

LEGAL ACTION GROUP (LAG)
(A Charity)
28a Highgate Road, London NW5 1NS
Telephone: 01-485 1189; 01-267 0048

Aims	A group of lawyers and others who are concerned to improve legal services to the community, particularly people living in deprived areas.

Officers

Director and PR	Susan Marsden-Smedley
Assistant Director	Clive Morrick
Chairman	Walter Merricks
Advertising	Jean Dyer

Staff 6

Membership 2,500

Fees £10 for firms, libraries, local authorities; individuals and charities £5.75.

Publications *LAG Bulletin of Social and Welfare Law* (m); pamphlets on aspects of legal aid, directories etc.

History Formed in 1971. A grant was made by the Nuffield Foundation for an information service to lawyers in the field of social and welfare law. First monthly bulletin published in February 1973. Members are involved in projects to provide fuller legal services in many parts of the country. Recent activities include surveys of duty solicitor schemes, and of LAG solicitor members on the use of the Green Form Legal Aid Scheme. Organise lectures, courses for members and others on housing, welfare etc.

NATIONAL ASSOCIATION FOR THE CARE AND RESETTLEMENT OF OFFENDERS (NACRO)
(A Charity)
125 Kennington Park Road, London SE11
Telephone: 01-735 1151

Aims Part of a national network of help and support for voluntary groups working with offenders, their families and others at risk; the development of alternatives to prison, and the prevention of crime by a national strategy to tackle its roots in society.

Officers	*Chairman*	Anthony Christopher
	Treasurer	Ronald Soothill
	Secretary	Robert Beech
	Director	Nicholas Hinton
	Press and PR	Gerry Northam
	President	Lord Donaldson
	Council Members	include Charles Irving MP, Mark Carlisle MP

Staff 153

Membership 1,000 individuals and organisations.

Fees Ordinary bodies actively involved in crime prevention etc £6 p.a.; Associate £2.50 p.a.

Regional Offices Manchester; Bradford; London; Birmingham; Bath.

Publications *Frontsheet* (bi-m); *Directory of Projects* (a); many books and pamphlets.

Connections Sister bodies in Scotland and Northern Ireland (SACRO and NIACRO (6)).

History Formed in 1966 when the National Association of Discharged Prisoners Aid Societies handed over its responsibilities for prison welfare work to the expanded Probation and After-Care Service. Became the new national body to represent and service voluntary effort. Recent activities include establishment of projects to cover accommodation, work training, needs of those at risk and ex-offenders etc. Plans include development of a multi-professional crime prevention strategy in pilot areas following national conferences held in 1975 with many professions.

NATIONAL CAMPAIGN FOR FIREWORK REFORM
15, 118 Long Acre, Covent Garden, London WC2E 9PA
Telephone: 01-836 6703

Aims To amend the 1875 Fireworks Law; to seek fresh legislation which would ban the retail sale of fireworks and place them under licence to be purchased directly from manufacturers or gunshops, essentially for display purposes only; thereby to remove the danger of children obtaining fireworks and eliminate the accidents that are caused because these explosives are available.

Officers		
	Director	Noel Tobin
	Treasurer	Henrietta Goldstein
	Secretary	Geraldine Tobin
	Press	John McCullogh, Regina Dollar

Prominent Members Include (all MPs) James Johnson, Andrew Faulds, Peter Archer, Janet Fookes, Gwilym Roberts

Membership 1,000 plus petition support of 100,000.

Fees 25p life membership.

Branches Southport; Hull; S Petherton, Somerset; Gourock, Renfrew; Blackpool.

Publications *Newsletter* (twice yearly); *Information Sheet* (a); *International Firework Report*, and other pamphlets.

Connections Member organisation include ILEA; Fire Brigades Union; British Safety Council etc. Also links with other bodies. including Women's Institutes (7).

History Formed in November 1969 by the amalgamation of various groups in the regions with the London group. First year campaign helped reduce accidents by 40%. On 10 March 1970, presented petition of 32,000 signatures, in association with *Mother* magazine, to the Home Office. At invitation of Lee Valley Regional Park Authority drew up safety document for firework display. A code was produced April 1973, and at the invitation of the Home Office, it amalgamated with that of manufacturers. Accepted and circulated by Home Office to all local authorities. Accidents have been reduced by about 18% over past two years.

NATIONAL COUNCIL FOR CIVIL LIBERTIES (NCCL)
186 Kings Cross Road, London WC1X 9DE
Telephone: 01-278 4575   Cables: Civlib London

Aims To assist in maintaining and extending civil liberties, particularly freedom of speech, expression and association, within the UK.

Officers		
	Chairman	Jack Dromey
	Vice-Chairman	Henry Hodge
	Treasurer	John Tuchfield
	General Secretary	Patricia Hewitt

Staff 12

Membership   5,000 plus 500 affiliated organisations

Fees   Individual £3.25; Couple £4.25.

Publications   Annual Report; *Civil Liberty* (bi-m).

Connections   Works closely with Cobden Trust; contact with parliamentary civil liberties group (Chairman: Fred Willey MP); also many law centres, women's groups, immigrants groups etc.

History   Founded in 1934. Prominent early officers included E M Forster, Julian Huxley, Harold Laski, H G Wells, Aneurin Bevan and Bertrand Russell. Recent activities include monitoring of administration of justice in Northern Ireland; a new women's rights campaign (succeeded in change of immigration rules to give foreign husbands of British women right of entry to UK); publication of report on conspiracy laws; a successful campaign to renew right of individuals to bring complaints to the European Commission on Human Rights. Plans the formation of women's rights unit to undertake test cases in anti-discrimination and equal pay complaints; safeguards to protect individuals' rights to privacy, particularly in censuses; campaign on prisoners' rights, continued lobbying through press and parliament on all matters of individuals rights.

NATIONAL COUNCIL FOR THE DIVORCED AND SEPARATED
(A Charity)
c/o 13 High Street, Little Shelford, Cambridge CB2 5ES

Aims   To promote the interests and welfare for all whose marriage has ended in divorce or separation; to make known the views of members on legislation concerning them; to offer free welfare and legal advice and assist in all problems arising from being divorced or separated.

Officers   *Chairman*   George Mawer
Secretary and PR   Mrs Sara Hanney

Prominent Members   Leo Abse MP, Dame Joan Vickers, R V Banks

Membership   4,000. Open to anyone who is or has been divorced or separated. 10% widows/widowers.

Fees   £1 p.a.

Regional Offices   Regional representation in Yorkshire, London, Sussex, Kent and Severnside. 80 clubs throughout Great Britain.

Publications   *NCDS News*, (bi-m).

Connections   Gingerbread; One Parent Families (Joint Action Committee on Finer).

History   Formerly National Federation Clubs for Divorced and Separated. Renamed March 1974 to extend welfare work; organises conferences and provides assistance and advice. Plans include training of welfare officers for spot assistance; lobbying of MPs particularly on Finer report; representation in custody courts; review of maintenance laws.

NATIONAL VIEWERS AND LISTENERS ASSOCIATION (NATIONAL VALA)
Far Forest, Kidderminster, Worcestershire
Telephone: Rock (by Kidderminster) 266 260

Officers   *President* — Chief Constable L Barnett (Rtd)
Honorary General Secretary and PR — Mrs Mary Whitehouse
Treasurer — Harold Thuft

Membership 31,000   **Fees:** Minimum 25p p.a.

Publications   *The Viewer and Listener* (q).

History   Originally set up as Clean Up TV Campaign in January 1964. National VALA launched in November 1966. Plans to work for Indecent Displays Bill; restructuring of broadcasting to give more independent 'say' to viewers and listeners; building international co-operation with other viewer/listener groups.

NORTHERN IRELAND ASSOCIATION FOR THE CARE AND RESETTLEMENT OF OFFENDERS
(A Charity)
41 Donegal Street, Belfast BT1 2FG
Telephone: 0232 20157

Aims   To encourage the public to assist with the rehabilitation of offenders and their families; to advocate penal reform.

Officers   *President* — Lord Dunleath
Chairman — Miss Bessie H Maconachie
Organising Secretary — R J Byers

Staff   2

Membership	300	**Fees:** £1.10 p.a.

Publications Annual Report, free.

Connections Other voluntary organisations represented on Executive Committee include Samaritans; Northern Ireland Council for Social Service.

History Established 1971 with government grant-in-aid, it has recruited support from Protestant, Roman Catholic and Jewish communities. Activities have included Wives and Families Centre established at Belfast Prison; volunteers recruited and trained; lodgings scheme initiated. Plans include recruitment of full-time organiser for employment agency and part-time staff member to organise volunteers, during 1975. NIACRO works very closely with its sister organisations in Scotland and England and Wales, SACRO and NACRO (6).

OUTSET LTD
(A Charity)
30 Craven Street, London WC2N 5BR
Telephone: 01-930 4255

Aims To encourage and enable individuals of all ages, and the community at large, to assist those who are homeless, lonely, neglected, old or handicapped.

Officers
Chairman Peter Ryan
Secretary Jack Sultzberger
Public Relations Nicholas Blake

Staff 3

Branch Offices Blackpool; Stafford; Leicester; Hammersmith; Southwark; Oldham.

Publications Reports on projects to identify disabled people; annual reports.

Connections National Council of Social Services; National Association of Voluntary Hostels; NACRO (6); Campaign for the Homeless and Rootless (6); Voluntary Movement Group.

History Founded 1970. Activities include mobilising 20,000 volunteers to do a wide range of projects. Hope to develop skills in setting up young volunteer groups; to persuade local authorities to use Outset's skills on surveys to discover chronically sick or disabled people and locating low cost accommodation.

PRESERVATION OF THE RIGHTS OF PRISONERS (PROP)
339a Finchley Road, London NW3 5HE
Telephone: 01-435 1215

Aims	Total reform of the penal system including rights of prisoners to union representation within prisons; votes in national and local elections; parole; communicate freely and be visited freely by the press and public; send and receive letters without censorship; to enter into marriage; adequate and humane visiting facilities; to own and sell products of leisure time activities; the removal of many other restrictions and independent inspection of prisons.

Officers   *London Organiser*
              and PR   E C Ward
              Secretary   G Sugden

Staff	2
Membership	60. Full membership only to present or past inmates of penal institutions.
Fees	£2 p.a.
Publications	Various books and reports.
Connections	NCCL (6); Radical Alternatives to Prison (6); Howard League (6); NACRO (6) and with prison unions in USA, Denmark and Sweden.
History	Prison strike 4 September 1972. Plans to work for a Royal Commission of Enquiry into Prisons in this country.

PROGRESSIVE LEAGUE
Albion Cottage, Fortis Green, London N2
Telephone: 01-452 8358

Aims	For economic and social reforms to banish fear, superstition and misery from the world; for international co-operation and understanding to end the risk of war; the repeal of all laws that impose unnecessary restrictions on freedom in personal life and the repudiation of all customs having that effect; for education to develop mature, responsible personalities and to provide for the fullest intellectual, artistic and emotional growth.

153

Officers	*President*	High Jenkins MP
	Chairman	Dr Ben Roston
	Secretary and PR	Dr Ernest Seeley
	Treasurer	Tom Graham
	Advertising	Mrs Mary Barnes
	Vice-Presidents	Dr James Hemming, Mrs Lena Jeger MP, H J Blackham

Membership 400

Fees London £2.25 p.a.; elsewhere £1.25 p.a.

Publications *Plan* (m).

Connections Affiliated to National Peace Council (5); NCCL (6); British Humanist Association; Conservation Society (11).

History Formed 1932 as Federation of Progressive Societies and Individuals as an attempt to secure unity among progressives to promote peace, oppose Fascism and protect individual liberty. Hold meetings for members and also public meetings on subjects such as battered wives, National Health Service etc.

PUBLIC INTEREST RESEARCH CENTRE LTD
(A Charity)
9 Poland Street, London W1V 3DG
Telephone: 01-734 0314

Aims To raise and examine issues of relevance and importance to those affected by decision-making in government, corporate and other major bodies; specifically, it is concerned to carry out research into the organisation and activity of government, industry, business, trade, the professions and the services and to calculate their effect upon the environment and life of the community — and to make the results of such research available to and for the benefit of the public.

Officers	*Chairman*	Christopher B Zealley
	Directors	Andrew Phillips, Oliver Thorold
	Secretary	Peter MacMahon

Staff 7 part-time.

Publications See Social Audit (6).

History   Set up late 1971 by Dr Michael Young, William Osborn and
                 Charles Medawar. Registered as a charity 1973. Reports
                 published through Social Audit on issues such as company law
                 reform, secrecy in government, advertising control and standards,
                 arms manufacture and export control, and shareholder participa-
                 tion in business. Has compiled social audits on three major
                 companies — Tube Investments, Coalite and Avon Rubber Co.

RACE TODÁY
74 Shakespeare Road, London SE24
Telephone: 01-737 2268

Aims   To publish journals and other publications contributing towards
                 the achievement of racial equality and the elimination of racial
                 discrimination.

Officers   *Editor*   Darcus Howe

History   Formed by the Institute of Race Relations in 1973. Magazine
                 and other publications now independently produced.

RADICAL ALTERNATIVES TO PRISON (RAP)
Eastbourne House, Bullards House, London E2
Telephone: 01-981 0041

Aims   The abolition of imprisonment; to change people's attitudes
                 towards the 'criminal'.

Staff   One full-time, one part-time.

Membership   500   Fees: £2 p.a.

Branches   West Horrington, Near Wells, Somerset; and Bradford.

Publications   (Distributed by Christian Action Publications Ltd) Newsletter (m);
                 various pamphlets.

History   Formed in 1970 by prison workers and ex-prisoners who felt a
                 need to break with traditional reform groups and create an
                 abolitionist platform; the group became an official project of
                 Christian Action in 1972. It mounted a campaign against re-
                 building of Holloway and imprisonment of women; started the
                 Newham Alternatives Project — a deferred sentence support
                 scheme; forged working links with various professional and
                 grassroots organisations. Lobbies official policy makers,
                 professionals working in the penal field.

RELEASE
(A Charity)
1 Elgin Avenue, London W9
Telephone: 01-289 1123

Aims	To advise and assist with: legal problems concerned with drugs and otherwise, providing information on everything from landlord/tenant disputes to do-it-yourself divorce, women's problems including contraception, abortion etc; psychiatric and medical problems concerned with drugs and otherwise; to assist at events such as pop festivals where medical, psychiatric and legal problems may arise; to provide information and support in specific fields of the use and abuse of drugs; to assist in building a network of alternative agencies and organisations in Britain and abroad; to assist and advise relatives and friends of people held in foreign prisons with specific reference to drug charges.
Officers	Run by a collective which makes joint decisions.

Press and Liaison	Roger Lewis
Information and Research	Don Aitken

Staff	14
Membership	No formalised membership. Almost 150 financial donors and a regular mailing list of 5,000.
Publications	*Newsletter* (m); *Connection* (bi-m).
Connections	Supported by Princedale Trust; members include Lord Melchett; Michael Schofield, Sonia Orwell, Caroline Coon, Rufus Harris, Diana Melly. Keeps in touch with about 300 UK organisations and 50 elsewhere. Represented on many bodies including NCCL (6), Festival Welfare Services Committee, Standing Conference on Drug Abuse etc.
History	Founded 1967 by Coon and Harris. 1969 women's abortion, contraception, Festival welfare advice and other services started. 1971 first full-time psychiatric worker. 1973 six-month exchange with US organisation. 1974 official recognition with Home Office Services Unit grant. Release residential house started. Plans include development of non-charitable subsidiary Release Publications for education, information and research. Free, confidential drug analysis. To campaign for de-criminalisation of cannabis. The vast majority of its work is unspectacular day-to-day counselling, advice, assistance etc.

ROYAL BRITISH LEGION (A Charity)
49 Pall Mall, London SW1Y 5JY
Telephone: 01-930 8131   Cables: Britegion London

Aims	To promote the welfare by charitable means of men and women who have served and of the widows, children, and dependants of those who have served in HM Forces or auxilliary forces or in the mercantile marine during hostilities afloat or in any Red Cross organisation whilst serving with our armed forces.
Officers	*President* General Sir Charles Jones *Chairman* Colonel J Hughes *General Secretary* D E Coffer *Public Relations* Braban PR Ltd
Staff	198
Membership	750,000 (including the Royal British Legion Women's Section).
Fees	Subscription varies by branches; amount of affiliation fee payable annually to headquarters: 30p per ordinary member, 15p per associate member. Membership qualifications: ex-servicemen and women who have served at least seven days with the colours and received seven days' pay in the Forces.
Regional Offices	11 Area Offices, including Northern and Southern Ireland but excluding Scotland.
Publications	*The Royal British Legion Journal* (m).
History	Formed 1 July 1921. Royal charter in 1971. Holds Remembrance Day on second Sunday in November with Poppy Day on Saturday preceding. Plans include development of membership and charitable activities.

ROYAL SOCIETY FOR THE PREVENTION OF ACCIDENTS (ROSPA)
Royal Oak Centre, Brighton Road, Purley, CR2 2UR
Telephone: 01-668 4272

Aims	To provide education in accident prevention.
Publications	*Occupational Safety and Health; Care in the Home; Care on the Road.*
History	Founded 1916.

SCOTTISH FOOTBALL ASSOCIATION LTD
6 Park Gardens, Glasgow, Scotland
Telephone: 041-332 6372   Telex: 778904   Cables: Executive, Glasgow

Aims	To promote, foster and develop Association football in Scotland.
Officers	*President* R G Grimshaw *Secretary* W P Allan
Staff	14
Membership	72 full member clubs.
Fees	Members: Entrance fee £3.00. Annual Fee: £1.00.
Publications	Annual Handbook; *One Hundred Years of Scottish Football.*
Connections	Closely related to the FA of England; the FA of Wales; the Irish FA. Member of Federation of international Football Association, FIFA and Union of European Football Association, UEFA.
History	Founded 1873.

SCOTTISH MINORITIES GROUP
60 Broughton Street, Edinburgh EH1 8SB
Telephone: 031-556 3673

Aims	The establishment for the same legal rights of homosexual people as currently apply to heterosexual people.
Officers	*Chairman* Ian C Dunn *Deputy Chairmen* Jean Polson, Michael Coulson *Treasurer* James L Halcrow *Secretary* Derek A Ogg *Honorary Officers* Robin Cook MP, David Steel MP, Prof G M Carstairs, Dr Keith Wardrop, Bailie Janey Buchan, Rev Tom Scott, Ray Carmichael
Membership	400
Fees	Ordinary £3 p.a.; Students, apprentices, elderly £1.
Branches	Glasgow; Dundee; Aberdeen; Inverness; Edinburgh; Carlisle (jointly with Campaign for Homosexual Equality).
Publications	*SMG News* (m).
Connections	Friendly co-operation with CHE (6), through Carlisle Branch and all-UK Law Reform Campaign. Affiliate of NCCL (6).

History	Founded in May 1969. Grew rapidly during 1971—2. Many 'homosexual firsts' in Scotland including right to hold gay dances etc without harassment. New HQ opened 1975 which is intended to become a Gay Community Services Centre. Seeking to win Post Office permission to advertise branches and address in all Post Offices.

SHELTER: NATIONAL CAMPAIGN FOR THE HOMELESS
(A Charity)
86 The Strand, London WC2
Telephone: 01-836 2051

Aims	To provide assistance for people in Britain without proper homes or without homes at all by promoting housing associations, housing aid centres, city improvement projects, influencing policy and public education.

Officers		
	Director	Douglas Tilbe
	Deputy Director Admin	Richard Blake
	Deputy Director Housing Policy	Chris Holmes
	Press and PR	Bobby Vincent-Emery
	Advertising	Richard Blake
	Information Officer	Joanna Roosevelt
	Projects Director	Michael Wright
	Research Director	Moira Constable
	Field Director	Terence Finley
	Board of Management	Lord Soper (Chairman), Lord Harlech, Viscount Simon of Garmoyle, Bruce Douglas-Mann MP

Staff	Approximately 70.
Membership	Not a membership organisation.
Offices	Welwyn Garden City; Newbury; Tenterden; Newcastle; York; Manchester; Birmingham; Ipswich; Bristol; Edinburgh.
Connections	Informal, sometimes bands together with organisations such as Child Poverty Action Group (6) on one particular issue.
History	Formed 1 December 1966. Des Wilson was first Director. Since then, Shelter has raised over £4 million and rehoused over 20,000 people. Money raised by donations and a wide variety of activities.

SIMON COMMUNITY TRUST

(A Charity)

Challenge House, 118 Grove Green Road, London E11

Telephone: 01-539 0541/3

Aims	To assist and care for homeless and rootless people who have additional social problems — mental illness, recidivists, sexual deviants, drug dependency etc.

Officers

Founder	Anton Wallich-Clifford
Chairman	John Jennings
Secretary and Treasurer	Austin Williams
Press and PR	John James

Prominent Members	Include Archbishops of Canterbury and Westminster, Greville Janner MP, Mrs Mary Wilson, Lord Beaumont, Bishop Trevor Huddleston, Lord Longford, Robert Mellish MP, Jeremy Sandford, Lord Avebury, Jeremy Thorpe MP, A Stallard MP
Branches	Hastings; London; Canterbury; Belfast; Cheltenham.
Publications	*Simon Star* (m); *No Fixed Abode* by Anton Wallich-Clifford.
Connections	With similar organisations in Liverpool; Glasgow; Ireland; Kenya; Dorothy Day Advice Centre.
History	Founded 1 September 1963 by founder who quit his job as probation officer because of concern with lack of facilities for homeless and rootless. First house of hospitality set up in Kentish Town in April 1964. Became independent at St Mungo Community in 1969. Centrepoint, Soho set up 1969. Companions of Simon became independent as The Cyrenians 1970. Recent activities include opening of new flat and house in London; neighbourhood advice centre opened in Hastings; community opened in Duldalk.

SOCIAL AUDIT LTD

9 Poland Street, London W1V 3DG

Telephone: 01-734 0561

Aims	Campaigns on two main issues — the abuse of secrecy in decision-making bodies; and social accountability in decision-making bodies. Acts as the publishing arm of Public Interest Research centre.

160

Officers	*Chairman*	Christopher Zealley
	Directors	Andrew Phillips, William Osborn, Charles Medawar (Executive)
	Secretary	Peter MacMahon

Staff   7 part-time.

Publications   *Social Audit* (q).

Connections   Associated with Public Interest Research Centre Ltd (6).

History   See Public Interest Research Centre. Was set up with the help of a grant from the Joseph Rowntree Social Service Trust and is otherwise financed by sales, donations and fees.

SOCIAL CREDIT CENTRE
Montagu Chambers, Exborough, South Yorkshire, S64 9 AJ
Telephone: Filey 2170

Aims   To further the spread of those ideas of C H Douglas (1879– 1952) which have become known as Social Credit. 'Systems were made for man, not man for systems, and the interests of man, which is self-development, is above all systems, whether theological, political or economic.' Believes that Social Credit has the philosophy and the monetary technique to produce in man — the unique creative animal — an infinite variety of physical, intellectual and cultural development; that it can also distribute wealth among all peoples of the world without war and without the necessity for a campaign to wage war on want.

Officers	*Honorary Secretary*	V R Hadkins
	Honorary Treasurer	Miss V Paley

Membership   200

Fees   According to means — average £2 per member.

Publications   *Abundance* (q).

Connections   Social Credit Party (1); exchanges with similar associations in Canada, Australia and New Zealand; National Campaign Against Inflation.

History   A nucleus formed in the early 1920s around C M Hattersley which led to founding of Social Credit Co-ordinating Centre in 1948. Name changed in 1974. Circulate MPs, local authorities and companies on Social Credit view of current affairs. Plans to urge the establishment of a 'National Discount' to bridge the gap between total prices and total incomes; to divorce money from gold, in order to ensure a stable exchange medium, in place of a depreciating medium of exchange.

UNITED KINGDOM ALLIANCE
12 Caxton Street, London, SW1H 0QS
Telephone: 01-222 4001

Aims	To eliminate from the nation the evils of drinking of alcoholic liquors by removing the cause.
Membership	6,000
Publications	*Alliance News*
History	Founded 1853.

VOICE OF THE INDEPENDENT CENTRE
(formerly MIDDLE CLASS ASSOCIATION)
c/o John Gorst MP, 35 Connaught Square, London W2
Telephone: 01-723 4836

Aims	To represent the interests of individuals who are self-employed, or in professional, creative or managerial occupations, (whether apprenticed, active or retired); to pursue these matters, either separately or in co-operation with other bodies, in whatever legal manner seems appropriate for their achievement.	
Officers	*Co-Founders*	John Gorst MP and Capt L P S Orr
	Membership Secretary	Mark Elwes
Staff	3	
Membership	Undisclosed.	Fees: £5.00 p.a.
History	Formed 11 November 1974 as Middle Class Association. Became Voice of the Independent Centre in May 1975.	

BRITISH HOUSEWIVES' LEAGUE LTD
33 Ashley Road, Epsom, Surrey
Telephone: Epsom 28000

Aims
: To provide British housewives with an effective voice in all matters concerning the welfare of themselves and their families; to give information and advice; to show that overall control by the State is not in the interests of a free and happy homelife and the development of personality in accord with Christian tradition; to encourage housewives to take their place as such, as MPs, local government councillors and representatives on other bodies.

Officers
: | *President* | Mrs M Blakey |
Chairman and Hon	
Company Secretary	Mrs J Mew
Hon Treasurer	Mrs M Martin

Membership
: Not disclosed   **Fees**: 50p p.a.

Publications
: *Housewives Today* (m except September)

Connections
: Excluded by Articles of Association, except overseas.

History
: Founded 1945. Immediate aims include an ample supply of food at reasonable price together with good houses and clothes to maintain a decent standard of living; the right of the individual to contract out of the National Health Service; opposition to rationing by coupon or price. Non-party and non-sectarian, the League upholds the British Constitution, namely, the rule of the Queen, in and through Parliament.

MARRIED WOMEN'S ASSOCIATION
87 Redington Road, London NW3 7RR
Telephone: 01-435 2281

Aims
: To promote recognition of a wife as a legal and equal financial partner during marriage and thereby strengthen the family as a unit; to end discrimination against women within marriage in all spheres.

Officers	*President*	Juanita Frances
	Chairman	Dorothy Wilson
	Secretary	Nora Bodley
	Vice-Presidents	include 106 members of all political parties

Membership 1,500 – 2,000   Fees: £1 p.a.

Publications Bi-monthly journal (free to members, to public on request)

Connections Council of Married Women, Washington DC; Married Women's Association, New Zealand; Status of Women Committee.

History Began in 1938 with small committee organised by Juanita Frances and supported by Baroness Summerskill (then an MP). Mainly operates in London. Tries to influence public opinion, parliament and government departments including the Home Office.

MOTHERS IN ACTION
9 Poland Street, London W1V 3DG

Aims To assist unsupported mothers regardless of race, colour or nationality.

History Founded 1967.

MOTHERS' UNION
(See Section 10)

NATIONAL BRITISH WOMEN'S TOTAL ABSTINENCE UNION INC
23 Dawson Place, London W2
Telephone: 01-229 0604

Aims To promote total abstinence by education and other means amongst all society, regarding the dangers of alcohol.

Officers *Secretary*   Mrs Kathleen W Sharp

Publications *The White Ribbon*

History Founded 1876. The union works among mothers and babies, and young people of both sexes to age 30; it is also concerned with anti-gambling, moral welfare, and world peace.

NATIONAL COUNCIL FOR THE SINGLE WOMAN
AND HER DEPENDANTS
166 Victoria Street, London SW1E 5BR
Telephone: 01-828 5511

Aims	The welfare of the woman who has never married, and who has or has had the care of elderly or infirm dependants.

Officers

President	Dame Flora Robson
Chairman	Baroness Seear
Director	Miss Roxane Arnold
Deputy Director	Miss Margaret Lofthouse

Vice-Presidents and Sponsors: The Archbishop of Canterbury, Baroness Emmet, Rev John Huxtable, Christopher Mayhew, Rev Mervyn Stockwood, Baroness Bacon, Baroness Harwood, Baroness Phillips, Miss B Harvie Anderson MP, C N Lippard, Dr Shirley Summerskill MP, Mrs Myra Sims, Dame Irene Ward

Staff 5

Membership 6,000

Fees (minimum) 25p for single women (as aims); 50p for all others

Branches 38 throughout the UK

Public Relations: Group 70, 69 Fleet Street, London EC4

Publications Newsletter (bi-m); also occasional reports

Connections National Association for Mental Health (8); Age Concern (6); National Council of Women of GB; National Federation of Housing Societies; National Council of Social Service.

History Registered as charity in 1965. National activities began at end of 1967 when funds became available. The founder, Rev Mary Webster, died in 1969. The organisation is now also a housing association and company limited by guarantee. Since formation, has actively and successfully campaigned to extend full social security benefits to single women with elderly or infirm relatives regardless of contributions. Has also set up a fund for loans or grants to assist in emergency. Plans sheltered housing for the single woman going out to work leaving elderly dependant at home. Legislation to ensure continued occupation of the family home when relative dies.

NATIONAL FEDERATION OF WOMEN'S INSTITUTES (A Charity)
39 Eccleston Street, London SW1W 9NT
Telephone: 01-730 7212

Aims	To provide a democratic, non-sectarian, non-party political, educational and social organisation for countrywomen, giving them the opportunity of working and learning together to improve the quality of life in the community and to enable them to develop their own skills and talents.

Officers

National Chairman	Mrs Pat Jacob
National Treasurer	Mrs K M Foss
General Secretary	Mrs A Ballard
Press and PR	Miss Carol Blaywire

Staff	50
Membership	442,158 (women only) **Fees:** £1 p.a.
Publications	*Home and Country* (m, circulation 150,000); also many other information sheets, pamphlets etc.
Branches	61 County Federation of Women's Institutes Offices; 9,318 Institutes
Connections	Official representation on many official and semi-official bodies; affiliated to many welfare and interest groups.
History	First Women's Institutes in England and Wales was started in September 1915 in Anglesey and a National Federation was formed 1917 when there were 137 WIs, with the first County Federation in Sussex in the same year. *Home and Country* first published in 1919. NFWI College of Further Education (Denman College) opened in Oxfordshire in 1948. Recent activities include celebration of Silver Jubilee of Denham College, 1975, a competitive Crafts Exhibition at Commonwealth Institute in March 1975 and celebrations to mark Diamond Jubilee in 1976.

NATIONAL HOUSEWIVES REGISTER
c/o Josephine Jaffray, Holmshaw, Moffat, Dumfriesshire DE10 9SQ
Telephone: Beattock 422

Aims	To provide a meeting point for lively-minded women who enjoy discussion on non-domestic topics. To promote friendship, mutual help and other activities among such like-minded people.

166

Officers	*National organisers*	Pat Williams and Josephine Jaffray
Membership	20,000	**Fees:** 35p p.a.
Publications	*NHR Newsletter* (spring and autumn)	
Connections	Close contact with many bodies but no affiliations.	

History   Formed 1960 by Maureen Nicol and called Housebound Housewives Register; by 1962 about 4,000 members; by 1970, 10,000 in 300 groups. Groups have always been autonomous. and whole organisation informal but in 1970 it became necessary to appoint two national organisers. Does itself not act as a pressure group, but helps fulfil a tremendous need by providing an organisation to give housewives some mental stimulation.

WOMEN IN MANAGEMENT
4 Mapledale Avenue, Croydon, Surrey CRO 5TA
Telephone: 01-654 4659

Aims   The better utilisation of the country's womanpower, through the provision of information, guidance and training.

Officers   *Director*   Eleanor Macdonald

Membership   Informal

History   Started 1969 by Eleanor Macdonald. Acts as a voluntary research and advisory body, and a training consultancy (E M Courses). The groups see the implementation of equal pay and opportunities legislation vital for the cost effective use of human resources.

WOMEN'S ABORTION AND CONTRACEPTION CAMPAIGN
c/o Women's Centre, 11 Waverley Road, Redland, Bristol BS6 6ES
Telephone: 0272 38120

Aims   'Women have the right to control their own lives. This is impossible unless we can control our fertility, we must be able to choose if we have children and when we have them. This means: free, safe and reliable contraception available to every woman on the National Health Service; abortion — a woman's right to choose — any woman who is unwilling to continue her pregnancy should have the undisputed right to a free and safe abortion; no forced sterilisation; pressure should not be put on any woman to accept sterilisation as a condition for abortion.'

167

Officers	None — all members of equal status.
Membership	At least 200, must be women. **Fees:** none
Publications	*WACC Newsletter* (3—6 monthly); *Women and Abortion*
Connections	Friendly informal relations with Abortion Law Reform Association (8); Broook Advisory Clinic; NCCL (6).
History	Formed as a result of a national meeting called by the London Abortion Action Group in January 1972. National newsletter had already been started by then by women in Nottingham and has since been produced by London and Bristol branches. Merseyside WAAC arranged first national conference in January 1973. Most activity takes place at the local group level including public meetings, demonstrations, etc as well as provision of free pregnancy testing services. Plans to be discussed on ideas about national activity.

WOMEN'S INTERNATIONAL LEAGUE FOR PEACE AND FREEDOM
29 Great James Street, London WC1N 3ES
Telephone: 01-242 4817

Aims	To bring together women of different political and philosophical tendencies united in their determination to study: to make known and help to abolish the political, social, economic and psychological causes of war and to work for a constructive peace. The primary objectives are total and universal disarmament, the abolition of violent means of coercion for the settlement of all conflicts, the strengthening of a world organisation, the institution of international law and for the political, social and economic co-operation of all peoples.	
Officers	*President*	Mrs Agnes Stapledon
	Chairman	Mrs Ruth Osborn
	Hon Secretary	Mrs Carmel Budiardjo
	Hon Treasurer	Mrs Ilse Singer
	General Secretary and PR	Miss Rose-Marie Adams
Prominent members	Include Mrs Joyce Butler MP, Mrs Maureen Colquhoun MP	
Staff	1	
Membership	600	**Fees:** £3.50 p.a.

Publications   *Peace and Freedom* (q); Newsletter (9 issues p.a. only to members

History   Founded 1915. International organisation with headquarters in Geneva. 21 national sections. Last triennial International Congress held in 1974 in Birmingham.

WOMEN'S LIBERAL FEDERATION
(See Section 1)

WOMEN'S NATIONAL CANCER CONTROL CAMPAIGN
44 Russell Square, London WC1B 4JP
Telephone: 01-580 3322

Aims   Early detection and prevention of cancer in women.

History   Founded 1965

WOMEN'S REPORT
2 Sherriff Court, Sherriff Road, London NW6 2AT

Aims   Exists to produce a magazine and through this to spread feminist information and ideas. The magazine is a combination of brief news items and feature articles dealing with important current events, giving a feminist analysis.

Publications   *Women's Report* (bi-m)

History   Grew out of a group called Women's Lobby (1971) whose aims were to campaign via parliamentary pressure for women's rights. As the group became more radical, it concentrated its energies on producing the magazine and working independently of the Fawcett Society which originally donated £100 to the magazine's production. Reconstituted as the Women's Report Collective in November 1973. This collective is composed of about 15 women who share between them all the work of producing the magazine.

WOMEN'S RIGHTS CAMPAIGN
Flat 2, 40 Menelik Road, London NW2
Telephone: 01-794 9510

Aims	To fight for equal rights for women; to make people aware that sex discrimination affects both men and women; legislation to grant women equal rights in education, employment, credit facilities, social security etc; improved child care facilities; equal representation of women in national life; to free women from the sole responsibility of caring for the family and men from the sole responsibility of supporting the family.

Officers   *Committee* (1975)   Carolyn Faulder, Tamar Karet, Una Kroll, Wanda Moore, Mary Stott, Barbara Todd, Angela Wyatt

                          Treasurer   Pamela Robinson

Membership	Open to all men and women concerned with equal rights for women
Fees	£1 p.a.
Publications	Newsletter (irregular)
History	Created by members of Women in Media's Anti-Discrimination Bill Action Group (ADBAG) in August 1974. First major action was to support the candidature of Dr Una Kroll as independent candidate at Sutton and Cheam in the October 1974 General Election. Action will be aimed at increasing the number of women in public life specifically at securing equal representation of women on national and governmental bodies and commissions.

WORKING WOMEN'S CHARTER CAMPAIGN
29 Lowther Hill, London SE23 1PZ
Telephone: 01-690 5518

Aims	To agitate and organise to achieve the rate for the job regardless of sex; equal opportunity of entry into occupations and professions: equal education; working conditions without deterioration to be the same for women as for men; the removal of all legal and bureaucratic impediments to equality; provision of free nurseries; eighteen weeks maternity leave with full net pay; free contraception and abortion; increased family allowances; to campaign amongst women to take an active part in trade unions and political life.

170

Officers   *Secretary*   Elizabeth Hambledon
                   Treasurer   Dian Booth
                   Information Officer   Mandy Snell
                   Convenor   Jane Leggett

Membership   None as such

Fees   Affiliation £1; mailing list fee 1975, £1.

Publications   Newsletter (2/3 weeks, mailing list only); other literature available

History   WWC introduced by women's subcommittee at a special meeting of London Trades Council in March 1974. Co-ordinating committee established 7th December 1974 to co-ordinate activities in London area. Over 35 branches have now been set up all over the country. Conferences held at Birmingham, Leeds, Cambridge, Brent, Ealing, as well as LSE. London area and SE Regional Council pressed TUC to adopt the charter.

ABORTION LAW REFORM ASSOCIATION
186 King's Cross Road, London WC1X 9DE
Telephone: 01-278 4575

Aims	To campaign for every women to have the right to control her own fertility through contraception, and, if she becomes pregnant, to end or continue her pregnancy as she wishes; for a legal right to medical abortion; free and comprehensive facilities for abortion through the NHS; free and readily available contraception and sterilisation; and counselling services.	
Officers	*President*	Professor Glanville Williams
	Vice-Presidents	include: Lord Boothby, Lady Gaitskell, Lena Jeger MP, Lord Molson, John Parker MP, Rev John Robinson, Sir George Sinclair MP, Lord Soper, David Steel MP, Lord Willis.
	Campaign Organiser and General Secretary	Sally Hesmondhalgh
Staff	1	
Membership	Not available.	**Fees:** £2.50 p.a.
Publications	*Why we must fight the Abortion (Amendment) Bill; Working of the Abortion Act.*	
Connections	Two members of executive committee appointed to National Council for Civil Liberties (6) in 1974 in connection with A Woman's Right to Choose Campaign.	
History	Formed 1936. 1967 saw passage of Abortion Act following introduction by David Steel in 1966 of ALRA's draft bill. Activities include adoption of abortion-on-request as policy following report of Lane Committee vindicating the 1967 Act. Now conducting major campaign against Abortion (Amendment) Bill.	

ACTION ON SMOKING AND HEALTH (ASH) (A Charity)
Margaret Pyke House, 27–35 Mortimer Street, London W1N 7RJ
Telephone: 01-637 9843

Aims	To mobilise, encourage and co-ordinate action throughout the UK to mitigate the damage to health caused by smoking, to discourage smoking, and to create an atmosphere in which smoking is seen as an unnecessary and harmful habit.

Officers

Chairman	Professor Charles Fletcher
Hon Secretary	Dr Keith Ball
Executive Director	Mr Mike Daube

Membership Not disclosed.

Fees Individual £5 p.a. Corporate £20 p.a.

Regional Offices Scottish Committee ASH at Royal College of Physicians, 9 Queen Street, Edinburgh EH2 1JQ.
ASH Northern Ireland, c/o Ulster Cancer Foundation, 43 Eglantine Avenue, Belfast BT9.

Publications *ASH Newsletter;* various leaflets.

Connections ASH receives an annual grant from the Department of Health and Social Security; subscriptions from area health authorities, close co-operation with health and health education organisations, and with Members of Parliament.

History Founded in 1971 under the Royal College of Physicians after their report, as 'Smoking and Health Now'. It campaigns to put pressure on government and tobacco and allied industries; produces publicity on the hazards of smoking; holds conferences; maintains a register of smoking withdrawal centres; and acts as an information centre for the press and public. It has campaigned for an increase in non-smoking accommodation; hopes for further restrictions on tobacco advertising and promotion, and for legislation to include tobacco products in the Medicines Act.

ALBANY TRUST (A Registered Charity)
31 Clapham Road, London SW9 0JD
Telephone: 01-582 0972

Aims	To promote psychological health in men and women in respect of the whole spectrum of psycho-sexual problems; by providing and promoting counselling services; running training courses

acting as a referal agency; undertaking and participating in educational and research activities, including publication of suitable material.

Officers

Managing Trustee	Antony Grey
Secretary	David Bernard

Membership None. Supporters welcome to donate funds including by Deed of Covenant.

Publications *Man and Society* (occasional).

Connections Direct participation and links with various bodies including the National Council for Social Service.

History Founded in 1958. Principally concerned with the problems of the homosexual. Developed into a major direct counselling agency but in recent years has done less direct work and more promotion and support for both voluntary and statutory bodies. The Trust receives a grant from the Voluntary Services Unit of the Home Office but other finance comes solely from trusts and individual contributions.

ASSOCIATION FOR THE PREVENTION OF ADDICTION (A Charity)
9 James Street, London WC2
Telephone: 01-836 1373 (Ansafone)

Aims To prevent the spread of drug abuse by educational and social means.

Officers

Chairman	Dr George Birdwood
Vice-Chairman	Dr Elizabeth Tylden
Hon Secretary	Mrs M Craven
Hon Treasurer	J A Dick

Staff 1 + 3 part-time.

Membership 600

Fees Central members £5 p.a.; Branch £1.50 p.a.

Offices Admin & Literature Centre — 11 Grosvenor Street, Canton, Cardiff. 15 branches throughout England and Wales.

Publications *APA Newsletter* (q), pamphlets on various topics.

Connections Representative on Executive Committee of Standing Conference on Drug Abuse. Working relationship with other bodies.

History   Formed after an appeal in *The Guardian* April 1967. First national charity to work with drug addiction both in practical social work, a pressure group and as an educational body. Branches have been busy with local counselling projects — Esher APA has established a residential hostel for 12 ex-narcotic users and has successfully rehabilitated several young men. The Association has pioneered many achievements but has found difficulty in attracting funds following the growth of other similar organisations. Its plans include developing work with schools and training teachers. Believes that the destructive effect of drug abuse can be largely prevented by imaginative educational work based on sound sociological principles. Also carries out counselling work.

BRIGHTON AND DISTRICT ANTI-FLUORIDATION CAMPAIGN
76 Osborne Villas, Hove, Sussex BN4 2RB
Telephone: 0273 737392

Aims   To consider and execute legitimate actions for the purpose of discouraging and/or preventing the artificial fluoridation of the public water supply in the Brighton area and the UK; to inform and educate the general public on matters relating to fluoridation.

Officers   *President*   Andrew Bowden MP
             Chairman   David Fletcher
             Hon Secretary   Miss Sue Evelyn

Membership   Full — open to persons normally resident in the Brighton area; associate membership for others.

Fees   50p p.a.

Connections   Affiliated to National Pure Water Assoc (11).

History   Founded in 1966 by Andrew Bowden MP.

BRITISH ANTI-SMOKING EDUCATION SOCIETY (A Charity)
125 West Dumpton Lane, Ramsgate, Kent CT11 7BH
Telephone: 0834 55036

Aims   To deter the public — especially the young — from the smoking habit.

Officers   *President*   Dr Howard Williams
             Chairman   T W Hurst
             Secretary   Rev Hubert Little

Prominent Members	Sir Adrian Boult, Yehudi Menuhin, Steve Race, Derek Nimmo, Ken Dodd, Lord Soper, Lord Arran, Clement Freud MP, Sir Cyril Black, David Hemery, Barry John, Gordon Banks, Dr Shirley Summerskill MP, John Parker MP
Staff	1
Membership	1,000 plus corporate bodies. Individuals must be non-smokers.
Fees	7 year Deed of Covenant.
Publications	*The Case against the Cigarette* and other pamphlets.
Connections	Collaborates with Council for Health Education. Closely linked with National Society of Non-Smokers (8).
History	Formed in 1967 by the National Society of Non-Smokers to finance, as a charity, its anti-smoking campaigns in schools started in 1955. Recent activities include a London display of scholars' anti-smoking posters; leaflets circulated to every scholar in some counties; publishing a selection of best limericks received in 20 years of school contests. Plan to celebrate in 1976 the national society's Golden Jubilee and 21st birthday of schools contests.

BRITISH MEDICAL ASSOCIATION
(See Section 2)

CENTRAL COUNCIL FOR THE DISABLED (A Charity)
34 Eccleston Square, London SW1V 1PE
Telephone: 01-834 0747/8

Aims	Concerned with all matters which affect, or may affect, the disabled, including causes of disability and their elimination; is a central co-ordinating body for all organisations concerned with welfare; maintains relationships with government and public authorities and with the progress of work on behalf of the disabled throughout the world.
Patron	HRH The Queen Mother

Officers	*President*	Sir Harry Platt
	Chairman	Duke of Buccleuch
	Chairman of	
	Executive Committee	Lady Hamilton
	Director	George Wilson
	Press and PR	Mary Morgan
	Advertising	Richard Freeman
	Housing	Jane Ribbens
	Welfare	Kay Kitching
	Holidays	Wendy Francis
	Access	Capt G Welch

Staff 20

Membership Not a membership organisation.

Publications *Bulletin* (m); *Contact* (bi-m); many leaflets etc including a series of town guides.

Connections Affiliated societies include many local and national organisations concerned with the disabled, and most local government authorities. Affiliated to International Society for Rehabilitation of the Disabled.

History Founded 1919 as Central Committee for the Care of Cripples working in conjunction with the Central Council for Infant and Child Welfare. In 1927 it became Central Council for the Care of Cripples and in 1941 it was incorporated as a company limited by guarantee. In 1962 the name was changed. The organisation has continued to work for improvement in facilities for the disabled; has published further town guides and generally increased the level of casework and activities. It claims that the appointment of Alfred Morris MP as the first Minister for the disabled in 1974 was in no small way due to its activities.

DISABLEMENT INCOME GROUP (DIG) (A Charity)
Queens House, 180–182a Tottenham Court Road, London W1 0BD
Telephone: 01-636 1946/7

Aims To secure for all disabled people a national disability income and allowance for the extra expense of disablement; to co-operate with other bodies for the improvement of the economic and social position of disabled people and the chronic sick; to promote research into the economic and social problems of disablement.

Patrons   Professor B Abel-Smith, John Astor MP, Baroness Masham,
Lord Bishop of Bristol, L Carter-Jones MP, Bishop of Southwark,
Sir George Edwards, Lady Hamilton, A Morris MP, Rabbi
M Nemeth, Dr D Owen MP, Rev K Slack, Professor P Townsend,
Dame Joan Vickers MP

Vice-Chairmen   Mrs L Chalker MP, J Pardoe MP

Officers   *Chairman of DIG*
Pressure Group   Miss Betty Veal
Chairman of DIG
Charitable Trust   C S S Lyon
Chief Executive   Miss Rosemary Till
(General Secretary
and PR)

Staff   7

Membership   15,000

Fees   Minimum 25p p.a. (subject to revision).

Publications   *Progress* (q). An ABC of Services and General Information for
Disabled People, and various other reports and leaflets.

Connections   Affiliated to National Council of Social Service; Central Council
for the Disabled (8); National Council of Women; member of
Disability Alliance.

History   Founded in 1965 by two disabled housewives, the late Mrs Megan
Du Boisson and Mrs Berit Thornberry. The charitable trust was
registered in March 1967. Recently DIG has played a leading part
in bringing about The Chronically Sick and Disabled Persons
Act 1971, which introduced the attendance allowance for people
so severely disabled that they require assistance from another person by day and/or by night. Its plans include pressing for further
legislation to increase pensions and allowances for all severely
disabled people.

FAMILY PLANNING ASSOCIATION LIMITED (A Charity)
Margaret Pyke House, 27–35 Mortimer Street, London W1A 4QW
Telephone: 01-636 7866

Aims   To preserve and protect the good health, both physical and
mental, of parents, young people and children and to prevent
the poverty, hardship and distress caused by unwanted
conception; to educate the public in the field of procreation,
contraception and health, with particular reference to personal

179

responsibility in sexual relationships; to give medical advice and assistance in cases of involuntary sterility or of difficulties connected with the marriage relationship or sexual problems for which medical advice or treatment is appropriate.

Officers	*Chairman*	Lady Tewson
	Deputy Chairman	Lady Houghton
	Hon Treasurer	Sir Robin Brook
	Director and Secretary	Vacant
	President	Vacant

Prominent Members   Lord Boothby, Lady Gaitskell, Sir Cyril Kleinwort, Lord Bishop of London, Lady Stocks

Staff   190

Membership   6,500

Fees   £4 p.a. Subscriptions may be waived for voluntary workers.

Branches   25 branches covering all Great Britain.

Publications   *Family Planning Journal* (q); *Medical Newsletter* (q); *EP News*, (10 issues p.a.).

Connections   County Council Association; International Planned Parenthood Federation and many others.

History   Incorporated in September 1966 as FPA. Originally set up as National Birth Control Council established in 1930. Present name adopted in 1939. Is the largest health service outside the NHS employing approximately 1,500 doctors, 2,000 nurses and 11,000 layworkers. Over 1,000 clinics set up by 1972, now being handed over to NHS. Achievements include free family planning from 1974. Activities have included use-effectiveness trials of contraceptives, and education and information services. Future plans will concentrate on information services, experimental projects, and establishment of regional development centres.

FEDERATION OF MENTAL PATIENTS UNIONS

c/o Mental Patients Union (Hackney), Robin Farquarson House, 37 Mayola Road, Clapton, London E5
Telephone: 01-986 5251

Aims   Concerned with the dignity and human rights of society's so-called mental patients; challenges repressive psychiatric practice and its ill-defined concept of 'mental illness'; believes that admission to a mental hospital arises primarily from social problems of inequality, poor housing, poverty and unemployment; aims to set up local groups working to guard the rights and welfare of mental patients in hospitals throughout the country.

Officers	*Chairman*	Valerie Roberts
	Secretary	Joan Martin
	Treasurer	Andrew Roberts

Staff 1

Membership No national membership record. Restricted to mental patients and ex-mental patients for full membership.

Fees Vary with local group.

Publications *MPU News*, irregular, circulated by MPU Hackney; *Declaration of Intent*, and various other leaflets.

Connections Affiliated to NCCL (6) and Campaign for Homeless and Rootless (6).

History Founded in London, March 1973, as the Mental Patients Union. General meeting held in Manchester, 1974, after establishment of several MPUs, and re-organised as a federation. All groups are autonomous with Hackney acting as central information centre. Recognised in Hackney by hospital authorities and runs two democratic households for members. Has concentrated on establishment of new groups, the right of members to meet on hospital premises etc. Will continue to challenge in day-to-day practice the use of mental hospitals as prisons, and to demand the abolition of compulsory treatment and hospitalization.

FLUORIDATION SOCIETY LTD
40–43 King Street, London WC2E 8JH
Telephone: 01-240 1127

Aims To improve dental health by securing the optimum fluoride content of water supplies.

Membership 1,000

Publications *Fluoridation Newsletter* (q).

History Founded 1969.

HUMAN RIGHTS SOCIETY
(See Section 6)

MIGRAINE TRUST (A Charity)
23 Queen Square, London WC1
Telephone: 01-278 2676   01-637 0741

Aims	Provision of assistance in research, propagation of information and making of grants for research into causes, alleviation and treatment of migraine.
Patron	HRH Princess Margaret
Officers	*Chairman* Sir Thomas Holmes Sellors *Information Officer* David Gordon
Staff	10
Membership	No membership but people requiring *Migraine News* give donations.
Publications	*Migraine News* (q), available to all donors. *Focus on Migraine, Hemicrania* (q), to GPs on request.
History	Formed 1965, it has been responsible for the establishment of the Princess Margaret Migraine Clinic (Charterhouse Square, London) and clinics at Charing Cross Hospital (London) and Southern General Hospital (Glasgow).

MIND/NATIONAL ASSOCIATION FOR MENTAL HEALTH (A Charity)
22 Harley Street, London W1N 2ED

Aims	Concerned with those suffering from any form of mental illness or severe stress — with children and young people who are maladjusted, emotionally disturbed or mentally handicapped in any degree; with mentally handicapped people who need training and assistance if they are to lead as full a life as possible; with the preventive services including child guidance, education in schools and colleges, and tackling the problems of poverty and deprivation; with stress at work; and with rehabilitation of those disabled by mental illness or handicap; to draw attention to these matters and to see that proper help is provided; to take action or to press for action at governmental level; to spread knowledge about the true facts of mental disorder and to work to overcome the stigma still attached to it.
Patron	HRH Princess Alexandra

Mind (continued)

Officers	*President*	The Rt Hon Lord Butler
	Chairman	Christopher Mayhew
	Vice-Chairman	Charles Clark
	Director	Tony Smythe
	Treasurer	Michael Edwardes-Evans
	Medical Advisor	E F Carr

Staff 68

Membership 11,200

Fees Full member £5 p.a. Associate member: £3.

Regional Offices Leeds; Cardiff; 127 Local and branch associations throughout UK.

Publications *Mind Out* (bi-m); *Information Bulletin* (m); occasional reports and papers.

Connections With 350 affiliated bodies comprising other National voluntary organisations and professional bodies in the Mental Health field.

History Found 1946 by amlgamation of three voluntary mental welfare bodies, the Central Association for Mental Welfare, the Child Guidance Council and the National Council for Mental Hygiene. Renamed in 1973 as MIND. It has submitted evidence to Commons Select Committee on Children and Young Persons Act, to Warnock Committee on Special Schools, to DHSS working party on Behaviour Modification Programmes and to Select Committee on Abortion (Amendment) Bill. It also runs conferences, and courses on mental health issues.

MULTIPLE SCLEROSIS SOCIETY OF GREAT BRITAIN AND NORTHERN IRELAND (A Charity)
4 Tachbrook Street, London SW1V 1SJ
Telephone: 01-834 8231

Aims To promote research in co-operation with the medical profession to find the cause and cure for multiple sclerosis; to help all those who suffer from multiple sclerosis.

Patron Princess Alice, Duchess of Gloucester

Multiple Sclerosis Society (continued)

Officers		
	President	Countess of Limerick
	Chairman	R P Cave
	General Secretary	A C Waine
	Press and PR	Mrs Ann Darnbrough
	Organising Secretary for Scotland	I C Cameron
	Admin Director Northern Ireland	Dr Wilson Johnson

Staff   12

Membership   30,000   Fees: Minimum of 25p p.a.

Branches   242 throughout the United Kingdom.

Publications   *M S S Bulletin* (m); *M S News* (q).

Connections   Affiliated to International Federation of Multiple Sclerosis Societies; National Council of Social Service; Central Council for Disabled (8). Affiliated societies include Multiple Sclerosis Societies in Ireland, Australia, Auckland, New Zealand, Rhodesia.

History   Founded 1954. Activities in past three years have included over £800,000 made available for research and a fleet of 100 ambulances/vehicles; two housing schemes completed at Liverpool and Nottingham adjacent to day-care centres; 4 day-centres, 3 full time holiday centres, plus other facilities. Plans include further research projects and formation of more branches in those areas presently without one.

NATIONAL ANTI-FLUORIDATION CAMPAIGN
36 Station Road, Thames Ditton, Surrey KT7 0NS
Telephone: 01-398 2117

Aims   The provision of national legislation to prohibit the employment of public water supplies for conveying any substances which has been deliberately added to the water for the purpose of influencing directly the growth, development or functioning of any part of the human body, nervous system or mind.

Officers		
	Chairman and Hon Secretary	P Clavell Blount
	Hon Treasurer	Miss E L Keeler
	Other Committee members	P J Macdonald, Mrs J C MacKillop, G J A Stern

184

Membership   Not given.   **Fees:** 25p minimum p.a.

Publications   Several hundred pamphlets and circulars have been produced.

History   Campaign officially launched on 4 July 1963 as London Anti-
Fluoridation Campaign. Name changed in July 1971. Has briefed
many groups of councillors when fluoridation has been advocated
and had considerable success in defeating proposals. Recent activities have been building up of body of MPs against fluoridation. In
June 1974 Chairman invited to appear before special committee
set up by Royal College of Physicians. It works closely with
Andrew Bowden MP who is chairman of the all-party group of
MPs opposed to fluoridation which by 1975 had 85 supporters.

NATIONAL PURE WATER ASSOCIATION
223–225 Newton Road, Worcester WR5 1JB
Telephone: Worcester 353184

Aims   To oppose the use of public water supplies for the purpose of
mass medication and, in particular, to oppose the fluoridation
of such supplies; to promote the protection of public water
supplies from any form of pollution or contamination.

Officers   *President*   Lord Douglas of Barloch
Chairman   R A Reid
Hon Treasurer   Mrs W M Sykes
Secretary   Mrs A R Cooper
Vice-Presidents   Viscount Bledisloe, Earl of Bradford,
                     Mrs Joyce Butler MP, Earl of Yarborough

Staff   4

Membership   Confidential

Fees   Full £2 p.a.; Students £1 p.a.; Associates 25p p.a.

Publications   Members' Notes (q); many pamphlets, reprints etc (between
6 and 10 produced each year).

Connections   Founded March 16, 1960 at House of Lords by invitation of
Lord Douglas of Barloch. Has always opposed fluoridation on
various grounds: it is an unwarranted violation of rights of the
individual; does not prevent tooth decay; dangerous and
medically unsound and contrary to medical ethics; of doubtful
legality; unscientific and haphazard etc. Main activity consists
of making views known to decision-making bodies. Speakers are
provided for a variety of organisations. The association supports

demands for higher financial allocations for genuine dental services including educational campaigns on nutrition and the dangers of excessive sugar consumption. It works closely with scientists who draw public attention to specific instances of water pollution, both deliberate and accidental.

NATIONAL SOCIETY OF NON-SMOKERS
125 West Dumpton Lane, Ramsgate, Kent CT11 7BH
Telephone: 0843 55036

Aims	As for the British Anti-Smoking Education Society (qv).
Membership	1,000 individuals. Must be non-smokers.
Fees	£1 p.a.
Publications	Newsletter (q); various pamphlets including *The Tyranny of Tobacco, Fifty Years Fight for Fairplay.*
Connections	Collaborates with Health Council.
History	Formed in 1926. In 1930 absorbed the Anti-Tobacco Society which in 1876 warned of numerous cases of smoker's cancer. Has secured no smoking amenities in public places. In response to appeals from 10,000 smokers, pioneered Stop Smoking clinics in Liverpool and London in 1957. In 1967 formed the British Anti-Smoking Education Society to finance anti-smoking campaign in schools which started in 1955. Plans include Golden Jubilee clebrations in May 1976.

PATIENTS' ASSOCIATION
335 Gray's Inn Road, London WC1X 8PX
Telephone: 01-837 7241

Aims	To represent and further the interests of patients; to give help and advice to individuals; to acquire and spread information about patient's interests; to promote understanding and goodwill between patients and everyone in medical practice and related activities.	
Officers	*President*	Dame Elizabeth Ackroyd
	Chairman	Jean Robinson
	General Secretary and PR	Kate Patrick
Staff	1	

Membership   1,000   **Fees:** £2 p.a.

Publications   Newsletter (q). Annual Report; various pamphlets.

History   Founded 1963 as a result of concern about unethical experiments on patients without their knowledge and consent, and the tragedies following the use of thalidomide. Campaigns have led or contributed to action in such areas as: appointment of NHS ombudsman, a code of practice for the medical profession in using patients during teaching, improved hospital visiting hours, improvements in drug safety, reductions in hospital waiting lists. The association is run by a committee of 8 people elected by members.

POPULATION COUNTDOWN (A Charity)
P.O Box 2LB, 24/30 Great Titchfield Street, London W1A 2LB
Telephone: 01-580 7331

Aims   To encourage the attitudes that all peoples should have the knowledge and the means of family planning as a basic human right; to support projects that work towards the stabilisation of the world population by means which also promote human welfare, personal freedom and the quality of life; to encourage voluntary family planning programmes that seek to establish a balance between the population of the world and its natural resources; to raise funds in the UK for the support of voluntary family planning programmes throughout the world.

Officers   *Chairman*   Lady Tewson
              Director   Ronald Dick
              Public Relations   Eileen Ware
              Appeals Officer   Richard Harris

Membership   Not applicable.

Publications   Newsletter (3 times p.a.); *Youth Campaign Leaflet,* (a); various pamphlets.

Connections   Strong links with Family Planning Association (8) and the International Planned Parenthood Federation.

History   Present campaign founded in November 1973, springing from previous efforts during 1962–72, under various names, (including Family Planning International Campaign). Activities include establishment of 50 local activist groups. Launched a youth campaign in schools and youth clubs throughout Britain, and has growing support in these areas. Plans include maintenance of the growth of local groups, encouraging the development of their fund-raising and local pressure activities; development of educational activities for all age groups, including the publication of special reports etc; increase of funds raised for family planning and educational projects overseas.

POSSUM USERS ASSOCIATION (PUA) (A Charity)
Copper Beech, Barry's Close, Stoke Bishop, Bristol BS9 1AW
Telephone: 0272 683596

Aims	To unite into one body of people the very severely physically handicapped who use special electronic equipment; to promote the social wellbeing, interests and welfare of all disabled members and to support similar organisations in establishing improved conditions, accommodation and services for the disabled.
Officers	*Hon Secretary and PR* D Hyde *Hon Editor/Chairman* K R Bowell *Vice-Presidents* Sir Adrian Boult, Cliff Morgan Lewis Carter-Jones MP is a member
Staff	1
Membership	1,350 Fees: Full: 50p p.a.; Associate £1 p.a.
Branches	Wharfedale.
Publications	*Possability* (q)
History	Formed October 1968. Activities have included Charity Concerts, appeals and the Association has assisted about 60 severely disabled people. A concert will be held in October 1976 at the Royal Albert Hall.

Note: The title name is derived from a mechanical aid known as the patient operated selector mechanism.

ROYAL COLLEGE OF NURSING AND NATIONAL COUNCIL OF NURSES OF THE UK (A Charity)
1a Henrietta Place, Cavendish Square, London W1M 0AB
Telephone: 01-580 2646   Cables: Remedial London

Aims	To promote the science and art of nursing and the better education and training of nurses and their efficiency in the profession of nursing; to assist nurses who by reason of adversity, ill-health or otherwise are in need of assistance of any nature.

Royal College of Nursing (continued)

Officers	*President*	Miss W E Prentice
	General Secretary	Miss C M Hall
	Chief Press and	
	PR Officer	Lt Col D C de Cent
	Other Press and PR	Miss V O'Connor, D Russell, M Palmer

Staff 100 approximately.

Membership 100,000

Fees Full £10.50 p.a.; Students £2.50 p.a. Open to all qualified nurses, students and pupils undertaking a statutory training.

Offices National Boards in Edinburgh; Cardiff; Belfast. Area officers in Darlington; Chorley; Birmingham; Bath; London.

Publications *Nursing Standard* (bi-m)

Connections With 70 bodies in UK including representation on staff side of Nurses and Midwives Whitley Council. Represents nursing profession within International Council of Nurses; European Group of Nursing Associations; Permanent Committee of Nurses in liaison with the EEC.

History Registered as a company and held its first meeting on 1 April 1916 as College of Nursing, standing for professional advancement and certification. In 1919 produced the 'Nurses Charter' which called for a 48-hour week, proper accommodation, systematic training, adequate salaries and a pension scheme. Incorporated by Royal Charter in 1928 and title Royal was granted in 1939. In 1963, amalgamated with National Council of Nurses. Student nurses admitted in 1968, and enrolled and pupil nurses in 1970. 1971 pay rise was largest in history and was largely due to the 'Raise the Roof' campaign: a deputation to Secretary of State for Social Services led to setting up of Lord Halsbury independent inquiry into nurses pay, which led to largest single increase since the inception of NHS. It plans to campaign for a new deal for nursing including better salary and career structures.

SOCIALIST MEDICAL ASSOCIATION
14/16 Bristol Street, Birmingham B5 7AA
Telephone: 021-622, 2020

Aims   The abolition of all health charges; a general practitioner service working from well-equipped Health Centres; an occupational Health Service; a democratic system of adminstration within the National Health Service.

Officers
President	Dr John Dunwoody
Hon Secretary	Dr R K Griffiths
Hon Treasurer	Mrs J Sohn-Rethel

Hon Vice-Presidents (MPs) L Abse, J Ashley, A Blenkinsop, Mrs J Butler, Mrs G Dunwoody, R Edwards, M Foot, W Hamling, J Hart, R Hughes, Mrs L Jeger, Miss J Lestor, Dr D Mabon, Dr M Miller, A Morris, S Newens, E Ogden, M Orbach, S Orme, A Palmer, L Pavitt, Dr J Powell-Evans, J Richardson, P Shore, Mrs R Short, J Silken, J Silverman, Dr S Summerskill

Staff   1

Membership   2,000

Fees   (all p.a.). Full £8, £6, £4, according to qualifications; associate £2; students 50p; affiliated organisations: national £10; local £2.50.

Branches   Wales; Bristol; Edinburgh; Harlow; Leeds; London & Home Counties; Merseyside; Nottingham; Sheffield; Teeside; West Midlands; International.

Publications   Several leaflets.

Connections   Affiliated to Labour Party (1) and NCCL (6).

History   Formed in 1930. Contributed to blueprint which was largely adopted as the NHS Act 1946. Past President Dr David Stark Murray moved resolution at Labour Party Conference on NHS. Has campaigned for increased democracy in NHS and for the institution of an occupational health service as well as campaigning for changes such as the abolition of private practice.

SOCIETY FOR THE PROTECTION OF UNBORN CHILDREN (SPUC)
9a Brechin Place, London SW7 4QB
Telephone: 01-373 7306

Aims	To bring to an end abortion and to protect the rights of children before as well as after birth.

Officers

Chairman	Rt Hon the Viscount Barrington
Treasurer	Peter W West
Director	Mrs Phyllis Bowman
Co-ordinator	Derek L Murray
Secretary	Mrs Jennifer Murray

Membership   17,000 individual members plus various organisations who hold group membership.

Fees   £1 p.a.; widows, pensioners and students 25p. Life membership £10; group membership from £2.20.

Branches   150 throughout the United Kingdom.

Publications   Bulletin (2/3 p.a.); various leaflets and medical reports.

History   The Society for the Protection of Unborn Children was formed January 1967, with the support of a number of Fellows of the Royal College of Obstetricians and Gynaecologists, in order to organize opposition to the new abortion law, inside and outside parliament, at the time it was being debated. After this was passed as the Abortion Act 1967, SPUC continued to oppose it and has been involved in attempts made in parliament for its reform and for an official enquiry into its working. The society organizes meetings on abortion throughout the country and sends speakers to meetings and debates in schools and universities. It keeps a register of private families willing to shelter girls under pressure to have abortions.

THE OPEN DOOR
4 Manorbrook, Blackheath, London SE3
Telephone: 01-852 8651

Aims   Self-help organisation and information service for those suffering from agoraphobia.

Officers   *Founder Secretary*   Alice Neville

Membership   4,000   **Fees:** £1 p.a. voluntary.

Branches   50 area secretaries throughout Great Britain.

Publications   Bi-monthly newsletter.

History   Formed 1965. Activities include many research projects.

THE SPASTICS SOCIETY (A Charity)
12 Park Crescent, London W1N 4EQ
Telephone: 01-636 5020

Aims   The welfare, treatment, education and advancement of spastics.

Membership   203 Institutions.

Publications   *Spastics News* and *Special Education.*

History   Founded 1952.

VASECTOMY ADVANCEMENT SOCIETY OF GREAT BRITAIN (A Charity)
1 Ravenscroft Court, London NW11 8BA
Telephone: 01-455 6541

Aims   The provision of training in vasectomy counselling and techniques for any medical practitioner; the promotion and co-ordination of research in the field of vasectomy.

Officers

President	Philip Whitehead MP
Chairman	Dr Michael Altman
Treasurer	Dr Michael Klinger
Secretary and PR	Mrs Marion Altman

Prominent Members   Baroness Birk, Dr S Carne, Dr M Smith (Chief Medical Officer FPA), Dr D Ralphs, Dr R Snowden

Membership   300. Full members: doctors only. Associate members: interested people with Advisory Board approval.

Fees   £10 joining subscription; Associate mebers £8. No annual fees.

Publications   Videotape and 16mm film *Vasectomy.*

Connections   National Association of Family Planning Doctors; Family Planning Association; Marie Stopes Memorial Clinic.

History   Founded in 1972 to provide instruction in vasectomy for any medical practitioner. Activities include continuing instruction courses and symposia and plans include medical students essay competition.

VOLUNTARY EUTHANASIA SOCIETY

13 Prince of Wales Terrace, Kensington High Street, London W8 5PG
Telephone: 01-937 7770

Aims	Legislation to permit voluntary euthanasia, so giving to an adult, in carefully defined circumstances and with proper safeguards, the choice between prolonged suffering and gentle, dignified death.	
Officers	*President*	Earl of Listowel
	Vice-Presidents	Sir George Thomson, Dr Eliot, T O Slater
	Secretary and PR	C R Sweetingham
Sponsors include	Sir Guy Nott-Bower, Rev L Weatherhead, Lord Ailwyn, Dame Peggy Ashcroft, Lady Bliss, Aleck Bourne, Lord Brown, Lawrence Cadbury, Prof Anthony Flew, Arthur Koestler, Prof Hyman Levy	
Staff	1+	
Membership	2,000	**Fees:** 50p p.a.; Life £5.25.
Branches	Brighton	
Publications	*Euthanasia and the Right to Death*	
Connections	With similar organisations in Netherlands, South Africa, Australia and USA.	
History	Formed 1936 as Voluntary Euthanasia Legislation Society; activities include publicity and campaigning against medicated survival against patients wishes. While the main objective is the necessary legislation, its interim aim is to reduce suffering in terminal illness.	

WOMEN'S ABORTION AND CONTRACEPTION CAMPAIGN
(See Section 7)

WOMEN'S NATIONAL CANCER CONTROL CAMPAIGN
(See Section 7)

ASSOCIATION FOR SCIENCE EDUCATION (A Charity)
College Lane, Hatfield, Herts AL10 9AA
Telephone: Hatfield 67411

Aims	To promote education by improving the teaching of science, by providing an authoritative medium through which opinions of teachers of science may be expressed in educational matters, and by affording a means of communication among people concerned with the teaching of science in particular and with education in general.
Officers	*Chairman* A A Bishop *General Secretary* B G Atwood
Staff	4 plus 11 part-time
Membership	14,000. Open to any person who is a teacher of science, or any person specially interested in the advancement of science teaching.
Fees	1st year £2.50; ordinary £5 p.a.; joint £6 p.a.; student £2.50 p.a.; overseas £4 p.a.
Offices	Network of 17 Regions in UK
Publications	*School Science Review* (q); *Education in Science* (5 p.a.); also other occasional publications.
History	Association of Public School Science Masters founded in 1900 led to Science Masters Association in 1919 and had 7,000 members in 1962. Association of Women Science Teachers was formed in 1912 and by 1962 had 2,000 members. Links between these two organisations began in 1922 and led to merger in 1963.

BRITISH ASSOCIATION FOR THE ADVANCEMENT OF SCIENCE
23 Savile Row, London W1
Telephone: 01-734 6010

Aims	To promote general interest and understanding in concepts of language, methods and applications of science by means of lectures, meetings etc.
Membership	4,540
History	Founded 1831.

BRITISH INTERPLANETARY SOCIETY LTD. (A Charity)
12 Bessborough Gardens, London SW1V 2JJ
Telephone: 01-828 9371

Aims	To promote advancement of knowledge relating to space research technology and applications including interchange of information etc.
Officers	*President* K W Gatland
	Secretary and PR L J Carter
Staff	4
Membership	3,000
Fees	Membership £5.50 p.a.; senior membership £6; Associate Fellows £6.50; Fellows £7.
Publications	*Spaceflight* (m); *Journal* (m)
Connections	International Astronomical Federation
History	Founded in 1933 to explore the possibilities of interplanetary flight and to promote relevant engineering technology and scientific research. Activities include meetings, presentation of annual and special awards and presentation of information to those concerned with space policy.

BRITISH SOCIETY FOR SOCIAL RESPONSIBILITY IN SCIENCE
9 Poland Street, London W1V 3DG
Telephone: 01-437 2728

Aims	To increase the awareness among scientists and the public of the social and political consequences of scientific activity, and to bring about social changes to ensure that science is used for the welfare and benefit of all mankind.
Membership	1,500
Publications	*Science for People*
History	Founded 1969.

196

BRITISH THEATRE LEAGUE
9 Fitzroy Square, London W1P 6AE
Telephone: 01-387 2666

Aims	To promote the development of the art of theatre both in education and the community.
Officers	*Director* Walter Lucas
Publication	*Drama*
History	Founded 1919. Provides information services, education, national festival of plays.

BRITISH UNIDENTIFIED FLYING OBJECTS RESEARCH ASSOCIATION
15 Freshwater Court, Crawford Street, London W1H 1HS
Telephone: 01-723 0305

Aims	To encourage and promote unbiased scientific investigation and research into unidentified flying object phenomena; to co-ordinate UFO research nationwide and co-operate with others engaged in research abroad; to collect and disseminate evidence and data.	
Officers	*President*	G G Doel
	Vice-Presidents	L G Cramp, G F N Knewstub, R H B Winder, Brinsley Le Poer Trench
	Chairman	R H Stanway
	Vice-Chairman & PRO	Lionel Beer
	Hon Secretary	Miss B Wood
Membership	600	
Fees	£4 p.a.; reduced rates in special circumstances. Also life membership available.	
Branches	Halifax; Newcastle-under-Lyme; Newtonabbey (N Ireland)	
Publications	*BUFORA Journal* (bi-m, free to members only)	
History	In July 1959, four researchers founded London UFO Research Organisation. One aim was to start national body and in September 1972 eight UFO societies set up British UFO Association. In January 1964, British UFO Association amalgamated with London UFO Research Organisation to form the present body. Regular meetings and conferences are held, and annual skywatch exercise. Active steps being taken to incorporate BUFORA as a company limited by guarantee, when charity status will be applied for.	

197

CENTRAL COUNCIL OF PHYSICAL RECREATION
70 Brompton Road, London SW3 1HE
Telephone: 01-584 6651

Aims	To constitute a standing forum where all national governing and representative bodies of sport and physical recreation may be represented and may formulate and promote measures to improve and develop sport and physical recreation; to support the work of specialist sports bodies and to bring them together with other interested organisations; to act as a consultative body to the Sports Council and other representative or public bodies concerned with sport and physical recreation.

Officers

Patron	HM The Queen
President	HRH Prince Philip, Duke of Edinburgh
Chairman of Executive Committee	Mrs M A Glen Haig MBE
Hon Treasurer	Sir Robin Brook
General Secretary	Peter Lawson
Information Officer	Patrick Cheney

Prominent members	Include The Rt Hon Lord Aberdare, the Marquess of Exeter, Denis Follows, Sir Charles Forte, Sir Reg Godwin, Denis Howell MP, the Bishop of London, Sir Jack Longland, Sir Stanley Rous, Lord Wakefield, Lord Wolfenden.
Membership	300 national governing bodies of sport and recreation.
Fees	By donation.
Organisation	A Regional Committee and Regional Standing Conferences; divisions for games and sports, movement and dance, outdoor pursuits, water recreation; interested organisations, major spectator sports committees.
Connections	It enjoys the closest contacts with all interested government departments; Sports Council; local authorities; industrial and commercial sponsors; its members represent organisations across the whole field of sport and recreation; sporting organisations in Europe, Australia, Canada, New Zealand, USA.
History	Formed in 1935, to encourage participation in sport and recreation and to provide a forum for discussion. In 1966 Denis Howell MP, as Minister with special responsibility for sport, set up the Sports Council; the CCPR has become recognised as its consultative body as provided for in the Sports Council's Royal Charter and is partly financed by the Council. Its activities include publicity, commercial sponsorship of sport,

coaching services, conferences for administrators, involvement with parliamentary legislation, legal and financial matters, and developing regional and international contacts as well as pursuing many special interests. It claims that as the collective voice of sport, it relates the views of the governing bodies to the government, the Sports Council, local and other authorities, to each other and to the nation. The CCPR is now indeed the national voice of sport and recreation in this country.

CONFEDERATION FOR THE ADVANCEMENT OF STATE EDUCATION (CASE)
81 Rustlings Road, Sheffield S11 7AB
Telephone: 0742 662467

Aims	To secure improvement in the quality and scope of the education provided by the central government and by local education authorities. Specifically: the abolition of selection; the introduction of fully comprehensive system of comprehensive education; furtherance of co-education throughout the system; urge that teachers, parents and pupils should all be involved in decisions about their schools; end to further subsidies to Direct Grant schools; abolition of corporal punishment; ending of compulsory religious instruction.

Officers

Chairman	Eddie Altman
Vice-Chairman	Bill Kirby
Hon Secretary	Barbara Bullivant
Hon Treasurer	Alan Fabb
Press and PR	Kathleen Hartley

Prominent members	Include Rt Hon Reg Prentice MP, Tyrrell Burgess, Professor Maurice Peston, Rt Hon Edward Short MP
Membership	Estimated that CASE associations probably total about 10,000 individuals.
Fees	Associations pay per capita fee of 20p; individuals (national) £1 p.a; publications subscribers (m) £3 p.a.
Regional organisations	North East; North West; Merseyside and N Wales; Yorks; Midlands; East; ILEA; Outer London; South East; Surrey; South.
Publications	*Parents and Schools* (bi-m, newsletter); CASEviews (occasional, usually on one topic); agents for *Home and School Working Papers* (3 times p.a.); also other occasional publications.

Connections   Founder member of Home and School Council. Informal links
              with STOPP (9); NCCL (6); Campaign for Nursery Education;
              Advisory Centre for Education; National Children's Bureau.

History   Formed in 1961. CASE is confederation of about 100 local
              groups. CASE committee co-ordinates, services, heads deputa-
              tions to ministers etc, encourages local groups to present well-
              informed cases. Became pro-comprehensive in mid-1960s, and
              a member was appointed to Plowden Council which reported
              in 1967. Most activity is at local level. Recent national activity
              has included presentation of evidence to Bullock Committee.
              Local successes have included increased parental representation
              on governing bodies; holiday activities for children; provision of
              local advisory services; schemes to reorganise secondary education.
              Plans include further campaigns on main aims including more
              finance for education, and ending of 11+ selection.

COUNCIL FOR BRITISH ARCHAEOLOGY (A Charity)
7 Marylebone Road, London NW1 5HA
Telephone: 01-486 1527

Aims   To press for improved legislation; encourage preservation and
              recording of sites; raise archaeological standards; to represent
              archaeology by appropriate means; to increase public awareness;
              encourage responsible and informed teaching and research and
              publish.

Officers   *President*   Nicholas Thomas
              Director   H F Cleere
              Admin Secretary   P A Marchant

Staff   6

Membership   350 institutions, societies etc (by recommendation)

Fees   Sliding scale £2–£12 p.a.

Branches   Regional groups covering all Great Britain

Publications *Calendar of Excavations* (m); *Archaeology in Britain* (annual
              report); various other publications available.

Connections   Representation on various bodies including National Trust (11) and Joint Committee of Amenity Societies. Also has links with Museums Association and the Department of the Environment.

History   Formed in 1945, previously Congress of Archaeological Societies (1888). Full-time secretariat established in 1949.

CYMDEITHAS YR IAITH GYMRAEG (WELSH LANGUAGE SOCIETY)
5 Maes Albert, Aberystwyth, Dyfed
Telephone: Aberystwyth 4501

Aims   To give to the Welsh language its rightful place as the national language of Wales and to create the social conditions which will realise this objective.

Officers   *Cadeirydd/Chairman*   Ffred Ffransis
Is-Cadeirydd/
   Vice-Chairman   Wayne Williams
Ysgrifenyddion/   Trebor Roberts
   Secretaries and PR   Marc Philips
Hon President   Saunders Lewis

Staff   2

Membership   3,000   **Fees: £1 p.a.**

Branches   60 with part-time officers in 10 regions

Publications   *Tafod y Ddraig* (m); various occasional publications, including some in English.

History   Formed 1962 with the short-term aim of achieving full official status for the Welsh language. Decided to adopt methods of protest through non-violent means, eschewing 'violence of the fist, heart and tongue'. First protest was in 1963 against Post Office refusal to use Welsh. Continuing protests have led to 800 members appearing in court for obstruction, conspiracy, etc, and resulting in some imprisonments. Major campaigns have been to gain recognition by public bodies and to obtain road signs in Welsh, education in Welsh at all levels, and to oppose the market in second homes in Wales except in Welsh interests. Achievements have included Bowen Commission, which came out in favour of bi-lingual road signs, and the Crawford Committee, which accepted some of the Society's views on fourth broadcasting channel in Welsh, with the BBC accepting the Committee's recommendations to provide Welsh language wavelength on VHF. Plans to campaign for Welsh priority on road signs; an Independent Welsh Broadcasting Authority, with continuing campaigns on education, housing and employment in interests of Wales; and organising courses for learners in Welsh and negotiating for workers day release courses at established centres.

ECONOMICS ASSOCIATION (A Charity)
Room 340, Hamilton House, Mabledon Place, London WC1H 9BH
Telephone: 01-387 6321

Aims	To promote the study of economics and kindred subjects in schools and colleges; to provide means for the exchange of views on teaching methods and syllabuses; to act as a representative body on occasions when educational interests of economics and kindred subjects are involved.

Officers	*President*	Professor Sir Austen Robinson
	Chairman	V S Anthony
	General Secretary and PR	R F R Phillips
	Prominent members	Michael Stewart MP, Sir Arnold Plant, Professor R C Tress, Professor C Harbury

Staff	1
Membership	2,215 **Fees:** Subscription £3; students £1
Regional branches	London; Southern; West Midlands; East Midlands; North Western; Yorkshire; North Eastern; Scotland; Wales
Publications	*Economics* (q)
History	Formed 1946 after discussions since 1939. Grant from Fairbairn Trust in 1970 enabled establishment of office in London. Activities include publications, film strips etc and conferences.

EDUCATIONAL DEVELOPMENT ASSOCIATION (A Charity)
8 Windmill Gardens, Enfield, Middlesex EN2 7DU
Telephone: 01-363 2659

Aims	The in-service training of teachers and adult education.

Officers	*Chairman*	Idwell Owen
	Secretary and PR	Arnold W Zimmerman

Membership	4,000. Open to teachers and others interested in education.

Fees   75p p.a.

Branches   Sunderland; Manchester; Birmingham; Havant; London;
                  Radnor; King's Lynn; Bury St Edmunds; Preston

Publications *Educational Development* (2 issues p.a., free to members)

History   Formed as the Educational Handwork Association in 1888
                  and changed its name in 1946. Started first summer school,
                  1903.

FELLOWSHIP OF INDEPENDENT SCHOOLS
33a High Street, Billingshurst, Sussex
Telephone: Billinghurst 2290

Aims   To promote the cause of independent schools.

Officers   *Organiser*   Miss E N Perkin

Membership   200

HELP ORGANISE LOCAL SCHEMES (HOLS)
56 The Glade, Stoneleigh, Epsom, Surrey KT17 2HB
Telephone: 01-393 5867

Aims   To encourage parents, teachers, social workers and other
                  volunteers to consider children's leisure needs in their own
                  locality and to help improve play facilities for over-fives after
                  school and during school holidays.

Officers   *National Correspondence Organiser*   Wendy Whitehead

Membership   370 correspondents

Publications Introductory leaflet (sent free on request with SAE); *Home
                  for the Holidays*, Wendy Whitehead, published by Paul Elek Ltd.

Connections   Members include National Council of Social Service; Toc H.
                  Links with many bodies including CASE (9); ACE; National
                  Housewives Register (7) and National Council of Women.

History   Operates as a correspondence exchange to compare experiences
                  and problems. Started by Wendy Whitehead in December 1969.
                  Hopes to develop links with playgroups to use premises as a base
                  for HOLS activities after they close for holiday periods.

NATIONAL ADULT SCHOOL UNION (A Charity)
Drayton House, Gordon Street, London WC1H 0BE
Telephone: 01-387 5920

Aims	Adult schools are groups which seek to deepen understanding and to enrich life through friendships, study, social service, and concern for religious and ethical values.

Officers
Chairman of Council	Leonard C Dale
Hon Treasurer	Redford Crosfield Harris
General Secretary	Leonard A Sanders
Press and PR	Roy F Plucknett

Staff	5

Membership 2,500   **Fees:** £2.50 p.a. — voluntary quota target

Branches	Midland Union, NASU Centre, Gaywood Croft, Cregoe Street, Birmingham B15 2ED 16 County Unions, and approximately 200 Adult Schools throughout England.
Publications	*One and All* (m); Study Handbook 1975 — *The Pursuit of Peace* (a)
Connections	Affiliated to National Council of Social Service; National Peace Council (5); Workers Educational Association (9).
History	1798 first Adult School in Nottingham followed by Bristol, Midlands, London, mainly to teach reading, writing; 1899 National Council of Adult Schools; 1914 National Adult School Union. Groups meet weekly or fortnightly to discuss wide range of subjects. All are self supporting, meeting either in own premises, hired rooms or members' homes. Recent activities have included support of Indian villages through War on Want. NASU provides holidays in Morecambe for elderly folk from Belfast. Plans include further summer schools, foreign visits and international summer school in London, August 1976.

NATIONAL HERITAGE: THE MUSEUM ACTION MOVEMENT
P.O. Box 689, Wandsworth, London SW18 2PD
Telephone: 01-228 0151

Aims	The support and promotion of all museums and art galleries in the United Kingdom.

Officers
Chairman	John Letts
Secretary	Mrs D Muirhead

204

Membership   1,200   **Fees:** £3 p.a.

Publications   *Museum News*, twice yearly, 10p

Connections   Affiliations with approximately 100 Friends' Associations
of various museums.

History   Founded 1970. Promoter and fund raiser of an annual Museum
of the Year Award.

RESEARCH DEFENCE SOCIETY LTD
(See Section 12)

ROYAL INSTITUTION OF GREAT BRITAIN (A Charity)
21 Albemarle Street, London W1X 4BS
Telephone: 01-493 0669

Aims   Through research, lectures and publications to advance the
general understanding of science and technology, and to provide
a medium for communication between science and the humanities,
as well as between different scientific disciplines and technologies.

Officers | | |
|---|---|
| *President* | Lord Kings Norton |
| *Treasurer* | Sir Gordon Cox |
| *Secretary* | J S Porterfield |
| *Director* | Professor Sir George Porter |
| *Professors* | Ronald King, M F Perutz, |
| | Sir Fred Hoyle, E R Laithwaite |
| *Reader* | Frank Greenaway |
| *Press and PR* | J F Friday |

Membership   2,000   **Fees:** Joining £3.15; £7.35 p.a.

Publications   *Proceedings* (a) (Applied Science Publishers Ltd); Annual Report.

History   Founded 1799. Granted a Royal Charter in 1800. Activities
include evening discourses and Christmas lectures for children
initiated by Michael Faraday. For 70 years the Institution was
virtually the only body in UK maintaining a laboratory with
equipment and assistance for research in the physical sciences.

SIMPLIFIED SPELLING SOCIETY
83 Hampden Road, London N3

Aims
: To do, and have done, research into the provision of a suitable alphabet for the English language and to educate the public into the findings of research.

Officers
: *President* — Professor John Downing (University of Victoria, Canada)
: *Hon Treasurer* — Leslie Blake
: *Hon Secretary and PR* — George O'Halloran

Membership 100   **Fees:** £1 p.a.

Publications
: News Sheet (q, members only); *The Pioneer* (irregular)

History
: Founded 1930s. Society has recently been reorganised and its plans include propaganda in schools and colleges; lectures, talks, meetings, annual conference and summer school.

SOCIALIST EDUCATIONAL ASSOCIATION
62 Thornhill Road, Heaton Mersey, Stockport SK4 3HL
Telephone: 061-432 1409

Aims
: To work for an education service which embraces all the nation's children and is capable of developing the full potential of each individual; to enlist the support of the Labour, Trades Union and Co-operative movements and to promote legislation for this purpose and to ensure its implementation.

Officers
: *President* — Caroline Penn
: *Chairman* — Norman Morris
: *Vice-Chairman* — John Hamilton
: *Organising Secretary* — Dr W Ross
: *Treasurer* — Mrs M Dixon
: *General Secretary* — David Robinson
: *Vice-Presidents (all MPs)* — Anthony Crosland, Tam Dalyell, Martin Flannery, Roy Hattersley, James Johnson, Joan Lestor, Fred Peart, Edward Short, Michael Stewart, George Thomas
: Also: Lady Alice Bacon, C B Johnson, Eric Robinson, Sir Harold Shearman

Membership
: 1,000 individuals approximately plus affiliated organisations

Fees
: Full £2.50 p.a.; joint £3; student /OAP 50p

Publications   *Socialism and Education*, 3 times p.a., 15p; many other pamphlets available

Connections   Affiliated to Labour Party (1). Founder member of International Union of Social Democratic Teachers; member of Commission of Socialist Teachers in EEC.

History   Founded 1927 as National Association of Labour Teachers and took present title in 1960 to admit non-teachers, some as associates. Meetings organised at Labour Party and NUT conferences etc. Many members active in local government education committees etc. Organised 1974 Conference of International Union of Socialist Teachers. Main contribution has been promotion of concept of comprehensive education. Currently producing second edition of *Guide to Comprehensive Education* and undertaking in-depth studies into topics such as community schools, democracy in education, examinations.

SOCIETY FOR THE PROTECTION OF SCIENCE AND LEARNING LTD
(A Charity)
3 Buckland Crescent, London NW3 5DH
Telephone: 01-722 2095

Aims   To assist refugee scholars by relieving poverty among them and their dependants and securing for them employment or other facilities whereby their special knowledge and abilities may continue to be used for the benefit of mankind.

Officers   *President*   A V Hill
Chairman of Council
of Management   Lord Ashby
Hon Treasurer   Lord Kahn
Hon Secretaries   Dame Honor Fell and
Professor W K Hayman
Secretary   Esther Simpson

Staff   1

Membership   No members, only donors and subscribers

Connections   Co-operation wherever relevant with other refugee organisations e.g. World University Service; British Council for Aid to Refugees; Jewish Refugees Committee; Academics for Chile.

Society for the Protection of Science and Learning (continued)

History   Founded 1933 as Academic Assistance Council after Hitler came to power in Germany. Its name was changed in 1957. Fascism and World War II brought many academic refugees from overrun countries. SPSL assists scholars displaced from university teaching or research positions for reasons of racial origin, political or religious opinion. Support has been given to others in recent years from countries such as Uganda, Czechoslovakia, Greece, Chile and Brazil. Activities and plans concern continuance of award of research and maintenance grants. Society has subsisted on results of financial appeal in 1939.

SOCIETY OF CHEMICAL INDUSTRY (A Charity)
14 Belgrave Square, London SW1X 8PS
Telephone: 01-235 3631

Aims   To advance applied chemistry in all its branches and to afford opportunities for the interchange of ideas with respect to improvements in the chemical industry, and for the discussion of all matters bearing on the practice of applied chemistry and the publication of information thereon.

Officers   *President*   Dr E L Streatfield
General Secretary and PR   Dr D H Sharp

Prominent members   include Lord Kearton, R S Wright

Staff   30

Membership   5,000   **Fees**: £7 p.a.

Publications   *Chemistry and Industry* (twice each month); many other publications of a specialist nature.

Connections   Chemical Society; Institute of Chemical Engineering; Chemical Industries Association and others

History   Formed in 1881 and received Royal Charter in 1907. Annual meeting in 1974 in Brussels on the theme 'Six into Nine'; in 1975 in Nottingham on 'Industry and Society — a study of the impact of the science-based industries'.

SOCIETY OF TEACHERS OPPOSED TO PHYSICAL PUNISHMENT (STOPP)
12 Lawn Road, London NW3

Aims   To seek the abolition, by legislation, of corporal punishment in the schools of England and Wales.

Membership   600

History   Founded 1968.

TH INGLISH SPELING ASOESIAESHAN
11 First Street, London SW3
Telephone: 01-584 1848 (evenings only)

Aims   To propagate a more rational spelling of English for any appropriate purpose.

Officers   *Acting Secretary/Treasurer*   S S Eustace

Membership   30   Fees: Not fixed

Publications *A More Rational Spelling for English* (1974)

History   Formally instituted November 8th 1974 after many years of deliberation. It is developing its relations with major type-founders, typewriter manufacturers and academic bodies. Plans include the relief of illiteracy, general availability of an extra alphabetic letter, linguistic education and conservation.

WORKERS' EDUCATIONAL ASSOCIATION (A Charity)
9 Upper Berkeley Street, London W1H 8BY
Telephone: 01-402 5608

Aims   To stimulate and to satisfy the demand of adults, in particular members of workers' movements, for education by the promotion of courses and other facilities, and generally to further the advancement of education to the end that all children, adolescents and adults may have full opportunities of the education needed for their complete individual and social development.

Officers	President	H D Hughes
	Deputy President	Dr Elizabeth Monkhouse
	Hon Treasurer	C T H Plant
	General Secretary and PR	R J Jefferies
	Vice-Presidents	include Lord Boyle, Lord Feather, the Rt Hon Edward Heath MP, the Rt Hon Sir Harold Wilson MP

Staff 200

Membership 130,000 individuals; 2,000 corporate

Fees Variable

Publications *WEA News* (September and January); pamphlets.

Connections Links with many voluntary groups including NCCL (6); Oxfam (5); Mind (8).

History Founded 1903 by Albert Mansbridge as an association to promote the higher education of working men. William Temple and R H Tawney were important influences during its formative years. It played an important role in agitation for 1944 Education Act and in formation of Campaign (later Council) for Educational Advance. Plans include development of work in education for the disadvantages, social and political education and education for trade unionists. The WEA is grant-aided by the Department of Education and Science and by local education authorities.

YN CHESHAGHT GHAILACKAGH (THE MANX GAELIC SOCIETY)
c/o 31 Glen Vine Park, Marown, Isle of Man

Aims The preservation and rehabilitation of the Manx Gaelic language.

Officers	Chairman	D C Targher
	Secretary	A J Pilgrim

Membership 200   **Fees:** 50p p.a.

Publications *Coraa Ny nGael* (free, bilingual)

History Formed 1899. Activities include re-publication of Gaelic literature and teaching of the language.

BUDDHIST SOCIETY (A Charity)
58 Eccleston Square, London SW1V 1PH
Telephone: 01-328 1313

Aims	To publish and make known the principles of Buddhism and to encourage the study and practice of these principles.
Officers	*Patron* His Holiness, the Dalai Lama *President* Christmas Humphreys *Vice-President* Lt Col R Gunter-Jones *Secretary and PR* Burt Taylor
Staff	3
Membership	3,000
Fees	London and Home Counties £3.30 p.a.; elsewhere £2.75 p.a.
Publications	*The Middle Way* (q); also books on Buddhism
Connections	With 30 Buddhist groups in UK affiliated to society, and with various Buddhist temples, also affiliated.
History	Founded in 1924 by current President. For many years it has been the largest Buddhist society in the West, and maintains close contacts with Buddhist organisations throughout the world. It is non-secretarian and conducts classes in all three main schools of Buddhism, Theravada, Mahayana and Zen. Celebrated Golden Jubilee in November 1974.

CATHOLIC TRUTH SOCIETY LTD (A Charity)
38/40 Eccleston Square, London SW1V 1PD
Telephone: 01-834 4392   Cables: Apostolic London SW1

Aims	To publish and disseminate low-priced devotional works; to assist all Catholics to a better knowledge of their religion; to spread amongst those who are not in full communion with the Catholic Church better information about the faith, and to assist the circulation of Catholic books.

Officers	*Chairman*	Rev Alan Clark
	Secretary and PR	David Murphy
	Treasurer	Michael Dalglish
	Membership	Nicholas Parker
	Advertising	George Broughton

Staff 35

Membership 40,000   Fees: Annual £1; Special £2; Life £30

Regional branches Newcastle; Cardiff; Manchester; Birmingham; Liverpool

Publications *Catholic Truth* (June and November); books, pamphlets etc: about 500 titles in print.
Bookshop: 201 Victoria Street, London SW1

Connections Connections with societies with similar objects in Canada, Scotland, Ireland, New York, Australia, India and Hong Kong.

History Founded 1868. Refounded 1884. Incorporated 1898. Appointed publisher to the Holy See 1964. During 1974, number of publications distributed increased to over 2 million. CTS Bible is the cheapest complete Bible in the world and sales increased by over 25% 1974–75. Society has been active in work for Christian unity. Members include a number of Christians of other churches. In 1974 Chairman addressed General Synod of the Church of England. Plans include publication of series of short illustrated statements of Christian doctrine.

LORD'S DAY OBSERVANCE SOCIETY
Lord's Day House, 55 Fleet Street, London EC4Y 1LQ
Telephone: 01-353 3157

Aims To preserve Sunday from commercial activity as a national Day of Rest; to promote the observance of Sunday as the Christian Sabbath by publications, meetings etc; to proclaim the scripture teaching about the Lord's Day and the message of the risen Saviour.

Officers	*President*	J Neville Knox
	Chairman	Rev J D Cuthbertson
	Secretary and PR	H J W Legerton

Staff 24

Membership No general membership. Support comes from individuals and churches.

Branches	Brighton, Bristol, Northampton, Lancashire, Yorkshire, Leicestershire, Edinburgh, Belfast.
Publications	*Joy and Light* (3 issues p.a.); many leaflets etc.
Connections	Incorporated in Society: Working Men's Lord's Day Rest Association. Lord's Day Association of Scotland; Imperial Alliance for the Defence of Sunday. Links with similar organisations in USA, Canada, Holland, Australia, Nigeria.
History	Founded in 1831. In recent years has organised opposition to Sunday Threatre Bill and attempted repeal of acts relating to other entertainments. Protested against League football on Sundays during 1973—74 fuel crisis. Consistently opposed Sunday markets.

MOTHERS' UNION
The Mary Summer House, 24 Tufton Street, London SW1
Telephone: 01-222 5533

Aims	A society within the Anglican Communion formed to strengthen, safeguard and promote the Christian family life.	
Officers	*Secretary*	Mrs H J Shepherd
Membership	Approximately 335,000 in UK	
Publications	*Mothers Union News* and *Home and Family*	
History	Founded 1876	

NATIONAL ASSOCIATION FOR THE PROTECTION OF FAMILY LIFE
39 Whittle Street, Walkden, Lancashire.
Telephone: Walkden 790 5749

Aims	To combat permissiveness and anti-family humanism and secularism.	
Officers	*Co-founders*	Frances and Ernie Morris
	President	Edith Urch
	Secretary	Fred Lamb
Membership	1,000. Members must favour sound moral family life.	
Fees	50p	
Publication	Newsletter (q — only to members)	

Connections   Family Rights of New Zealand; leading families of America; Catholic families of France.

History   Founded 1970. Public pressure against abortion, euthanasia, atheism. Plans include campaigning for a 'Minister for the Family' to protect family life.

NATIONAL CLEANSING CRUSADE
Merrow, 212 Darlington Lane, Stockton-on-Tees, Durham
Telephone: Stockton 65050

Aims   The safeguard of our Christian heritage, restoration of capital punishment, the outlawing of sodomy, penalties to fit the crime including recompense and corporal punishment, opposition to all pacts, agreements and treaties that may weaken, destroy or nullify our national heritage based upon common law; wants 'thinking people willing to participate actively in our desperate cause to help stem the flood of Godlessness engulfing our beloved homeland'.

Officers   *General secretary*   Vera Fletcher

Membership   'Without number'   **Fees:** has never asked for any

Publications   *Mothers of Britain — Wake up; Christian Manifesto Proclamation* of 1972

Connections   National Association for Teachers of Religious Knowledge; Anglo-Rhodesian Society (5); Mothers' Crusade Inc. for Victory over Communism (Arizona); National Equine Defence League.

History   March 1966 NCC council campaigned on capital punishment issue. General Secretary stood as an independent candidate for Teesside (Stockton) at October General Election 1974, but lost her deposit.

NATIONAL SOCIETY (Church of England) FOR RELIGIOUS EDUCATION
(A Charity)
Church House, Deans Yard, London SW1 3NZ
Telephone: 01-222 1672/3

Aims   The promotion and development of religious education in all educational activities especially in voluntary and state educational institutions as well as within Christian communities at home and abroad.

Officers	*Chairman*	The Right Rev the Lord Bishop of Blackburn
	General Secretary and PR	The Rev Canon R T Holtby
Staff	14	
Membership	2,000	**Fees:** £1 p.a.

Publications Durham Report *(The Fourth R)*, with the Society for Promoting Christian Knowledge. Various booklets etc.

Connections Church of England Synod Board for Education.

History Charter 1811. Recent activities include opening of Religious Education Centre; plans include a further centre at York. The society has stimulated education in schools, youth work, adult education and the training of teachers.

PROTESTANT ALLIANCE (A Charity)
112 Colin Gardens, London NW9 6ER
Telephone: 01-205 0489

Aims The support and maintenance of the Protestant evangelical faith both in the established church and nonconformity, the preservation of religious liberty and the assistance of Protestants in any part of the world.

Officers	*General Secretary and PR*	Rev A G Ashdown
	Treasurer	A N R Gutteridge
	Branches Secretary	Miss P J Henderson
		53 Upper Lewes Road, Brighton
	Prominent members	include Rev Ian Paisley MP, Sir Cecil Wakeley

Membership 1,500. Must be members of protestant churches and fellowships.

Fees 40p p.a.

Publications *The Reformer* (bi-m); various pamphlets in opposition to RC-dominated Common Market.

Connections Members of the United Protestant Council.

History   Founded in 1845 (by Anthony Ashley Cooper — Lord Ashley, who later became seventh Earl of Shaftesbury). Began with opposition to Catholicism and the effects of the RC Relief Act of 1829. At one time was largest Protestant society and has now begun once again to expand its activity, including lectures, preaching, providing speakers for meetings. Opposed to EEC and to the opening of office of Lord Chancellor to a Roman Catholic.

SOCIETY FOR PROCLAIMING BRITAIN IS ISRAEL (A Charity)
Brith Lodge, 87 St Barnabas Road, Woodford Green, Essex IG8 7BT
Telephone: 01-504 3737

Aims   To proclaim the counsel of God; personal salvation through our Lord Jesus Christ; the inspiration and absolute authority of the holy scriptures; the coming of the Kingdom of God under the rule of Christ; the identity of the Celto-Anglo-Saxon peoples with the Israel of the Old Testament as distinct from Judah.

Officers

President	J W Gray
Chairman of Council	H J G Harris
General Secretary and PR	Rev Francis Thomas

Staff   2

Membership   1,200   Fees: none; relies on donations

Fees   None; relies on donations and offerings.

Publications   *BRITH* (monthly)

Connections   The Covenant People of South Africa.

History   Founded in April 1945. Approximately 36 regular monthly meetings in various parts of the country. Special meetings held at Caxton Hall in May and September with an annual summer convention at Hoddesdon, Herts each July.

SOUTH PLACE ETHICAL SOCIETY
Conway Hall, Red Lion Square, London WC1R 4RL
Telephone: 01-242 8132/3

Aims   The study and dissemination of ethical principles and the cultivation of a rational religious sentiment.

Officers	*General Secretary*	Peter Cadogan
	Hall Manager	Miss Iris Mills
Members	Include Harold Blackham, Lord Brockway, Richard Clements	
Staff	2	
Membership	800	**Fees:** £1 p.a.
Publications	*The Ethical Record* (10 times p.a.)	

History Founded 1793 as a Philadelphian Church. 1802 became Unitarian. 1834/7 independent religious society. 1869 stopped praying. 1888 took present name. Always committed to free enquiry, civil and religious liberty all over the world, it remains a private religious society with trust deed. Activities include regular Sunday meetings and concerts of chamber music, Tuesday discussions and many social activities including art exhibitions, lunches, parties.

SPIRITUALIST ASSOCIATION OF GREAT BRITAIN (A Charity)
33 Belgrave Square, London SW1 8QB
Telephone: 01-235 3351/4

Aims To hold religious and healing services, to seek, collect and obtain information respecting, and generally to investigate, the phenomena commonly known as psychical or as spiritualistic second sight and all matters of a kindred nature, and to disseminate the knowledge gained.

Officers	*President*	W Hunter Mackintosh
	General Secretary	Thomas M Johanson
	Treasurer	John McAlpine
Membership	7,000	

Fees Full £2.10 p.a.; Patrons £5.00 p.a.; Associates £1.05 p.a.; Life £15.00. Other fees for psychic and other services.

Publications *Spiritualist Gazette* (m); *Service* (q)

History Founded in 1872. The largest and oldest spiritualist organisation in the world. It caters for approximately 150,000 people each year. Interdenominational with no creed. Annual meeting held at Albert Hall for past 25 years.

UNITED SOCIETY FOR THE PROPAGATION OF THE GOSPEL
(A Charity)
15 Tufton Street, Westminster, London SW1P 3QQ
Telephone: 01-222 4222   Telegrams: Gospelize London

Aims	To spread the message of the Christian gospel throughout the world, through living agents such as priests, doctors, teachers, nurses, agriculturists who not only presch but live the Christian message through service; to give financial aid to schools, hospitals, hostels and other institutions.

Officers

President	The Archbishop of Canterbury
Secretary	The Rev Canon James Robertson
Overseas	Rev George Braund
Home	John Dudley Nixon
Finance	Frank Chappell
Appointment and Training	Rev Michael Hardy
Press Officer	Stanley Ebdale

Staff   HQ and Area, 150

Membership   Supported by many hundreds of Anglican parishes, by voluntary donations, offerings etc.

Branches   30 area secretaries

Publications   *Network* (m); *Adventurer* (m) (a children's magazine); *Friends of USPG* (q newsletter); other occasional leaflets.

Connections   The Conference of British Missionary Societies.

History   Founded in 1701 and granted Royal Charter by King William III in same year as Society for the Propagation of the Gospel. Work has extended into over 40 countries. Annual budget is now over £1¼ million and some 100 dioceses receive aid in some form. Over 500 men and women serve overseas, from nurses and doctors to administrators and maintenance men. Universities Mission to Central Africa and SPG together formed USPG and later joined by Cambridge Mission to Delhi.

ANTI-CONCORDE PROJECT
70 Lytton Avenue, Letchworth, Herts
Telephone: Letchworth 2081

Aims	As part of the world movement against supersonic transport, to oppose the development, manufacture and operation of supersonic transport aircraft.
Officers	*Secretary/PR* Richard Wiggs *Assistant Secretary* Nigel Haigh
Staff	1
Membership	3,000 in more than 300 countries.
Fees	Voluntary contribution.
Publications	*Concorde: the case against supersonic transport* (Pan Books 1971); frequent newsletters and pamphlets and reprints of press adverts.
Connections	Affiliated to Conservation Society (11); Noise Abatement Society; Federation Against Aircraft Nuisance in UK; overseas links include European Union Against Aircraft Nuisance; Coalition Against SST (USA); Project to Stop the Concorde (Australia).
History	Founded 1967 by individuals whose main concern initially was prospect of uncontrolled supersonic operations over this country. The groups have since opposed Concorde on the complete range of environmental and economic grounds, and are at the centre of world-wide anti-supersonic information network. They aim to achieve bans at key airports and to have Concorde banned from flying supersonically over land, and to continue to work for the complete cancellation of the Concorde project.

ARBORICULTURAL ASSOCIATION (A Charity)
(inc. Association of British Tree Surgeons and Arborists)
c/o Merrist Wood Agricultural College, Worplesdon, Nr Guildford, Surrey GU3 3PE
Telephone: Worplesdon 2424

Aims	To advance the general interest, profession and practice of arboriculture, the cultivation of trees; to promote planting and care of trees for amenity purposes and to heighten public awareness and appreciation of trees.	
Officers	*President*	Lord Kennet
	Chairman	F T Wilson
	Vice-Chairman	A R Haigh
	Treasurer	D V Wells
	Secretary and PR	P H Bridgeman
	Vice-Presidents	John Parker MP, Sydney Chapman, Lord Cranbrook

Membership 1,000

Fees (all p.a.). Fellows: £7; Associates: £4; Ordinary: £3; Student: £1.50; Corporate: £7. (Fellows and Associates must be professionally concerned with arboriculture).

Regional Branches Bristol; Northwood, Middlesex; Stafford; Wakefield; Lasswade, Midlothian.

Publications Newsletter (q); Journal, (2 p.a.).

Connections Representation on Tree Council and British Standards Institution (2). Co-operation with all allied bodies.

History The Arboricultural Association originally was formed in 1964 mainly by local authority staff. Developed over 10 years as main organisation representing arboriculture. The former, Association of British Tree Surgeons and Arborists was set up in 1963 by main commercial tree surgery companies. These two bodies formally merged in Spring 1975 to represent all interests. Activities include meetings, conferences, publication, training and education and research. Plans include development and consolidation of profession of arboriculture, to formulate policy and advise government departments on matters affecting national tree cover.

ASSOCIATION FOR THE PROTECTION OF RURAL SCOTLAND (A Charity)
20 Falkland Avenue, Newton Mearns, Renfrewshire G77 5DR
Telephone: 041-639 2069

Aims	To stimulate and guide public opinion for the protection of the Scottish countryside; to act as a centre for giving advice and information on matters affecting the general welfare of rural areas including towns and villages; to encourage suitable and harmonious development and ensure the rational enjoyment of the countryside.	
Officers	*President*	Sir Islay Campbell of Succoth
	Chairman	Alan Stewart-Clark
	Secretary	Richard Livingstone
	Council Members	include T G C Galbraith
Staff	2	
Membership	Over 1,000	**Fees:** Ordinary £2.50 p.a.; Life: £2.50.
Publications	Annual Report	
Connections	National Trust for Scotland; AA (4); RAC (4); Caravan Club; Royal Scottish Society for Protection of Birds; Council for the Protection of Rural England.	
History	Formed in June 1926 as the Association for the Preservation of Rural Scotland. Title changed 1974. Recent activities have included a careful watching brief on North Sea oil developments including the lodging of objections where appropriate; media coverage for subjects such as village development and expansion, re-opening of inland waterways and need for countryside parks.	

ASSOCIATION FOR THE REDUCTION OF AIRCRAFT NOISE
11 First Street, London SW3
Telephone: 01-584 1848

Aims	The reduction of aircraft noise by all reasonable means.
Membership	50
History	Founded 1964.

221

ASSOCIATION FOR STUDIES IN THE CONSERVATION
OF HISTORIC BUILDINGS
University of London, 31–34 Gordon Square, London WC1H 0PY

Aims	To collate data and keep members informed on all aspects of conservation relating to historic buildings and sites of archaeological interest.	
Officers	*President*	Ashley Barker
	Chairman	Professor W F Grimes
	Hon Treasurer	I C Bristow
	Hon Secretary	J N Elliott
Membership	180	**Fees:** £2 p.a.
Publications	*Transactions* (occasional).	
History	Formed 1969 by students of the diploma course in the conservation of historic monuments. Aims to increase membership considerably.	

ASSOCIATION OF RAILWAY PRESERVATION SOCIETIES
c/o Hon Secretary, 34 Templegate Road, Whitkirk, Leeds LS15 0HE
Telephone: Leeds 648939

Aims	To encourage high standards among member societies; to stimulate co-operation between them; to promote publicity for them and make representations to national bodies such as British Rail and the Department of the Environment.	
Officers	*Chairman*	Capt Peter Manisty
	Vice-Chairman	D A Ives
	Secretary	M D Crew
	Treasurer	R T Yates
	Publicity	J E Rumens, 31 Dornton Road, South Croydon, Surrey CR2 7DR
	Public Relations	J C Locke, 23 Faraday Avenue, Sidcup, Kent
Membership	Organisations: Full: 50, Associate: 50; Individuals: 263 Full membership only where constitutions satisfy all requirements of Code of Practice.	
Fees	(p.a.) Full £5; Associate £3; Individual £2.	
Publications	*ARPS Newsletter* (approximately m); *Railway Forum Steam,* (3–4 times p.a.); *Steam Trains in Britain* (a, published in association with Association of Minor Railway Companies).	

Connections	Close links with bodies such as British Tourist Authority; British Rail; Transport Trust; most railway preservation societies are full or associate members.
History	Originated in early 1960s and adopted present name and aims in 1965, when it had 9 members. Does not run any schemes itself but provides a free advisory service to members, ranging from accounts and legal matters to railway operating and safety.

BEAUTY WITHOUT CRUELTY LTD
(See Section 12)

BLACK COUNTRY SOCIETY
49 Victoria Road, Tipton, West Midlands DY4 8SW
Telephone: 021-557 4662

Aims	To promote the interests in the past, present and future of the Black Country region.	
Officers	*President*	Dr J M Fletcher
	Secretary	J Brimble
Prominent Members	include (all MPs) Peter Archer, Bruce George, Geof Edge, Peter Snape, John Gilbert	
Membership	1,800	**Fees:** £1 p.a. (joint £1.50).
Publications	*Blackcountryman* (q); also other pamphlets available.	
Connections	Affiliated to West Mid Arts. Work in conjunction with numerous other local organisations.	
History	Formed in January 1967. Future plans include even greater involvement in the work, life, culture and planning of local authorities in the region, involvement in the development of Black Country Museum.	

BLUEBELL RAILWAY PRESERVATION SOCIETY
Sheffield Park Station, Nr Uckfield, Sussex TN22 3QL
Telephone: Newick 2370

Aims	To preserve vintage steam trains and operate them in a vintage scene.	
Officers	*Chairman*	J E Potter
	Press and PR	B J Holden
Membership	1,700	**Fees:** £2 p.a.; Life £40.

Publications *Bluebell News* (q)

Connections Member of Association of Railway Preservation Societies (11); Transport Trust.

History Formed 1959. Railway between Sheffield Park and Horsted Keynes commenced operations in 1960. Now carries over 25,000 passengers annually and hopes to extend the system.

BRITISH ECOLOGICAL SOCIETY (A Charity)
c/o Department of Botany, The University, Manchester M13 9PL
Telephone: 061-273 3333

Aims To further the study of ecology.

Officers *President*   Dr G C Evans
Secretaries   Dr R R Askew and Dr J A Lee
Press Consultant   Jon Tinker

Membership 3,000

Fees £5 p.a. (entitles the receipt of one Journal).

Qualifications A professional qualification in ecology or a related discipline (usually a degree in botany, zoology, biology or ecology), is desired. Membership by people without this qualification is considered by the council of the Society.

Publications *Journal of Ecology* (3 issues p.a.); *Journal of Animal Ecology* (3 issues p.a.); *Journal of Applied Ecology* (3 issues p.a.); *Bulletin* (members only).

History Founded in 1913. Conducts meetings on a wide range of topics, with three main meetings a year and 6 discussion group meetings.

BRITISH NATURALISTS ASSOCIATION (A Charity)
Willowfield, Boyneswood Road, Four Marks, Alton, Hants GU34 5EA
Telephone: Alton 63659

Aims To encourage and support all schemes and legislation for the protection of wild life; the preservation of natural beauties and the promotion and maintenance of national parks, nature reserves, conservation areas and sanctuaries; to bring naturalists and nature-lovers into helpful communication with each other.

Officers	*President*	Alfred Leustcher
	Chairman	J L Cloudsley-Thompson
	Secretary and PR	Mrs K L Butcher
	Treasurer	V G Caine
	Editor	Anthony Wootton
	Members include	Sir Geoffrey de Freitas

Membership 2,500 **Fees:** £1.50 p.a.

Branches 19 mainly in the south and midlands.

Publications *Countryside* (3 times p.a.); booklets on various subjects.

Connections Council for the Preservation of Rural England (11); Nature Conservancy; British Museum (Natural History); with many overseas nature organisations.

History Founded in 1905.

BRITISH RESORTS ASSOCIATION
(See Section 2)

CAMPAIGN FOR REAL ALE (CAMRA)
94 Victoria Street, St Albans, Herts AL1 3TG
Telephone: St Albans 67201/2

Aims Preservation and promotion of traditional beer, ie stored and served without the addition of extraneous carbon dioxide, having been produced from natural and traditional ingredients.

Prominent Members include William Wilson MP, Roy Mason MP

Staff 6

Membership 30,000 **Fees:** £2 p.a.

Branches 100 throughout UK.

Publications *What's Brewing* (m); *Good Beer Guide,* (a).

History Formed March 1971 as Campaign for Revitalisation of Ale. Name changed in March 1973. Constant campaigning has led to CAMRA becoming accepted as a consumer force and claims that real draught beer availability is increasing and the trend to unnatural beers is being reversed. Activities include public protests at closure breweries, written recommendations to

Food Standards Committee on Beer. In 1974, it set up Camra (Real Ale) Investments Ltd, under the Chairmanship of Nicholas Winterton MP, to run a chain of model pubs selling traditional beer. First pub was White Gates, Hyde, Manchester. Plans include the possible purchase of a brewery.

CHANNEL TUNNEL ASSOCIATION
36 Wentworth Hill, Wembley, Middlesex
Telephone: 01-904 0427

Aims	To facilitate impartial study of all aspects of tunnel project.
Publications	*Eurotunnel News*
History	Founded 1963.

CHICHESTER SOCIETY (A Charity)
Bell House, Theatre Lane, Chichester, Sussex
Telephone: Chichester 89320

Aims   To stimulate public interest in Chichester; to promote high standards in planning and architecture; to secure the preservation protection, development and improvement of features of historic or public interest.

Patron   Earl of Bessborough

Officers   *Chairman*   David Goodman
             Deputy Chairman   Rev Keith Walker
             Hon Secretary and PR   Mrs Jane Colborne

Membership   3,000   Fees: 10p p.a.; £1 life.

Publications Newsletter, (bi-m); *A City in Balance?* and other pamphlets.

Connections   Working relationship with local authorities and officials; liaison with other historic cities and other amenity societies.

History   Formed October 1st 1973 as a result of serious alarm at increasing threat to Chichester's ancient form and character. The society recognises the need for change but deplores unsympathetic buildings proposed by property developers. It has held many public meetings. In June 1974, it convened an historic town meeting in the cathedral — first since Middle Ages — which received national publicity. Currently working with other similar cities in hope of persuading their MPs to form a lobby at Westminster.

226

COASTAL ANTI-POLLUTION LEAGUE
Alverstoke, Greenway Lane, Bath BA2 4LN
Telephone: Bath 64094

Aims	To stop pollution of beaches on the coast of England and Wales by local authorities discharging untreated sewage; to educate the public in respect of sewage disposal on the coast of England and Wales.

Officers	*President*	Viscount Norwich
	Chairman	J A Wakefield
	Company Secretary	Mrs D P Wakefield

Membership	400	Fees:	£1 p.a.

Prominent Members	Include Reginald Bennett MP.

Publications	*The Golden List of Clean Beaches in England and Wales*

Connections	The Solent Protection Society.

History	Formed in 1960 by present Chairman after death of his daughter from polio contracted after bathing in sewage-polluted sea water in Solent. Evidence given to various public enquiries and official committees and working groups. It is working on publication of series of 2½ inches to 1 mile maps of location of all outfalls.

COCKBURN ASSOCIATION (THE EDINBURGH CIVIC TRUST) (A Charity)
10 Albyn Place, Edinburgh EH2 4NR
Telephone: 031-225 5085

Aims	The maintenance and improvement of the amenity of the city of Edinburgh and its neighbourhood, and the protection of the city's landscape and historic and architectural heritage.

Officers	*President*	Lord Fraser
	Chairman	Charles Jauncey
	Secretary	Oliver Barratt
	Treasurer	Robin M Martin

Staff	1
Membership	900
Fees	Annual: £2; Corporate: £5; Life: £25.
Publications	*Cockburn Association Newsletter* (every 3/4 months); *Cockburn Guide to Edinburgh and Some Practical Good* (History of first 100 years of Association).

Connections   Corporate members of Association for Protection of Rural
Scotland (11); Scottish Association for Public Transport.
Represented on Scottish Georgian Society; Edinburgh
Architectural Association. 50 local amenity groups are
corporate members.

History   Founded 1875 to continue work of Lord Cockburn to preserve
character of his native city. Many successful campaigns over the
years and now a respected voice on amenity and physical planning.
The sub-title was added in 1968 to recognise a relationship with
the Scottish Civic Trust and a new role as co-ordinator of local
amenity societies. It has successfully objected to demolition of
16 buildings during past two years. Statements on transport have
led to rethink on role of public transport. Frequent meetings and
exhibitions held to stimulate interest in architecture and planning,
particularly during 1975, its centenary year and European
Architectural Heritage year.

COMMITTEE FOR ENVIRONMENTAL CONSERVATION (CoEnCo) (A Charity)
29–31 Grenville Street, London EC1N 8AX
Telephone: 01-242 9647

Aims   To provide a forum for discussion of all aspects of environmental
interest by the major voluntary conservation organisations in this
country; to promote concerted action by the voluntary groups; to
encourage the best use of existing resources.

Officers

Chairman	Lord Craighton
Vice-Chairman	Stanley Cramp
Secretary	F D Webber
PR and Press	John Yeoman, 4 Hobart Place, SW1

Staff   2

Members   Must be a voluntary body operating at national level.

Publications   Annual Reports; various reports on transport, and the environment; *Energy and the Environment* (published by Royal Society
of Arts, and compiled by RSA, CoEnCo and Institute of Fuel).

Connections   Professional Institutions Council for Conservation; Countryside
Commission; founder member of recently formed European
Environmental Bureau. Its Committee includes Civic Trust;
Council for Nature (11); National Society for Clean Air;
National Trust (11); Youth Hostels Association.

History   Formed 1969. Activities included submission of evidence to
Verney Committee concerning sand and gravel workings; reply
to Department of the Environment on Maplin Project; statement
on British Railways review of railway policy; and statement on
Channel Tunnel Project. Plans include production of a Guide to
Conservation for managers in industry, and the development of
the European Environmental Bureau.

COMMONS, OPEN SPACES AND FOOTPATHS PRESERVATION SOCIETY
166 Shaftesbury Avenue, London WC2H 8JH
Telephone: 01-836 7220

Aims   To secure the registration of commons and greens under the
Commons Registrations Act, 1965 in order to save the commons
for the enjoyment and recreation of the people.

Officers
President	Lord Chorley
Chairman	Carol Johnson
Press and PR	Mrs Mary McArevey

Prominent Members   Include Sir Felix Brunner, Patrick Cormack MP, Lord Molson,
J Parker MP

Membership   1,000 Local Authorities; 400 local associations and
1,500 individuals.

Fees   £1.50 p.a. — individuals; £2 p.a. for associations; local
authorities according to population.

Publications   Journal (3 times p.a.)

Connections   Linked with other amenity societies through the Central Rights
of Way Committee.

History   Formed 1865. Leading members in early days included Lord
Eversley, Sir Charles Dilke MP and John Stuart Mill. Its object
was to save remaining commons for enjoyment and recreation
of the people. Initial activities centred on London — Hampstead
Heath, Epping Forest and Wimbledon Common were among early
victories — and work then spread to rest of country. It secured
public right of access by law to all commons in urban districts,
and ensured continuation of right under new local government
system. Recent activities have been concerned with registering
commons and greens under 1965 Act. Society has itself registered
over 400 as well as assisting others. Plans include conference on
future of footpaths and defending future commons registration
cases.

CONSERVATION SOCIETY
12 London Street, Chertsey, Surrey KT16 8AA
Telephone: Chertsey 60975

Aims	To secure for humanity a way of life which shall satisfy human needs and aspirations, and be capable of indefinite continuance. For this purpose the Society is especially concerned with problems of population size, conservation of animal, vegetable and mineral resources, the protection of the environment and the prevention of pollution. It believes that these problems are of great magnitude and urgency and that their solution demands profound changes both in the outlook of individuals and in the political and economic structure of society.

Officers

Chairman	Irene Coates
Hon Secretary	P S Berry
Hon Treasurer	O Barraclough
Director	Dr John Davoll
Vice-Presidents include	Sir John Betjeman, Prof Fred Hoyle, Sir Julian Huxley, J B Priestley, Sir Peter Scott, Dame Joan Vickers, Dr M Winstanley, Douglas Houghton MP

Membership 6,500

Fees (p.a.) £4; Joint £4.40; Fellow £5; Students/OAPs £2.

Branches 60 throughout country.

Publications *Conservation News* (4—6 issues p.a.). Numerous reports.

Connections Members of CoEnCo (11), National Council of Social Service, European Environment Bureau, Transport 2000; affiliate of International Union for the Conservation of Nature and Natural Resources.

History Founded 1966 by Dr D M C MacEwan and Miss Edith Freeman. Organised Population Day, May 12th 1973, as a countrywide operation calling on government to make a specific declaration of population policy for UK. Plans to convince government that policy must now be directed to attainment of an economy which is sustainable, and not to the pursuit of continual expansion.

COUNCIL FOR NATURE
Zoological Gardens, Regents Partk, London NW1 4RY
Telephone: 01-722 7111

Aims	To co-ordinate the views and information of the unofficial bodies in the UK concerned with the conservation of nature and the study of natural history; to make representations to the government and others as necessary, and to act in a consultative capacity; to keep the need for nature conservation constantly before the public and increasingly to interest young people in safeguarding the country's heritage of natural beauty and wild life.
Officers	*Chairman* Edgar Milne-Redhead *Joint Hon Secretaries* P J Conder, G L I Lucas, A E Smith *Secretary* T S Sands *Assistant Secretary* Colin Mackintosh
Membership	Affiliated societies — 350 with about ½ million members; Individuals — 1,300.
Fees	Societies £3 — £10 depending on size; Individuals £1.50; Associates £5.
Publications	*Habitat* (m); *Natural History Newsletter;* Annual Report; many booklets.
Connections	Close contact with Nature Conservancy Council; Countryside Commission; Department of Environment; represented on many committees; member societies include Royal Society for the Protection of Birds (12); Field Studies Council; Scottish Wildlife Trust.
History	Founded in 1958 and re-constituted 1968. Organised National Nature Weeks in 1962 and 1966. Founded National Conservation Corps (now independent under British Trust for Conservation Volunteers). It has been developing closer links with government departments and parliament on wild plant legislation. Actively engaged in campaign on rabies; building closer links with local societies; monitoring of wildlife issues including effects of oil exploration, water resources etc. The information and co-ordinating activities are extremely important to its work.

COUNCIL FOR THE PROTECTION OF RURAL ENGLAND (A Charity)
4 Hobart Place, London SW1W 0HY
Telephone: 01-235 9481

Aims	To promote and encourage for the benefit of the nation the improvement, protection and preservation of the English countryside and its towns and villages and the better development of the rural environment; to educate, inform research and advise on these matters.
Patron	Her Majesty the Queen

Officers

President	Lord Molson
Chairman	Christopher Hall
Secretaries	M V Osmond, A F Holford-Walker
Press, PR and Advertising	J R H Yeoman
Fund Raising	B Arbery
Administration of Branches	C J Ringrose-Voase
Information Officer	R Grove-White

Staff	20
Membership	27,000 individuals; 200 affiliated organisations.
Fees	National £2.50 p.a.; Branch subscription varies.
Branches	One in each county of England.
Publications	*Background* (bi-w) available only to branches, affiliates etc; Bulletin (bi-m); various reports.
Connections	Large number of bodies are collectively represented on National Executive Committee such as Ancient Monuments Society; Automobile Association (4); National Trust (11); Selborne Society; Soil Association etc. CPRE is also represented on many government committees and working parties.
History	Formed 1926. Over recent years there has been a major expansion of national office activity and staff to cope with increasing commitments particularly in legislation, regional and local planning, and establishment of information unit. Plans include further activity resulting from national appeal coinciding with CPRE Golden Jubilee Year in 1976. Wishes to expand activities in fields of education, information, research and development, and casework.

232

COUNCIL FOR THE PROTECTION OF RURAL WALES (Limited company)
14 Broad Street, Welshpool, Powys SY21 7SD
Telephone: Welshpool 2525

Aims	To secure the protection and improvement of rural scenery and amenities in the countryside of Wales by means of annual study conferences, newsletters, exhibitions and other media.	
Officers	*President*	Baroness White
	Chairman	Wynford Vaughan-Thomas
	Vice-Chairmen	John H Barrett, C W Grove-White
	Hon Treasurer	Major E S Lowe
	Director	S R J Meade
	Admin Officer and PR	Ann Lawrence
Prominent Members	Emlyn Hooson MP, Geraint Howells MP, Gwynfor Evans MP	
Staff	3	
Members	4,300	
Fees	Individuals £2 p.a., joint £3; Life £40 +; Corporate £4; Schools £2 or above according to size; OAPs £1; Juniors 50p.	
Branches	In every county of Wales; run by volunteers.	
Publications	Newsletter (3 times p.a.); Annual Report.	
Connections	Close liaison with Council for Protection of Rural England (11); Corporate members include Caravan Club, Farmers Union of Wales (2) and National Trust (11). Representatives of CPRW sit on many bodies including CoEnCo (11), Council for Nature (11) and Nature Conservancy.	
History	Founded in 1928. Is the most widely-based environmental organisation in Wales. Activities are undergoing expansion under the auspices of a grant from the Carnegie Trust.	

DARTMOOR PRESERVATION ASSOCIATION (A Charity)

Aims	The protection, preservation and enhancement in the public interest of the landscape, antiquities, flora, fauna, natural beauty and scientific interest of Darmoor; the protection of public access to and on Dartmoor subject to the ancient rights of Commoners.

Officers	Chairman	Crispin Gill
	Hon Secretary and Chief Executive Officer (& PR)	Dr W F Beech
	Hon Treasurer	B J Rider
	Patrons	Lady Sayer, Vice-Admiral Sir Guy Sayer
	President	Prof W G Hoskins
	Member of Executive Committee	Lord Foot

Membership 1,5000   **Fees:** Minimum £1 p.a.; Life £10.50

Branches Many local groups especially in London.

Publications Newsletter £3 p.a. (circulation restricted); many other publications by Association and members.

Connections Both informal and official with many organisations such as Ramblers' Association; Youth Hostels Association; Council for Preservation of Rural England (11); Transport 2000. Represented on Standing Committee on National Parks of CPRE.

History Founded 1883. During past 10 years have actively opposed two major reservoir schemes at Meldon and Swincombe — in the latter case opposition was successful with the water authorities. Bill thrown out after 17 days hearing by Parliamentary Select Committee. Public inquiries fought against further china clay working, motorways and other mining and quarrying. Representatives have given evidence before several committees including Defence Lands Committee and Sandford Committee.

FRIENDS OF THE EARTH LTD
9 Poland Street, London W1V 3DG
Telephone: 01-434 1684

Aims To promote the conservation, restoration and rational use of the world's resources, including the recycling of materials, protection of endangered species and recognition of environmental considerations in energy policy.

Officers	Campaign Director	Graham Searle
	Admin Director and Secretary	Richard Sandbrook

Staff 14

Membership 5,000 plus members in over 120 local groups.

Fees   Minimum subscription £1.50 p.a.

Branches   Throughout the UK.

Publications   Variety of books, pamphlets, posters and campaign stickers.

Connections   Associated charity, Earth Resources Research Ltd. Member of an international organisation covering 12 national Friends of the Earth groups.

History   Formed 1970. Organisation and general nature imported from US. First major campaign involved return of thousands of bottles to Cadbury Schweppes in protest at their non-return policy. Then opposed plans of Rio Tinto Zinc for open-pit mine in Snowdonia National Park. Recent achievements include a ban on import of certain whale products. Have also campaigned through parliament for protection of endangered species. Specific future plans include promotion of public as opposed to private transport; opposition to nuclear power development on various counts; promotion of energy conservation and recycling.

FRIENDS OF THE LAKE DISTRICT
27 Greenside, Kendal, Cumbria LA9 5DX
Telephone: Kendal 20296

Aims   To protect and cherish the landscape and natural beauty of the Lake District; to unite those who share these aims, and to take common action with other societies when the need arises.

Officers   *President*   The Archbishop of Canterbury
                Vice-Presidents   Viscount Rochdale, Lord Chorley
                Chairman   Roland Wade
                Hon Treasurer   J C H Hopton
                Secretary and PR   Geoffrey Berry

Staff   2

Membership   Fees: Minimum 50p p.a.; Life £15 min.

Publications   Newsletter (2 issues p.a.)

Connections   Affiliated to Council for the Protection of Rural England (11); Commons Society; Ramblers' Association; other similar bodies. About 50 open air, rambling and climbing organisations are affiliated to FLD.

235

History   Founded in 1934, the society was an early advocate for
               creation of national parks. Despite Lake District becoming
               largest national park in 1951, work continued with problems
               of afforestation, water abstraction, overhead electric cables,
               commercial tourism, traffic etc. Activities include campaigning
               for transport management policy and restrictions on road
               building, including appearance at public inquiries; tree-planting
               schemes etc. Plans include campaigning for overall traffic policy
               for Lake District and to conserve the basic qualities for the
               enjoyment of this and future generations.

GREAT OUSE RESTORATION SOCIETY
River Cottage, Great Barford, Bedfordshire MK44 3LQ
Telephone: Bedford 870261

Aims   To further the restoration of the Great Ouse between Tempsford
               and Bedford as a navigable highway, and its repair and maintenance
               in its restored condition, and so preserve and develop the amenities
               of the river for the benefit of all people.

Officers   *President*   Sir Peter Scott
               Chairman   D K Cassels
               Hon Secretary   D J Kettle

               Vice-Presidents   include The Duke of Bedford,
                                   Viscount Boyd, Stephen Hastings MP,
                                   Arthur Jones MP, Trevor Skeet MP,
                                   Sir Ronald Stewart, Lord Thorneycroft

Membership 400   **Fees:** £1 p.a. minimum

Publications   *The Lock Gate* (q)

Connections   Associated with Inland Waterways Association; East Anglian
               Waterways Association; Great Ouse Boating Association etc.

History   Founded 1951. Bedford lock re-opened 1956; Cardington Lock
               1963; Roxton Lock 1972; Great Barford Lock now being
               re-built. Currently involved in money-raising. Plans include rally
               of boats at Great Barford in 1976.

GREAT WESTERN SOCIETY LTD
Didcot, Berkshire

Aims	To foster and encourage interest in the achievements of the Great Western Railway and, in a practical way, to keep in being selected items of historical importance which would otherwise disappear.	
Officers	*Chairman*	G A Perry
	Secretary	W J Smith
	Public Relations	Peter Hemy
	Advertising	F L Dumbleton
Membership	3,500	Fees: £3 p.a.
Branches	London; Reading; Oxford; Midlands; Taunton; Hampshire; Swindon; Bristol; South West	
Publications	*Great Western Echo* (q), 20p	
History	Formed in 1961 as the 48 Preservation Society. First locomotive purchased in 1964. Name changed to reflect a broadening interest in all things Great Western. Control of the growing number of railway vehicles required a change in structure and in 1967 Great Western Society Ltd was set up to run the society with Great Western Preservations Ltd as a holding company for the preserved items. British Railways Didcot depot was taken over in 1967 to house the collection and to serve as workshops. Also serves as centre for steam excursions over British Railways.	

GREATER MANCHESTER TRANSPORT ACTION GROUP
c/o K F Child, 102 Millgate Lane, Didsbury, Manchester M20 8SD
Telephone: 061-445 7328

Aims	To encourage high standards of transportation planning in Greater Manchester; encourage the preservation, development and improvement of transport facilities for the people of the area; promote public discussion and participation in the formulation of transport proposals; to pursue these means by meetings, publications, exhibitions etc.	
Officers	*Chairman*	J P Gill
	Secretary	K F Child
Membership	100 plus affiliated community groups.	
Fees	50p p.a.	
Publications	Newsletter (q); various pamphlets.	

237

Connections   Affiliated to Transport 2000. Represented on Council for Voluntary Service, Passenger Transport Advisory Committees and Transport Consultative Committee of Greater Manchester.

History   Formed 1972. Holds monthly discussion group. Publications have aimed at providing elected representatives with information to enable them to re-appraise present policies.

HISTORIC CHURCHES PRESERVATION TRUST (A Charity)
Fulham Palace, London SW6 6EA
Telephone: 01-736 3054

Aims   To assist with grants of money and technical advice where needed for the preservation of historic churches which are in need of essential fabric repairs, the cost of which is beyond local effort.

Officers
Chairman	Lord Ramsey
Hon Treasurer	S L Lloyd
Trustees	include the Rt Hon Edward Heath MP, the Rt Hon Lord Home, Sir John Betjeman, the Rt Hon Sir Harold Wilson MP

Staff   2

Membership   Not a membership organisation.

Publications   Annual Report

Connections   With autonomous county trusts, diocesan bodies and local amenity societies.

History   The Trust was established in 1952 for the purpose of raising funds by public appeal. So far, about £2 million has been raised by the parent trust and about £490,000 by county trusts. Grants have so far been given to about 2,700 historic churches. Work is continuous though it was intensified in connection with European Heritage Year 1975.

HISTORIC COMMERCIAL VEHICLES CLUB
Iden Grange, Cranbrook Road, Staplehurst, Kent
Telephone: 0580 892369

Officers
Chairman & Secretary	M Banfield
Vice-Chairman	G Beeston
Press and PR	L Falkson

	Prominent members	include Lord Montagu of Beaulieu

Membership 2,000   **Fees:** £3 p.a.

Publications Newsletter (m, members only); Quarterly magazine (members only)

History Formed 1958. Has acquired its own vehicles but the majority belong to individual members. Regular events include London—Brighton run on first Sunday in May and trans-Pennine (Manchester to Harrogate) run in August.

INTERNATIONAL TANKER OWNERS' POLLUTION FEDERATION LTD
(See Section 2)

KEEP BRITAIN TIDY GROUP (A Charity)
Bostel House, 37 West Street, Brighton BN1 2RE
Telephone: 0273 23585/8

Aims To protect and enhance the amenities of town and country in the UK by promoting the prevention and control of litter.

Officers
	President	Lady Brunner
	Chairman	A P de Boer
	Director General	D J Lewis

Staff 27

Membership Open to all. Supported by voluntary subscriptions and donations from industry, commerce, local authorities and individuals.

Publications *Tidy Times* (q, newspaper); *Business Bulletin* (q); Annual Report plus various booklets.

History Formed 1954. An independent, non-profit making public service organisation which is supported by private donations matched by government contribution. Is currently concentrating efforts to strengthen contact with local authorities.

LONDON AMENITY AND TRANSPORT ASSOCIATION
26 Elm Park Mansions, Park Walk, London SW10 0AW
Telephone: 01-352 5628

Aims	To promote improved transport facilities consistent with the attainment of a more attractive environment for London as a whole.	
Officers	*Chairman*	Harley Sherlock
	Vice-Chairman	James Ogilvy-Webb
	Treasurer	David Southron
	Hon Secretary	Tim Martin
	Press	Terence Bendixson
Membership	40 corporate, 60 associate (individual)	
Fees	Corporate £5 p.a.; associate £1 p.a.	
Publications	Newsletter (3 or 4 p.a.); *Motorways in London* and other pamphlets, booklets, etc	
Connections	Informal with Edinburgh and Greater Manchester groups and Alliance Against M16.	
History	Formed in 1967 by a group of people professionally involved in transport who had organised themselves into a group called Transport in London. It has exerted pressure on various authorities responsible for transport in London on a variety of matters including fare increases, financial policy, traffic restraint, pedestrian facilities, environmental schemes, public consultation, compensation for people adversely affected by transport schemes etc. Presented evidence to Greater London Development Inquiry opposing motorway building in Inner London and putting forward an alternative strategy. It has proposed many policies such as improved pedestrian and cyclist facilities, and hopes to attract outside funds to enable more research and pressure activity and to act as a more effective channel of communication between amenity and other groups throughout London.	

MAPLIN MOVEMENT
82 The Sorrells, Stanford-Le-Hope, Essex SS17 1DS
Telephone: Stanford-Le-Hope 74849

Aims	To promote the building of an airport/seaport complex at Maplin.	
Officers	*Chairman*	Peter Hart

Maplin Movement (continued)

Membership 4,000. No fees but donations invited.

Publications Occasional newsletter and other publications.

Connections Work with other organisations including groups campaigning against expansion of Irish airports.

History Formed September 1973. Has campaigned against cancellation of Maplin project and will continue to do so.

MEN OF THE STONES (A Charity)
The Rutland Studio, Tinwell, Stamford, Lincolnshire PE9 3UD
Telephone: Stamford 3372

Aims To stimulate public interest in architecture and good buildings of all periods; to advocate and encourage a greater use of stone and other natural and local materials in building; to work generally for the protection of buildings of good architectural and special merit.

Officers

President	Earl Spencer
Chairman	Alex T Brodie
Vice-Chairman	J L Barber
Hon Secretary and PR	A S Ireson
Hon Press Officer	John Slee

Membership 400   **Fees:** 50p p.a.; £5.25 Life.

Publications Annual Report

Connections With many organisations in conservation movement including Ancient Monuments Society; Society for the Protection of Ancient Buildings; National Trust (11); Countryside Commission.

History Founded on 26 May 1947.

MEN OF THE TREES (A Charity)
Crawley Down, Crawley, Sussex
Telephone: Copthorne 712536

Aims The encouragement of the planting and preservation of trees everywhere, and to promote interest in the knowledge and appreciation of trees, shrubs and similar plants and in the science of afforestation.

Officers	*President*	Earl of Bessborough
	Chairman	K J Signy
	Director for Administration	F T Wilson
	Vice-Presidents	include Duke of Bedford, Sir John Betjeman, Sir John Eden MP

Staff	2
Membership	5,000+
Fees	£2.10 p.a. (or £3.15 joint); £100 life.
Branches	13 branches in England and Channel Islands.
Publications	*Trees* (3 per annum) and leaflets.
History	Founded by Richard St Barbe Baker in 1922. Has saved for posterity many trees and woodlands besides influencing large-scale reafforestation both at home and overseas. Helped save the finest redwood groves in California from the axe. Now collaborating with representatives of 61 countries for a world organisation to fight the encroachment of desert conditions upon already inadequate food sources. Aims to reinstate the tree as a vital part of the world ecological system. Co-operates with all amenity and preservation societies.

NATIONAL COUNCIL ON INLAND TRANSPORT
Woodside House, High Road, London N22 4LJ
Telephone: 01-888 1282

Aims	To promote the development of an integrated transport system and the recognition of the real costs and social values in assessing comparative advantages of the various forms of transport.

Officers	*President*	Earl of Kinnoull
	Chairman	A W T Daniel
	Hon Secretary and PR	Roger Calvert
	Parliament	Ron Atkins MP
	Vice-Presidents	include Earl of Lanesborough, J B Priestley, Sir James Richards, G F Fiennes, Sir James Farquharson

Membership	Over 110 corporate bodies plus individuals.
Fees	Individuals £2.10 p.a.; corporate bodies £10.50 p.a.
Branches	Liverpool; Wolverhampton; Leyburn, Yorks; Dundee.

Publications   A variety of unions, local authorities, companies and associations who are members.

History   Formed 1962. Activities include meetings, conferences, briefings for MPs etc.

NATIONAL HERITAGE: THE MUSEUM ACTION MOVEMENT
(See Section 9)

NATIONAL PURE WATER ASSOCIATION
(See Section 8)

NATIONAL SOCIETY FOR CLEAN AIR (A Charity)
136 North Street, Brighton, Sussex BN1 1RG
Telephone: Brighton 26313

Aims   To promote public education in all matters relating to the value and importance of clean air; to initiate, promote and encourage investigation and research into all forms of pollution in order to achieve its reduction or prevention.

Officers

President	H B Greenborough
Secretary General	Rear Admiral P E Sharp
Chairman of Council	Miss M George
PR	Nicola Walters
Press	Sian Crowhurst
Advertising	Peter Mitchell

Staff   8

Membership   Corporate 140; Local Authorities 300; Individuals 430.

Fees   Not stated.

Regional Representatives: in Glasgow; Belfast; Newcastle; Manchester; Pontefract; Halesowen; Derby; Slough; Bristol; Port Talbot.

Publications   *Clean Air* (q); *NSCA Yearbook;* various books and pamphlets including some for children.

Connections   With many local authorities, Department of the Environment, Warren Springs Laboratories, Alkali Inspectorate; 6 members on Clean Air Council. Among the corporate members are British Gas Corporation, British Medical Association, CEGB, Institute of Fuel, Institute of Petroleum, NCB, Shell BP and Royal Society of Health.

History   Predecessor was the Coal Smoke Abatement Society established in London in 1899. This combined with the Smoke Abatement League in 1905 to form the National Smoke Abatement Society. It widened its horizons to cover all forms of air pollution and took its present name in 1958. It presented evidence to Royal Commission on Environmental Pollution in 1973 and had membership of special DoE working parties. Holds annual one week conference and four day seminars, the most recent of which was an international conference at Brighton in October 1975.

NATIONAL TRACTION ENGINE CLUB
127 Greensted Road, Loughton, Essex IG10 3DJ
Telephone: 01-508 4963

Aims   To assist and encourage the preservation, maintenance and operation of steam traction engines and other steam road vehicles including portable steam engines; to promote events, meetings etc, co-operate with other bodies, provide information etc., for the benefit of members.

Officers

President	S J Wharton
Chairman	AS Heal
Secretary	G F Beck
Press and PR	D Brandt
Editor	G R Hawthorne

Membership   3,000   **Fees:** £2 p.a.

Publications   *Steaming* (q); List of Approved Traction Engine Rallies (a); various leaflets.

Connections   50 clubs are affiliated. Affiliated to Transport Trust. Work closely with Historic Vehicle Clubs Joint Committee.

History   Formally inaugurated in 1954 by enthusiasts who had worked together informally.

NATIONAL TRUST
42 Queen Anne's Gate, London SW1H 9AS
Telephone: 01-930 0211

Aims   To preserve and safeguard places of historic interest and natural beauty for the nation for all time.

Officers

Chairman	The Earl of Antrim
Director-General	J D Boles
Press and PR	M V Beaumont

Prominent Members	include Sir John Betjeman, Duke of Grafton, Kenneth Robinson, Earl of Ross, John Parker, Sir Marcus Worsley
Staff	1,200 (approximately).
Membership	464,000
Fees	£3 p.a. (plus £1.50 for other family members at same address).
Branch Offices	16 covering the various regions of England, Wales and Northern Ireland.
Publications	*Properties Open* (a); list of properties (5 year intervals); also guide books to individual properties.
Connections	Many associated organisations concerned with conservation, historic buildings, arts, etc many of which nominate members to the Council of the National Trust.
History	Founded in 1895 and incorporated by Act of Parliament in 1907. Its original purpose was to acquire and preserve places of historic interest or natural beauty. One important provision was the unique power of the Trust to declare its property inalienable so that it would never be sold or given away. A further Act in 1937 allowed the Trust to hold country houses and their contents. The Trust now has 150 country houses and 377,000 acres of land and protective covenants over a further 61,000 acres. One of the most recent and major activities has been Enterprise Neptune, the extension of coastal land owned by the Trust.

NOISE ABATEMENT SOCIETY
6—8 Old Bond Street, London W1X 3TA
Telephone: 01-493 5877

Aims	To eliminate excessive and unnecessary noise from all sources.	
Officers	*Chairman*	John Connell
	Hon Secretary	Miss T Adler
	Hon Treasurer	Rev the Hon A C V Elphinstone
Prominent Members	Sir John Betjeman, Sir Ronald Howe, Dr Neville Coghill, J Chalmers Ballantyne, Dr W J Barry, Sir Michael Redgrave	
Membership	5,000	
Fees	(p.a.) £2; for corporate membership: £5.	
Publications	Various leaflets on noise.	

Connections   CoEnCo (11); Noise Advisory Council; also links with International Association against Noise (Zurich); Professional Institutions Council for Conservation; Institution for Environmental Sciences; National Council for Inland Transport (11).

History   Founded 1959. Influential in framing Noise Abatement Act 1960, Control of Pollution Act 1974 and many local bye-laws. Continuing campaign against aircraft, traffic and industrial noise. Advisory service to general public on noise nuisance. Technical, legal PR activities. Plans include children's paper on environmental subjects and setting up of local groups in each new District Council.

OFFA'S DYKE ASSOCIATION (A Charity)
Old Primary School, West Street, Knighton, Powys LD7 1EW
Telephone: Knighton 753

Aims   To promote public benefit in the area of the border counties of England and Wales, by securing the conservation, protection, development and improvement of ancient buildings, earthworks or similar natural and man-made features of historic or public interest, in particular those associated with Offa's Dyke or the Offa's Dyke Path.

Officers   *President*   Baroness White (1974)
                          Dame Kathleen Kenyon (1975)
            Chairman   H N Jerman
            Vice-Chairman and
            Press   Frank Noble

Prominent   include Chris Brasher, Leslie Alcock, Dr M Apted, Lady White,
Members   Lord Hunt

Membership   600   **Fees:** Full: £1.50; Associate £1.

Publications   Newsletter (3 issues p.a.).

Connections   With Tref-y-Clawdd; Countryside Commission.

History   Formed in 1969. Preceded by an Action Committee and various informal groups. Its first object was to secure official informal groups. Its first object was to secure official opening of Offa's Dyke Footpath which was done in July 1971, and has since expanded aims to cover whole Borders area. Produces maps, booklets and conducts regular surveys to report state of foot-path to responsible authorities. Comment on road proposals

Offa's Dyke Association (continued)

affecting route and succeeded in changing proposals affecting roadworks at Knighton. Opening information centre at Knighton in conjunction with Mid Wales Tourism Council.

ROYAL TOWN PLANNING INSTITUTE
(See Section 2)

SOCIETY FOR THE PRESERVATION OF BEERS FROM THE WOOD
c/o Ye Olde Watling, 29 Watling Street, London EC4M 9AY

Aims

To obtain legal definition of draught beer as opposed to keg or top pressure beer, and to seek maintenance of a ready supply of the traditionally-brewed and served beer as is widely preferred.

Officers

Chairman	J Morgan
Vice-Chairman	D Viner
Secretary	J Liffen
Treasurer	R Graham
PR Officer	O S Tillett

Membership   Over 8,000

Fees   None. Must be proposed, and sign two pledges.

History

Following a letter from a disgruntled bitter drinker, published in the *Financial Times,* in October 1963, seven men met in a public house at Epsom and became founder members. They handed full control to a national executive committee in April 1973. The Society is now recognised by Ministry of Agriculture and Food, and was invited in June 1974 by Food Standards Committee to submit evidence and comments for drawing up future laws regarding composition and labelling of beer.

SOCIETY FOR THE PROMOTION OF NATURE RESERVES LTD (A Charity)
The Green, Nettleham, Lincoln, LN2 2NR
Telephone: Lincoln 52326

Aims

To promote the conservation of wildlife, encourage a love of nature and a better understanding of its value to man.

Officers

President	J C Cadbury
General Secretary	A E Smith

Staff   13

247

Membership Limited by charter to 50 elected members. Approximately 80,000 Association (Trust) members. Associate membership through membership of a County Trust.

Publications *Conservation Review* (2 issues p.a.) and some technical conservation publications.

Connections The Society acts as the national body for all the County Naturalists' Trusts.

History Founded in 1912 by N Charles Rothschild. Incorporated by Royal Charter in 1916. Since 1958 mainly concerned with the support and development of the County Trusts.

TRANSPORT REFORM GROUP
Flat C, 2 Hyde Park Street, London W2
Telephone: 01-262 0505

Aims Concerned about the effects of the present transport policies on the environment and people.

History Founded 1973.

ANIMAL DEFENCE SOCIETY LTD and ANIMAL DEFENCE TRUST
(A Charity)
52/53 Dean Street, London W1V 5BJ
Telephone: 01-734 5922

Aims	Alleviation of all forms of animal suffering.	
Officers	*President*	Mrs Ruth Harrison
	Chairman	Mrs B MacDonald
	Secretary	Mrs J Cormack
	Chairman (Trust)	Mrs P Dain
Staff	4, 20 for the Society and 2 for the Trust	
Membership	Not disclosed	**Fees**: £1 p.a.; £10 Life
Publications	Annual Report; occasional booklets and leaflets	
Connections	With various organisations in the anti-vivisection field.	
History	Founded 1906 as Animal Defence and Anti-Vivisection Society to oppose all forms of cruelty to and exploitation of animals. Incorporated in 1964. Animal sanctuary separately established as a charity in 1966. Present title adopted April 1971.	

BEAUTY WITHOUT CRUELTY LTD
1 Calverley Park, Tunbridge Wells, Kent TN1 2SG
Telephone: 0892 25587

Aims	To bring to people a greater awareness of the state of the world, the pollution of earth, air and water, the plight of the endangered species and other animal suffering; and to endeavour to influence commercial firms and the general trend towards humane and non-harmful alternatives.	
Officers	*Founder Chairman*	Lady Dowding
	Executive Director	David Whiting
	Vice-Presidents	include Spike Milligan, Brigid Brophy
Staff	4	
Membership	6,000. Members must not wear any animal fur products.	

Branches	Edinburgh, Glasgow, Dundee, Fleetwood, Bramhall, Leeds, Bourne, Llandaff, Crosshaven (Eire)
Publications	*Compassion* (3 times p.a.); also data sheets as available.
Connections	In association with Compassion in World Farming; full voting member of International Society for the Protection of Animals.
History	Founded in 1959 by Lady Dowding, to give information against unnecessary cruelty in obtaining animal ingredients particularly in the fur and cosmetics industries and to provide viable alternatives. Activities have included fact-finding missions concerning seal hunting in Labrador; use of civet cat in Ethiopia which provides a fixative (this led to major manufacturer changing to non-animal fixative); musk deer in Himalayas; kurukal lamb in Afghanistan. It conducts a continuous campaign with film shows, fashion shows, etc throughout world, stressing the alternatives, itself producing a range of cosmetics, the profits from which are paid into an associated charity.

BRITISH NATURALISTS' ASSOCIATION
(See Section 11)

BRITISH UNION FOR THE ABOLITION OF VIVISECTION INC. (A Charity)
47 Whitehall, London SW1A 2BZ
Telephone: 01-930 7698

Aims	Dedicated not only to the abolition of vivisection but also to the active promotion of medical research that makes use of the many available substitutes for animals.
Secretary	Sidney A Hicks
History	Founded 1898.

CAPTIVE ANIMALS' PROTECTION SOCIETY
46 Pembroke Crescent, Hove, Sussex BN3 5DG
Telephone: Brighton 732363

Aims	To abolish performing animal exhibitions; to influence public opinion to work to this end through local authorities and parliament; to co-operate with other societies for the prevention of cruelty to animals.

Captive Animals' Protection Society (continued)

Officers	*President*	Andrew Bowden MP
	Hon Secretary and PR	Miss I M Heaton
	Hon Treasurer	Mrs E W Mitchell
	Press Secretary	Miss K Mitchell
	Asst. Press Secretary	Ralph Jones

Vice-Presidents include Peter Black, Antony Hopkins, Marcus Lipton MP, Dudley Smith MP, Andrew Bowden MP, Dirk Bogarde, Robert Brown MP, Fay Compton, the Bishop of Coventry, the Earl of Huntingdon, Edgar Lustgarten, Spike Milligan, Virginia McKenna, Lord Olivier, Dame Sybil Thorndike, Lord Willis.

Staff 3

Membership 400 **Fees:** £1 p.a.

Publications News Letter (published in January) and Annual Report (in July to members only); other leaflets freely available.

Connections World Federation for the Protection of Animals; National Council of Women; Conference of Animal Welfare Societies; Performing Animals' Defence League.

History Formed 1956. Promoted a bill in the House of Lords, February 1965. Continuous campaign against the use of performing animals and for improvement in conditions in zoos. General publicity includes press articles, television and radio appearances by members. Recent achievements include adding of several local authorities to list of those refusing sites to circus proprietors. Plans include stepping up work in public relations including press, meetings, talks to groups (including youth), and further efforts for fresh legislation.

CATS PROTECTION LEAGUE (A Charity)
29 Church Street, Slough SL1 1PW
Telephone: Slough 20173

Aims To do the greatest amount of good for the largest amount of cats.

Officers	*Chairman*	Mrs N de Clifford
	Secretary	A E Parratt
	Hon Treasurer	Miss E E Smith

Patrons Lady Strabolgi, Dame Anna Neagle, Katie Boyle, Margot Bryant, Lord Houghton, Ted Graham MP, Phillip Whitehead MP, Brian Vesey-Fitzgerald

Staff   18

Branches   26

Publications   *The Cat* (bi-m)

Connections   With all charitable animal organisations.

History   Founded 1927 in Slough as the first animal society solely for cats/kittens. Formerly known as Cats Protection League and Tailwavers. Amended titles agreed with Charity Commissioners in 1974. Recent activities include the formation of two new branches, a new property purchase for branch shelter facilities and the enrolment of 1,000 new members. During 1973/74 £68,000 spent on neutering cats and kittens at HQ; plans include opening of new shelters.

COUNCIL FOR NATURE
(See Section 11)

COUNCIL OF JUSTICE TO ANIMALS AND HUMANE SLAUGHTER ASSOCIATION (A Charity)
17 Bolton Street, London W1Y 7PA
Telephone: 01-493 6875

Aims   The promotion of humane methods of slaughter; reforms in cattle markets and the welfare of animals and birds in transit.

History   Founded 1911.

INTERNATIONAL LEAGUE FOR THE PROTECTION OF HORSES
(A Charity)
67a Camden High Street, London NW1
Telephone: 01-388 1449

Aims   To prevent cruelty to equine animals and to further their welfare by promoting legislation etc; to rescue and give sanctuary to horses in distress; to combat the traffic in live horses for butchery.

Activities   Maintains sanctuaries in Surrey, Norfolk, Bedfordshire and Sussex.

LEAGUE AGAINST CRUEL SPORTS LTD
1 Reform Row, London N17 9TW
Telephone: 01-801 2177/8

Aims	Abolition of hunting wild animals with hounds, i.e. beagling, deer hunting, fox hunting, hare coursing, hare hunting (harriers) and otter hunting.	
Officers	*President*	Lord Soper
	Vice-President	Eric Heffer MP
	Chairman	Raymond Rowley
	General Secretary	Mark Davies
Staff	4	
Membership	20,000	**Fees:** 55p p.a. or £11 for life membership
Branches	25 voluntary branches	
Publications	*Cruel Sports* (3 times yearly); various leaflets on hunting.	
History	Founded 1924. During past two years has created 500 acres of anti-hunt and wildlife sanctuaries. Campaigned for recent legislation which abolished hare coursing.	

NATIONAL ANTI-VIVISECTION SOCIETY LTD
51 Harley Street, London W1N 1DD
Telephone: 01-589 4034   Cables: Zoophilist, London

Aims	The eventual abolition of experiments on animals calculated to cause pain, suffering or distress. The promotion of research techniques not involving the use of live animals.	
Officers	*President*	Lady Dowding
	Chairman	Rev W H Barnard
	General Secretary	Colin Smith
	Vice-Presidents	include Captain Lord Ailwyn, R Body MP, Kenneth Lomas MP, Lord Houghton, Miss Brigid Brophy
Staff	10	
Branches	30 throughout UK	
Press and PR	Bullock and Turner Ltd **Advertising:** E John French	
Publications	*Animals' Defender and Anti-Vivisection News* (6 times p.a.)	

Connections   Founder member of International Association Against Painful Experiments on Animals, which has consultative status with UN Economic and Social Council.

History   Founded in 1875. Among its activities, the society sponsors medical and scientific research projects not involving experiments on live animals through its specially created department known as Air Chief Marshal the Lord Dowding Fund for Humane Research.

NATIONAL CANINE DEFENCE LEAGUE
10 Seymour Street, London W1H 5WB
Telephone: 01-935 5511

Aims   Care of lost and unwanted dogs and assistance to dog-owners.

History   Founded 1891.

RESEARCH DEFENCE SOCIETY
11 Chandos Street, Cavendish Square, London W1 9DE
Telephone: 01-580 1729

Aims   To emphasise the importance of animal experiments to the welfare of mankind and animals and the great saving of human and animal life and health and the prevention of suffering due to them; to publish the facts about research, conditions and regulations; to assist researchers in applications for licences and certificates and defend them from attacks by anti-vivisectionists. The society is in favour of alternatives to animal experiments whenever an alternative is genuinely effective.

Officers

President	Earl of Halsbury
Chairman	Professor W D M Paton
Hon Treasurer	F A Robinson
Hon Secretary	Professor Henry Barcroft
Secretary	Mrs Catherine Ewen
Vice-Presidents	include Lord Adrian, Lord Amulree, Lord Cohen, Sir Peter Medawar, Christopher Mayhew
Council members	include Tom Stuttaford, John Osborn MP

Membership   1,750   Fees: Full £1.05; student 25p; Life £10

Publications   *Conquest* (for members); newsletters (bi-a, members)

History   Founded in 1908 by Stephen Paget, under the presidency of Lord Coonier.

SOCIETY FOR THE PROMOTION OF NATURE RESERVES
(See Section 11)

THE ROYAL SOCIETY FOR THE PROTECTION OF BIRDS (A Charity)
The Lodge, Sandy, Bedfordshire SG19 2DL
Telephone: 0767 80551

Aims	To ensure the better protection of birds by developing public interest in them and in their place in nature.	
Officers	*President*	Robert Dougall
	Chairman	Charles Wilson
	Director	Peter Condor
Staff	About 180	
Membership	180,000	
Fees	Basic £3 p.a.; Fellows £6 p.a.; Life £100	
Press and PR	Peter Firth, John Moore Association, 71 Fleet Street, London EC4	
Regional Offices	Wales; Scotland; Northern Ireland; North of England; South-East England; South-West England	
Publications	*Birds* (bi-m to members); *Bird Life* (6 times a year to members of the young ornithologists club, the junior section of the RSPB).	
Connections	Works closely with other conservation bodies such as the Council for Nature (6) and the Nature Conservancy Council.	
History	Founded in 1889. Royal Charter 1904. Owns or manages 50 reserves covering more than 20,000 acres.	

VOLUNTARY ANIMAL WELFARE SOCIETY (A Charity)
92 Victoria Road, Portslade, Brighton, Sussex BN4 1XB
Telephone: Brighton 415145

Aims	Enlightenment, protection and reform.	
Officers	*President*	Jon Evans
	Hon Secretary	Mrs L Entwistle
Patrons	Include Richard Body MP, Andrew Bowden MP, Lord Houghton, Marcus Lipton MP, Kenneth Lomas MP, Spike Milligan, Harry Secombe	

WILDFOWLERS ASSOCIATION OF GREAT BRITAIN AND NORTHERN IRELAND (WAGBI) — for shooting and conservation
Grosvenor House, 104 Watergate Street, Chester CH1 2LF
Telephone: 0244 311466/9

Aims	To foster and safeguard sporting shooting with particular emphasis on wildfowling and roughshooting. To assist in the lawful preservation and conservation of wildlife, whenever possible making a practical contribution in terms of habitat improvement, and the rearing, ringing and release of both ducks and geese and also game birds. To suppress poaching and prevent the careless and dangerous use of sporting guns and rifles.

Officers

Patron	HRH Prince Philip
President	The Viscount Arbuthnott
Chairman	John Ruxton
Vice-Chairman	I W Bailey
Hon Director	
Conservation/Research	Dr J G Harrison
Director	John Anderton
Parliamentary	Ben T Ford *(Chairman)*, Peter Hardy,
Committee	John Farr, Stephen Ross, Hector Munro

Staff	24
Membership	35,000 (banned to anyone who has offended against the laws appropriate to the sport).
Fees	Full membership: 1st year £4, thereafter £3 p.a. Supporter: £1.50; Junior: £1; Trade: £5–£10; Life £75
Branches	310 affiliated clubs; 18 regional joint councils; 6 specialist groups
Publications	*WAGBI Magazine* (q, free to members); *Conservation* series (occasional); *Know Your . . .* series, includes wildfowling, geese, ducks etc.
Connections	Many international and national bodies including International Council for Game and Wildlife Conservation; International Council for Bird Preservation; Game Conservancy Council; British Field Sports Society; National Trust (11); Central Council for Physical Recreation (9).

History Founded 1908 by the late Stanley Duncan. 1953/4 concerned with Protection of Birds Act 1954. In 1967 fought a bill to prohibit punt gunning. Practical conservation activities have included Duck Conservation Scheme in 1954; reintroduction of greyleg geese 1956; establishment with Wildfowl Trust of experimental reserve at Sevenoaks, 1958. In 1973 successfully opposed proposals in a Green Paper, 'The Control of Firearms in Great Britain'. 172/74 provided funds towards Icelandic government research into pink-footed geese threatened by a proposed hydro-electric development.

FURTHER READING AND SOURCES

(a) Reference Works

Charities Digest (Family Welfare Association Ltd)

Directory of British Associations (edited by G P and S P A Henderson, CDB Research Ltd)

ANDREW ROTH, *The Business Background of Members of Parliament* (Parliamentary Profiles Ltd)

NICHOLAS SAUNDERS, *Alternative London* (Wildwood House)

The Times' Guide to the House of Commons (Times Publishing)

Voluntary Social Services Directory and Handbook (National Council of Social Service)

Whitaker's Almanac (J Whitaker and Sons)

Who's Who

(b) General Works and Case Studies

V ALLEN, *Power in the Trade Unions* (Longmans 1954)

S H BEER, *Modern British Politics: a study of Parties and pressure groups* (Faber 1965)

J BLONDEL, *Voters, Parties and Leaders; the social fabric of British politics* (Pelican original 1963, revised 1974)

J N BROWNE, *Insight into government: how the public can influence decisions and how officials can secure the co-operation of the public* (Pitman 1965)

J B CHRISTOPH, *Capital punishment and British politics* (Allen & Unwin 1962)

H A CLEGG, *General Union* (OUP 1954)

H H ECKSTEIN, *Pressure group politics: the case of the British Medical Association* (Allen & Unwin 1960)

S E FINER, *Anonymous Empire* (Pall Mall 1965)

I GILMOUR, *The Body Politic* (Hutchinson 1971)

A J KILLICK and R ADAMS, *Trade Union Officers* (Blackwell 1961)

R M MacIVER, *The web of government* (Macmillan, New York 1947)

G McCONNELL, *Private power and American Democracy* (Knopf, New York, 1966)

F J MUNGER and D PRICE, *Readings in Political Parties and Pressure Groups* Crowell, New York, 1964)

A POTTER, *Organised Groups in British National Politics* (Faber & Faber 1961)

P RIVERS, *Politics by Pressure* (Harrap 1975)

B C ROBERTS, *Trade Union government and administration* (Bell 1957)

P ROSE, *Politics in England Today* (Faber & Faber 1974)

P SELF and H STORING, *The State and the Farmer* (Allen & Unwin 1962)

J D STEWART, *British Pressure Groups* (OUP 1958)

H H WILSON, *Pressure Groups* (Commercial Television Campaign) (Secker & Warburg 1961)

J G G WOOTTON, *The politics of influence: British ex-servicemen, cabinet decisions and cultural change, 1917—1957* (Routledge and Kegan Paul 1963)

L H ZIEGLER, *Interest groups in American Society* (Englewood Cliffs N J Prentice Hall 1964)

ALPHABETICAL INDEX OF ENTRIES